Writing Online

Rhetoric for the Digital Age

Writing Online

Rhetoric for the Digital Age

George Pullman

Hackett Publishing Company, Inc.
Indianapolis/Cambridge

Copyright © 2016 by Hackett Publishing Company, Inc.

19 18 17 16   1 2 3 4 5 6 7

For further information, please address
        Hackett Publishing Company, Inc.
        P.O. Box 44937
        Indianapolis, Indiana 46244-0937

        www.hackettpublishing.com

Cover image: Shutterstock 131635 © jamie cross
Cover design by Deborah Wilkes
Interior design by Laura Clark
Composition by Aptara, Inc.

Library of Congress Cataloging-in-Publication Data

Names: Pullman, George, 1962– author.
Title: Writing online : rhetoric for the digital age / George Pullman.
Description: Indianapolis, Indiana : Hackett Publishing Company, [2016] |
  Includes index.
Identifiers: LCCN 2015041305| ISBN 9781624664588 (pbk.)
Subjects: LCSH: Language and languages—Study and teaching—Technological
  innovations. | Literature—Study and teaching—Technological innovations.
  | Academic writing—Study and teaching—Technological innovations. |
  Educational technology. | Web-based instruction. | Technical writing.
Classification: LCC P53.855 .P855 2016 | DDC 808/.0420285—dc23
LC record available at http://lccn.loc.gov/2015041305

For Leola

ACKNOWLEDGMENTS

I'd like to thank Deborah Wilkes for encouraging me to pursue this project and for having the foresight required to imagine what books and the book industry might be in the future. I'd also like to especially thank Sarah Murphy for tirelessly alpha testing both the website and the manuscript. I burned through no fewer than twenty-four drafts of *Writing Online,* and Ms. Murphy's sharp eye and critical-thinking skills improved each iteration significantly. She also wrote the Glossary, as if being user zero weren't enough.

CONTENTS

INTRODUCTION

Rhetoric is going digital. We're living at a moment in intellectual history when reading, writing, researching, learning, and communicating in general are moving online. The changes attending this transition from the literate to the digital are profound and far reaching, and it may be several generations before the social, economic, and educational significance of those changes will fully manifest. Nevertheless, enough has happened since the arrival of Mosaic[1] (1993) and the rise of the World Wide Web that we can start to develop a rhetoric specifically designed for the digital age. Using the project-based learning experience of designing and building a digital presence from the domain name up (your-online-self.com), this book will show you how to learn, think, and write digitally.

How to *use* this book

I don't want you to read this book. I want you to *use* it. *Writing Online* is a hybrid composition existing in the liminal space between the literate and the digital rhetorical worlds. It's a book written to mimic online rhetorical practices to the extent paper can, and it encourages you to put it down frequently to get online so you can directly experience the differences between literate and digital rhetoric—differences that you have to understand if you're going to write effectively online.

You want to *think* through an entire section and then *do* something online, either with the code I've given you or by seeking alternative code or supplementary explanations. The truth is everything I'm going to show you can be found for free online. Indeed, one of my goals is to convince you that you can (and must) become your own best teacher using free Internet resources. The value I'm adding to the Internet's cosmos of tools and techniques, how-to videos, glossaries, and repositories is a model of digital thinking and a re-vision of rhetorical practice designed to help you become a writer and a learner better equipped for the digital age. The value I'm adding to the thousands of books on rhetoric is a digital take on rhetoric and a new kind of book, one designed to accelerate your transition from the literate to the digital.

---

1. *Writing Online* has an extensive glossary of technical terms and phrases at the back of the book.

Throughout the book you'll see [[Search: . . .]]. This means search the Internet for whatever is in place of the three dots. Were this book digital, I'd provide links or a focused search box in such places. Because this is a book, links are impossible. I could supply universal resource locators (URLs), but they're impractical in print. Links rot faster than paper does. Transcribing a lengthy URL is tedious anyway. It's better to search for fresh content, especially as this isn't a book about how to follow a recipe so much as it is about how to think and learn and compose and communicate, in digital ways, and searching the Internet and making useful sense of what you find is a primary skill.

So ponder a section of this book and then search the Internet for inspiration and tutorials and further explanations. Make a digital asset or digitize a paper artifact. Reflect on the maker experience as well as the ways paper artifacts differ from digital assets and how each requires different composition and interpretative processes. Then come back to this book and think some more. You may want to review some sections of the book several times. I encourage you to dog-ear the table of rhetorical epochs in particular so you can return to it readily as your thinking about writing starts to change. The section on digital memory will likely require the most time and the most revisiting because it shows you how to make content management systems, the current state-of-the-art of digital rhetoric, the digital asset with the most moving parts, and a plausible successor to the (nonfiction) book.

In addition to the intentionally disruptive [[Search: . . .]] you'll see **bold lines**. This is a gesture in the direction of online delivery. It's a common place of digital rhetoric that users[2] don't read so much as skim, looking for the key feature of a section. By bolding the key sentence or phrase in a section, I'm offering to help you "read" in this way, a kind of prehighlighting, if you will. Rather than having to read line by line, you can flip through the pages to get the highlights. All the same, if you want to learn how to do anything in particular, you'll need to work with the words surrounding what's in bold.

Lastly, typography. I have occasionally wrapped text with `<tags></tags>`[3] as a way of helping you understand HyperText Markup Language (HTML) on a conceptual level, despite the fact that you're holding a book. Learning how to recognize tags and understand how they identify content is an important part of learning digital rhetoric. I've also used `Courier` font to indicate computer code.

---

2. One of the most profound and likely unsettling changes is that during the course of this book, you'll be moving from thinking in terms of a reader to thinking in terms of a user. I realize that "user" has negative connotations. As people often observe, the only two businesses that have users are drug dealers and software companies. "Client" might be better, and web-based companies prefer it. I'm using "user" just to differentiate the online person from the in-person "audience" and the literate "reader," and thus as a way to emphasize a task orientation. Connection still matters. Aesthetics still matter. But the focus in this book is on making information accessible and useful so that others can get what they need and get on with their tasks at hand.

3. Such tags, with a couple of exceptions, are not part of the standard HTML element set.

And on one occasion I used a cursive font to indicate a different, more traditional, <metaphor>voice</metaphor>. In that case I could have used <tags></tags>, but the subtle difference between digital and typographical representations of words highlights a primary difference between literate and digital composition, the technical separation of content, structure, and appearance.

Don't read: plunder and run.

About *Writing Online* online

Writing Online is also online (www.digital-rhetor.com) but the website is not the book digitized. The "e-book," like the web "page" of the 1990s, is an anachronism (an atrophic metaphor), the persistence of which impedes our understanding of how to write online. The website isn't exactly a companion to the book either. The book and the website intersect and diverge. In several places (all under Sections/Rhetoric) the website offers digital transformations of the text of *Writing Online* as a way of showing through comparison the different affordances of online writing, to help you start thinking about how pages differ from screens, how text differs from data, how artifacts differ from assets, how digital rhetoric differs from its predecessors, and how content providers differ from orators and authors.

Elsewhere, the book and the website parallel each other. The book offers code that you can copy and paste from the website, but reading it in the book first, where you can't make it work and so you can't as readily substitute working for understanding, will save you time in the long run because it will help you develop a mental model of computational thinking for communicative purposes. Once you think you have a handle on how a bit of code works, you can get it from the website and tinker with it to see if it works the way you think it does. While I've worked hard to make both the code I offer and my explanations of it intelligible, I've left some things unwritten for two reasons. I want you to puzzle over code the way you might puzzle over a challenging poem. I also want to create a learning experience that makes getting out on the web searching for supplemental ideas and code second nature—the digital equivalent of raising your hand in a classroom setting. Because of this I anticipate you'll sometimes find the experience of *Writing Online* frustrating. I'm not apologizing for that. Very little worth doing is easy to do. Teachers, in my opinion, all too frequently want to save students the struggle of figuring things out on their own, for fear the students will think them incompetent or because they want to make sure the students provide positive outcomes, by administration's standards. Any smart student quickly realizes this and so an environment of learned helplessness ensues. You need to struggle, and I need to resist the powerful urge to save you the trouble. I don't want to make your life easier; I want to make it better.

Although my goal with this *book* is to send you frequently into the neon night market of the Internet, foraging for explanations and examples and code, the website does offer a handful of layouts, menus, and applications that you can copy and paste and mix and match to get you started thinking in digital detail about how you want your-online-self.com to look and feel. While you can create a perfectly useful website with the pieces I'm giving you, I'm not giving you a complete website. I'm giving you a handful of blueprints and a bunch of parts. Not so much a jigsaw puzzle as an Erector Set.

[[Search: littleBits]]

And yet I've written the website for easy harvesting. When you click a link, it will open a new tab that doesn't have the main site's menu. This way when you reveal the source code (right-click Windows, two finger–click Mac), you won't see anything extraneous; only the code you need to replicate the effect will be present. You can copy the code, paste it into your editor, and start fiddling with it to make it do what *you* want it to do.

While you have to reveal the source code to copy and paste the Cascading Style Sheets (CSS) and HTML and JavaScript examples, the website has a number of files containing examples of programs written in the Hypertext Preprocessor (PHP) language. You don't have to reveal the source code with these files. The code is on the surface, ready to copy and paste. However, to get the PHP scripts working, you'll have to upload them to a server.[4]

Does *Writing Online* have a shelf life?

The current rate of technological change is such that parts of even this forward-thinking book may seem a bit stale a few years after publication because it shows you how to make an HTML/CSS/JavaScript/PHP/MySQL-based website, and some people are predicting mobile apps will replace websites in the near future. (Others are betting that since there's only room for a dozen apps or so on a screen and no one can choose from among the literally millions of apps available, the app business is terminal too. Still others are predicting that voice commands will replace the interface entirely.) Personally I think websites and their more sophisticated descendants, content management systems, will persist into the next decade. However, even if apps replace websites (or Apple Watch eliminates apps or Amazon's Echo eliminates all interfaces entirely), **the underlying practice of rhetorical problem solving using the creation of digital assets managed through effective interfaces remains permanently viable.**

The digital assets you make as you use this book, the online presence you fashion (your-online-self.com), will wither if you don't maintain them, but the digital literacy you acquire in the process of making version 1.0 of your-online-self.com will enable you to keep up with the times if you decide to accept the challenge of lifelong digital learning, a challenge that I think you have no choice but to accept.

---

4. We'll get to servers later. It's actually possible to get PHP programs to run on your desktop or laptop, but that is unnecessary for what we're trying to accomplish.

Autodidacticism is the new school

Over the course of your working life, if the predictions are accurate, you'll work for at least ten different companies. Many of you will be more or less contracting for life.

[[Search: the gig economy]]

An increasing number of companies keep the smallest possible real estate presence and the least possible number of permanent employees to minimize operating expenses and taxes. Not only will you be changing companies regularly, and freelancing between gigs, you may be working from home or from anywhere you want. The life of a digital nomad is exciting but it's also personally challenging, because while you'll have the spectacular joy of taking a client call via Skype or FaceTime while sipping an espresso on the Via Veneto, you'll have to fix for yourself anything that breaks down out there. You'll have to become your own geek.

You're also going to have to become your own teacher. In the past, when employees tended to work at a single corporation for life and job descriptions were relatively static, before software and hardware changed everything, a worker could rely on his or her corporation to provide the necessary technical training and professional development to remain current in his or her job. Today's corporations still have training programs, but few of these companies will want to invest significant time and money in an employee who won't be with them for life. This means that you'll need to accept full responsibility for your continuing education.

Taking an online program or getting a certificate or a badge, or even a whole degree online, might make sense in some circumstances, as long as you're adept at learning online and have the high level of self-direction, self-reflection, and project management skills that online learning requires (capacities using this book will help you achieve). But how do you know what you need to learn next?

Less than twenty years ago Google, Facebook, Twitter, LinkedIn, MailChimp, Airbnb, Uber, and all of the other well-known software enterprises didn't exist, nor did the jobs they created. Social media expert, data analyst, app designer, usability expert, usability design researcher, content strategist, content marketer, interaction designer, digital assets manager—the list expands almost daily—none of these jobs existed until recently, and no degree major prepares people to do them now. This means that anyone with a demonstrable and extensible skill set has as good a claim to work in these industries as any less articulate person with a purely technical degree. The people who get paid to do these jobs now are the people who hacked into the problems the burgeoning web economy was struggling with, figured out how to solve them, and got paid. **If you can learn to think digitally, you can create your own place in the world.** The truth is, by the time universities have caught up sufficiently to offer a degree in the next big thing, the world will have already moved on anyway.

Certificates, badges, even degrees are commodities. You can buy them. Education is not a commodity. You can't buy an education any more than you can buy health. You <emphasis>achieve and maintain</emphasis> an education by figuring out how things work, experimenting, hypothesizing, testing, reading, synthesizing, and talking with others who are both more and less experienced than yourself, in both your own realm and all of the realms contiguous with yours. You don't need to spend money to get an education. Today more than ever you have tools and information at your fingertips for free and you can meet and interact with people from all over the world for free online. The only problem with getting an education independent of a credential is that for a long time, many people were willing to take a degree (any kind of credential) as a proxy for learning, as a sign that the person whose name is on the paper can learn and therefore contribute value. But increasingly people are beginning to realize that a degree proves little.

[[Search: Google hiring college degrees]]

[[Search: death of the resume]]

By creating both the content and the interface for your-online-self. com you'll be presenting to the world a collection of digital assets that prove you have the intellectual skills digital communications require. Along the way you'll have developed new ways of writing and thinking and learning. You'll have become digitally literate.

Credentials will continue to matter for a while, but before long, **evidence of ability and potential will trump diplomas and badges,** especially in settings where knowledge becomes obsolete and ways of life go out of business every few years.

[[Search: Mike Rowe and the yellow pencil]]

Who needs to learn how to write online?

Anthropology, communication, English, history, philosophy, political science, and sociology majors

This book is intended for people majoring in any of the discursive disciplines descending from the liberal arts tradition, but it will be valuable for anyone whose love of reading and writing has led them to seek ways to write for a living. Being an excellent writer and a careful thinker versed in qualitative and quantitative research methodologies, and having a portfolio of work to prove it, is a great place to start a career in many different fields. However, the practices and abilities that make one an excellent writer today differ in significant ways from those of the past, and those differences have yet to be fully integrated into the curricula of the discursive disciplines because they continue to focus on the subject matter while largely ignoring the ways in which subject matter gets communicated, to say nothing of how the methods of communication in fact alter the subject matter and the way people value it.

Nearly everyone who writes for a living or uses writing regularly as a part of what they do for a living (nearly everyone) now writes online, and writing online is different from writing on paper. Don't interpret that literally. *Writing Online* isn't just about crafting prose for online delivery. Writing Online **is about the differences among traditional rhetoric (the practices and intellectual habits that lead to oratory), literate rhetoric (the practices and intellectual habits that lead to literature, journalism, and history), and digital rhetoric (the practices and intellectual habits that lead to content creation, sharing, and management).** If you want to write for a living in the digital age, you need to develop a skill set that extends far beyond the traditional—that is, oral and literate—rhetorical skill sets. You need to be able to think in computer-relevant ways. Because you need to be able to create both the content and the container, you need to know about usability, design, and databases. You need to know how content creation and management is different from writing, just as writing differs from public speaking and the literate world differed from its oratorical predecessor.

We liberal arts people are often quick to dismiss practice-oriented learning as vocational and beneath the objectives of higher education. Although practice oriented, *Writing Online* is no training manual. **Just as logic and rhetoric are disciplines of the mind, so the programming necessary for writing online requires higher-order thinking.** It just happens that the kind of thinking programming fosters now offers the kind of cultural capital that logic and rhetoric once offered on their own. Thus, just as one could find interesting work in a variety of settings with nothing more "vocational" than a quick mind and a ready tongue or precise pen, adding computer-relevant thinking into that mix will provide new opportunities, even if you never write a single line of code at work.

Digital humanists

Graduate students, postdoctoral fellows, and professors looking for a future in the digital humanities also need to learn how to write online. As more and more of the material generated by our ancestors gets digitized, as our own thinking is born digital, thoughtful ways of displaying, searching, and otherwise making effective digital use of all that digital material require that we content providers accept a greater responsibility for the ways our content gets provided.

Libraries of the future will be virtual archives, a nexus of digital content management systems designed to help people learn and share, many actually devoid of all but the few books most frequently circulated. These **content management systems will be far better if designed and written (coded) by content experts.** The current practice relies on programmers and designers to create and maintain the interface through which the content provided by the subject matter expert (SME) perpetuates the ancient, lamented rhetorical conundrum that separates knowledge from articulation, leaving professors who don't know how to design their own interfaces dependent on those designed by people who neither teach nor understand the subject matter. **Who controls the interface controls the information.**

Even if you don't consider yourself a nascent digital humanist, I think you should entertain the possibility that the discursive disciplines as we have known them are receding. Interdisciplinary, problems-based learning environments may well replace traditional, majors-based departments, meaning that those of us who are accustomed to single authorship and the rhetoric of the monograph are going to have to start thinking seriously about collaborative research and writing. As the book is replaced by whatever replaces it (we don't yet know what, the open-access journal perhaps), the people who have experimented with the elements and activities that will invent the post-codex will have valuable insight because they'll have direct experience informing their opinions. Making, after all, is a form of learning.

[[Search: Confucius on hearing, seeing, and doing]]

To accomplish this shift from analysis and consumption to production, you'll need to learn some basic programming. Don't panic. If you can write, you can write code.

I'm not talking about full-on programming anyway. If you've had a few years of foreign language study and ever had a chance to travel in the land of your target language, then you have a sense of a functional competence. You can order food, book and pay for a hotel, hail a cab, navigate the subway. You can get around and have a good time, but you can't engage the locals beyond small talk (they may courteously respond in English) and much of what happens in the local media eludes you. If you could just live there for a year you'd be fluent. That's me when it comes to programming. I can design and write a content management system, but I wouldn't dream of applying for a full-time job as a programmer. Nevertheless, if I can think of a digital asset, I can create a prototype in a few hours, and if the result seems worth the effort, I can make a production-quality example over a few weeks. I'll show you how it's done.

Alt-ac professionals

The expression *alt-ac* is an abbreviation for *alternative to academic*, and it's typically used as a heading for discussions about how someone with an advanced degree might find meaningful employment outside academe. In the past, people with advanced degrees were overwhelmingly headed for academe. To go into industry was often an admission of academic failure. Today, alternative paths are becoming the norm because decent academic jobs are increasingly scarce. As tenured professors retire, their lines are being converted to adjunct, postdoctoral, visiting, and other temporary positions that pay so poorly that 25% of contingent faculty require some form of public assistance to pay their loans and keep themselves and their families fed, according to a University of California at Berkeley study done in 2014 (retrieved April 15, 2015 from http://laborcenter.berkeley.edu/pdf/2015/the-high-public-cost-of-low-wages.pdf).

[[Search: professors on food stamps]]

As schools grow their enrollments to offset reductions in state funding, class sizes are growing while the number of literal seats in classrooms remains constant.

Thus, alternatives to traditional educational practice are being sought, while the nature of academic work is changing dramatically.

Given these narrowing job prospects and the profound changes coming to academic work, prudence demands you think outside the traditional lines, not just because a wider skill set will make you a more plausible hire in nonacademic settings, but also because learning to think and write in digital ways will give you a wider range of abilities to offer the traditional academy as well, to say nothing of a less contingent place in the new university should you decide to accept an opportunity to stay. You'll be able make the kind of digital assets and learning experiences that are replacing the library stacks.

Lifelong learners

Regardless of the kind of writer you are or what kind of content provider you want to become, I'm making several assumptions about you. I assume you have some familiarity with rhetorical tradition and that you've at least heard of the five canons of rhetoric (invention, arrangement, memory, style, and delivery). All the same, you don't *need* to be a student of rhetoric to benefit fully from this book.

I'm also assuming you don't use your cell phone[5] as your only interface to the web, but that you use a computer at least frequently if not always. I'm assuming that you know how to install software. More importantly, I'm assuming you enjoy puzzles and problem solving and tweaking settings to suit your preferences. I'm assuming, in other words, that you're discontent with life's defaults. I'm also assuming that you're persistent and flexible, that you can differentiate challenges from threats and therefore you're willing to put in some serious time without knowing for certain the results in advance.

If you're suddenly uncertain if you're the sort of person this book is asking you to be, let me assure you that *Writing Online* will help you become a do-it-yourself geek. Let me also encourage you with the promise that the intellectual journey you're embarking on contains many euphoric A-ha! moments. Crushing a bug in your code is instantly gratifying. When it's right, it runs.

[[Search: YouTube: Medieval helpdesk]]

Oral, literate, and digital rhetoric differentiated

Because we plan to spend a lot of time on the ground, tinkering with digital nuts and bolts, it might be a good idea to begin with a drone's-eye view of rhetoric, to give you a sense of where we came from, where we've been, and where we're going.

The term *rhetoric* has too many meanings to be meaningful, and this book isn't the place to ponder that legacy. Let's say for the sake of getting on with digital

---

5. It's odd that we persist in calling these handheld computers "phones." Many of us don't even make phone calls anymore.

writing and thinking that rhetoric **refers to a set of practices and intellectual habits that develop in a person the capacity to think clearly and communicate effectively in the dominant medium, leading to a level of civic engagement and social significance commensurate with a person's aspirations, abilities, and opportunities.** As the dominant medium changes, the rhetoric changes.

The following table differentiates the essential qualities of the three rhetorical epochs: oral, literate, and digital. The chart is schematic rather than representational because there are elements of the previous rhetorical traditions still relevant today, and because we have no way of knowing what truly prehistoric rhetoric was. Even when anthropologists have encountered nonliterate tribes, they've perceived them through the lens of literacy. At the same time, we don't yet know what digital rhetoric is because it's currently and perhaps permanently in a state of flux.

The timeline across the top of the table is also misleadingly coherent (i.e., <colloquial>rhetorical</colloquial>). We like to think of history as consisting of significant moments, but years aren't dominoes. Writing was developed long before the fifth century BCE and had different characteristics and purposes in different cultures. The idea that there's a single thing called "writing" is similarly simplistic. That rhetoric started in pre-Homeric times is a convenient fiction that excludes innumerable cultures and influences. The advent of movable type marks a readily identifiable moment in the spread of literacy, hence the nod to Guttenberg, but the Chinese had type 400 years earlier. Given the space constraints, however, it's impossible to do more here than acknowledge the implicit Eurocentricity of the headings chosen.

The encryption/decryption struggle between the combatants during World War II played a large part in the race toward computational dominance. Turing's machine is offered as the first functional computational device of the modern era and Vannevar Bush's MEMEX as the first theoretical description of what Tim Burners Lee turned into the World Wide Web. These moments can be said to demark seismic shifts in the ways we think, remember, and communicate. But both can be easily disputed. Moreover, the transitions took place over long periods of time at different levels of acceleration and different peoples reacted in different ways. It's not as though when Mosaic (1993), the first graphical user interface to the World Wide Web, replaced Lynx, the dominant textual user interface, digital rhetoric completely replaced literate rhetoric (Lynx still exists), nor did the spread of high-speed Internet connections instantly turn the world and human action into data. The transitions are still happening and reading and writing will persist, I believe, indefinitely into the future. But that future will look different from the past because its inhabitants will learn, write, think, and communicate digitally.

The following table might be more useful if it were available for crowd-sourcing on an open-access website. Were it digital, each cell could scroll in place or there might be layers revealing additional information, perhaps user-contributed information. In a digital space we could abandon the table in favor of a digital tool like Timeline.js, thus making an infinitely expansive visual representation of the transformative moments that lead from the oral through the literate to the digital.

But taking advantage of such digital affordances would eliminate the cognitive value of trying to compress complicated ideas into a tight, inflexible spot (not to mention the ideology implicit in the idea that change over time is linear). And after all, you're *reading* an artifact of the literate rhetorical tradition. So, a table it is. The + indicates that previous rhetorical features still apply.

Rhetoric	Oratorical (Speech)	Literate (Text)	Digital (Data)
Timeline	Pre-Homer to fifth century BCE	Fifth century BCE to Gutenberg to WWII	Turing's machine, the MEMEX, Mosaic
Sender	Orator	Scribe/Author	Content provider/presenter/author/programmer/algorithm
Receiver	Audience (voters)	Readers	Users: human, algorithmic
Medium	Dynamic event	Static artifacts: stone, wax, skin, cloth, paper	Dynamic assets: screen, speakers
Purpose	Decision/instruction/entertainment	Instruction/entertainment/influence	Instruction/entertainment, influence/decisions (closed-circuit court TV)
Mode	Embodied speech: political, legal, ceremonial, poetic, dramatic	Text: political, legal, ceremonial, poetic, dramatic, historical, journalistic, scientific	+ Audio, video, graphics, networked, data-enabled, computational
Duration	Ephemeral	Durable	Digital: plastic lasts indefinitely in the ocean but it's hard to identify one in a hundred million bottles
Context	Organic, synchronous, local	Crafted, asynchronous, global	Designed (CMS) or spontaneous (Twitter), sync(a), global
Place	Marketplace	Library	Anywhere
Barriers to entry	Gender, age, membership, education, wealth	Education, capital (often age and gender but a bit less so because not entirely face-to-face)	Access to the Internet, desire to make an asset of it
Boundaries	Walkable distance, the end of the day, how far sound can travel	Books available, the edges of a page	Virtually limitless given electrical power and translatable data formats

(continued)

Rhetoric	Oratorical (Speech)	Literate (Text)	Digital (Data)
Character traits fostered and required of sender and receiver	Deep focus, presence (of mind and body, a good memory), pragmatic, decisive, quick-witted, extroverted (good with people and crowds)	Deep concentration, absence (reflective, meticulous), resilient (to criticism), deliberate, conscientious (dedication required to learn letters and literature and history, but also writing is more durable than words), introverted (more scholar than politician), historical perspective	Shallow/broad awareness caused by constant stimuli (email, Twitter, Facebook), less reflective, more immediate, but not always present; focus and concentration still required of makers, much less so users, video games being liminal; networked: ambiverted
Ultimate attainment	Eloquence	Perspicacity	Usable, contagious
Audience	Present, empowered, homogenous, grouped, local	Absent, nonvoting, diverse, solitary, distributed across time and space	+ Bots and spiders, and algorithms that can read, write, and decide
Invention (sources of ideas)	Poetry/lore/current events/observation	+ Written records	+ Algorithmically generated data
Arrangement	Primarily but not necessarily linear, repetitive, potentially interactive, digressive	Primarily linear, less repetitive, static, noninteractive, but indexes and contents enable some reader control and one can dog-ear pages and write in margins	Linear, nonlinear, dynamic (can change in response to data), interactive (can change in response to user), location and time aware
Delivery	Appearance, voice, gesture, posture, eye contact, can respond to immediate feedback, reproducible by hearsay	Typography, binding, illustration, contents, index; nonresponsive or at least not immediately responsive (errata, subsequent editions)	+ Screens, speakers, searchable, readily repurposable, infinitely reproducible, automated, location, time and device aware

Rhetoric	Oratorical (Speech)	Literate (Text)	Digital (Data)
Memory	Natural, working, artificial (the memory palace)	+ Recorded history	+ Digital: potentially encyclopedic, dynamic, a digital variant of the memory palace
Style	Correctness, grammatical and regional, some acceptable distinction, often characterized as "manly"	Correctness, grammatical, and reflective of educational system; latinate, resistant to vernacular; of the writer but also of characters within work offer regional inflections; genders accommodated eventually	+ CSS; tendency toward abbreviation, clarity, often less overtly formal although exclusionary in its own ways (alphabet soup, memes)
Pedagogy	Conversation/ recitation	Lecture/reading/ writing	+ Autodidacticism, making (video/code/data)
Plagiarism	Acceptable practice (term didn't exist)	Indifferent at first but eventually adamantly opposed because of capitalization	A culture of sharing, mashups, sampling, remixing, copy/paste, crowd sourcing, possible death of copyright
Religion[6]	Pantheism	Monotheism	Atheism
Politics	Democracy	Meritocracy	Oligarchy (venture capitalism)

Remember, this is just a back-of-the-napkin sketch, a low fidelity mockup to get you thinking about how the oral, literate, and digital rhetorical epochs differ and overlap. You'll want to return to this table periodically. I encourage you to write in the margins, add your own ideas, and elaborate on and question mine. **You need to start making your own understanding of digital rhetoric.**

Getting digital

So how do we get from a literate to a digital rhetoric? Let's start by turning a paragraph into a digital asset. Our donor paragraph asks and answers questions

6. The last two dimensions are deliberately provocative. They're the paper equivalent of link bait or troll fodder, an obviously deliberate attempt to incite controversy in the comments section and thus increase traffic with the hope of maybe going viral. Because this is a book, of course, such provocation leads to I know not where. Regardless of whether you're liking or disliking at the moment, I hope you keep reading. Religion and politics have no presence in what follows.

to help a reader decide if he or she should keep reading the text offered. The paragraph will have to answer its own questions because, of course, when it was written, only the author was present and as it's being read, the author is gone. The dialogic format is a facsimile of conversation, a genre with rich rhetorical provenance. Were you and I meeting face-to-face, we could interview each other. With writing, pretense is necessary because we have to imagine each other.

> <u>Is this the right book for you?</u>
> Do you know how to reveal the source code in a browser?
> If not, this book is *definitely* for you because it will help
> you understand what's going on beneath the surface of
> the websites you admire, a critical first step. If you do
> know how to view the source code, do you know what
> `<link rel="stylesheet" type="text/css"`
> `href="style.css">` means? If your answer is no, this
> book will help you level up. If your answer is yes, then do you
> know about web forms and MySQL databases? If your answer
> is no, then this book will greatly advance your digital skills. If
> your answer is yes, then while the coding parts of this book
> may be redundant for you, you'll get something out of the
> discussions about digital rhetoric.

Notice the structure: question: if no, stop; if yes, continue questioning. If your answer to the first question were no, then you could have skipped the rest of the paragraph. Indeed, the author might have preferred that first-no readers stopped reading then because the remaining sentences might intimidate a novice. Even the most courageous (or arrogant) novice would find them mystifying. Were we trying to achieve the same rhetorical purpose—that is, help a person make a decision—using a digital asset we could redirect novices at the first no to the part best suited to their learning needs, while continuing the interaction for the others, letting them jump to the appropriate place as they find their level. Thus, a digital composition could reduce the instance of unintended consequences and shorten the time on task for all users.

Here's an example of the process I'd use to turn a literate artifact (in this case a paragraph) into a digital asset (in this case a JavaScript decision tree).

Digital composition in a nutshell: From pseudocode to real code

I know that decisions can be represented by a flowchart and that a digital flowchart can respond to user input, so I'd seek to create an interactive flowchart. I'd start with a pseudocode version of an interactive flowchart (a.k.a. a decision tree) and then I'd look online for actual code I could bend to my will.

Pseudocode is natural language prose that mimics the conventions of computer programming. It's written for people rather than computers, but because of the way it's written, it offers a kind of blueprint for actual code. It's also an effective way to write a first draft of anything digital, a hybrid born of a flowchart and an outline. There are no agreed upon rules about punctuation, but often each line has a number and the end of each expression is indicated, often with a semicolon, but people tend to mimic the punctuation of their dominant programming language, which means you might encounter many different forms. Here's what the pseudocode for "Is this the right book for you?" might look like.

```
What is a primary question the negative
answer to which clearly indicates the
utility of this book? Hmm, this isn't a
binary question. I need a continuum of
responses not an either or:

Do you know how to reveal source code in a
browser?
   1. if no,
      this book is definitely for you
   2. if yes,
      do you know what <link rel="stylesheet"
      type="text/css" href="style.css"> means?
   3. if no,
      this book has a number of useful
      things for you to learn
   4. if yes,
      do you know anything about web forms and
      MySQL?
   5. if yes,
      You will benefit from the rhetorical
      parts of this book
   6. if no,
      This book can teach you about dynamic
      website design and implementation
```

You'll notice that the text of the pseudocode isn't identical to the text of the paragraph. I could have copied, pasted, and reworked the original, but at this point in the process, structure matters more than presentation and reproducing the gist was quicker than reformatting the original. **Efficiency is a primary goal of digital rhetorical practice.**

So, how do I turn that pseudocode into real code? I know I want a user-responsive decision tree and therefore I know I want it written in JavaScript because JavaScript is designed for web browser/user interaction. I could go to a code-centric user group and ask for help, but because I don't have a specific technical question formulated yet, and I'm still a bit vague about my requirements, they'd likely just shrug. Instead of asking for help (or buying a solution at Freelancer.pk[7])

---

7. Were you looking at a website rather than reading a book, these sites would have working links. I've written this as though it is digital just to underscore a point about a basic difference between the literate and the digital. Go to Sections/ Rhetoric+/Digital Composition to get the digital reality.

I'd search Google for "JavaScript decision tree." I could search Bing or Yahoo! but Google is my default. It needn't be yours.

When I Googled "JavaScript decision tree," I got the following results:

> This looked intriguing but it also seemed like it might be a little more work than I was willing to put in for the goal I had in mind. Rapid prototyping is an important principle in digital rhetoric. While you're still in the early stages of digital learning, you have to be doggedly persistent, but once you have some skill you want to be able to anticipate the amount of work something will involve and balance that against the value of the asset obtained. So I made a quick mental note of it and moved on.
>
> This looked promising but it could only answer two questions and I couldn't understand it quickly enough to make it answer more given the time I was willing to allot. So I abandoned it and went back to Google.
>
> This time I found this and it I grokked well enough to serve my purposes, but it used links instead of checkboxes and I wanted checkboxes. At that point, an hour into my hunt and think process, a grad student stopped by and then I had to interview a job candidate and do some other professorial work for a couple of hours. So, later that day, I went back to Google and this time, having thought more about what I wanted in the process of working through what didn't work for me, and doing other things (parallel processing?), I entered "show hide JavaScript checkbox," and got something I could work with. This tiny bit of JavaScript made sense to me immediately and thirty minutes later I had what I wanted.

So, two sixty-minute fiddling sessions yielded a sharable (because on the web), reusable, and interactive (because digital) decision tree example. Two hours is a long time, I suppose. But now that I have a working example, the next time I need a decision tree, I won't have to search for the JavaScript. So I may get those two hours back over time. This is a significant difference between literate and digital composition. I don't know how many times I've spent several hours composing a paragraph I'll never be able to reuse. **Digital assets are recyclable.** A significant part of learning digital composition is realizing and making full use of the recyclable nature of digital assets.

If you go to the website and select Sections/Rhetoric+/Composition, you can copy and play with my decision tree. You'll also be able to click on the linked examples that are, of course, nonfunctioning in this paper environment. Comparing what you've just finished reading with a digital variation will foreshadow how literate rhetoric (both the composing and the interpreting sides of it) differs from its digital descendants.

I took you through this pseudo interior monologue as a worked example of the kind of digital thinking, writing, and learning you need to learn how to do if you're going to become comfortable and effective with communicating in digital domains. You'll need to strip your writing practices back to each one's fundamental rhetorical purpose and then recode to profit from the digital. Rather than thinking in terms of paragraphs, for example, you want to start thinking in terms of expanding and collapsing (dynamic) content that offers tailored experiences based on user preferences, stated or observed.

At this point you may be wondering if writing your own digital assets, even if based closely on readily available models, is necessary for rhetorical success in the digital age. <smile>I'm glad you asked.</smile>

Why learn about code when you can pour words into templates?

If our goal as writers in the digital age were merely to put our literate words online, then learning how to use a WordPress or Wix template would suffice. Learn the tool; use the tool. Done. Why reinvent the wheel? Why learn to fish when you can shop, or even more efficiently, why not just buy lunch at The Fish & Chips Truck?

The tool is not the craft

If you mistake a tool for the craft, then your job prospects are limited to places where that tool is used. If the tool breaks, you're done for the day. If the tool doesn't meet your needs, you can't customize it, which means you have to accommodate it rather than making it accommodate you. Even if the tool you learn is the industry standard, learning to use it doesn't set you up for life. Standards change because the work changes. When desktop publishing came on the scene, everyone was learning FrameMaker. A few years later the tool du jour was Page-Maker. A few years after that QuarkXpress took over. A few years after that InDesign took over. Now desktop publishing has been largely superseded by content management because fewer and fewer documents are actually getting printed and more and more documents are linked to other documents and designed for digital distribution and consumption, while a great many of the communication functions that text would have provided are now provided by dynamic data and video, none of which print. So people who have learned four different desktop publishing systems now need to retool and rethink the work those tools enabled. Now they have to learn how to use content management systems, an entirely different technology requiring a different rhetorical skill set producing a profoundly different kind of rhetorical experience. A screen is not a page. The same "page" can present different content at different times, to different users, in different ways. Files are not documents. Digital text is data.

A few years from now, content management systems like WordPress and Drupal will be replaced by other tools because the rhetorical practices they facilitate will be replaced by other rhetorical practices: as desktop publishing gave way to content creation and management so shall content creation and management give way to something else.

You could argue that people who focused on the writing, indifferent to the digital technology, were ahead of this curve because they never learned the tools of the publishing trade. They just wrote. I'd argue that being merely a writer, a subject matter expert, severely limits your employment options and your intellectual potential by trapping you in a literate mindset. To think digitally is to think differently. I'd also argue that control over the means of production is where the real power lies. A great turn of phrase will get you in the door, but it's the ability to anticipate, adapt, and learn that will move you from the vestibule to the elevator bank. You don't want to contribute to someone else's profit. You want to create value, not just content.

Here's where the argument gets disturbing. We have algorithms that write. You may have read some of their work without knowing it was written by computer code. There's an online *New York Times* article that offers samples of prose and asks you to identify if they were written by a machine or a person.

[[Search: *New York Times* interactive quiz human or computer]]

IBM's machine learning computer Watson just published a cookbook (*Cognitive Cooking with Chef Watson: Recipes for Innovation from IBM & the Institute of Culinary Education*). The *Los Angeles Times* published a computer-generated article about an earthquake *seconds* after the event, far faster than humanly possible.

[[Search: *Los Angeles Times* algorithm earthquake]]

Corporations like Narrative Science and Persado have written algorithms that can analyze data-rich sources of information, anything from stock market reports to sports scores, and write stories about that data in nanoseconds. Often a person reviews or edits the computer-generated prose before it hits the printing press or the website, but increasingly such editorial oversight is unnecessary. There are also algorithms that can read and make decisions based on their analysis, taking digital sources of information written by people or machines, searching for patterns and expressions and word clusters to determine if there's anything of interest, where interest can be anything from vulgar language to a business opportunity. In some cases, the algorithm's analysis triggers a further automated action, such as sell a stock, buy a ticket, or send a message.

Writing and reading are being digitized, which means that people who would have done that research and written those documents are no longer needed in that capacity. **It's not just that computer code can write convincingly now; code can read and make decisions, and so any job requiring thought patterns that can be regularized, from legal to medical to financial to actuarial to instructional decisions, realms far beyond reporting data, can be offloaded to algorithms.** Aren't people better writers than computer algorithms? Well, define "better." If cost effectiveness enters the definition, then no, human writers don't write better prose than algorithms. The people who write the code are worth paying because their code replaces the labor of untold numbers of people who require health insurance and family leave and decent working conditions.

[[Search: normalcy bias]]

People who have a great deal of time and effort invested in a tool (like desktop publishing or even a more fundamental tool like oratory or literacy) not only find it hard to retool, they resist seeing the need for change longer than is wise. They're trapped by legacy ways of thinking—a cultural lag.

One last argument and then I promise to drop the future shock <colloquial>rhetoric</colloquial>. The tools you use influence how you understand your work and thus constrain and enable the work you can do. Word processing software like MS Word or Pages enables a certain kind of writing practice, one designed originally with print in mind.[8] We aren't constrained by paper anymore. Writing online enables a different kind of writing and therefore a different kind of rhetoric, which means that **if you continue to use a word processor as the interface between your ideas and the people who might want to encounter them, your communications processes won't evolve to meet the needs of the digital age.** At the same time, however, just switching from a word processor to a "blog" tool like WordPress doesn't accomplish the necessary transformation. Switching your writing from word processor to a blog tool merely shifts your constraints from one enabler to another, albeit one more in tune with <emphasis>current</emphasis> digital communications.

De-professionalization happens in every industry when inexpensive technologies become available; whether it's journalism as a result of the cell phone and Twitter, or desktop publishing as a result of content management and the web, or big-box retailors as a result of Amazon, or record labels as a result of GarageBand, or media firms like Viacom (MTV) as a result of YouTube, once the equipment and the distribution processes are within financial reach of anyone who wants them, the profession is no longer controlled by credentialed and acknowledged experts. Workers who know how to use software are commodities. People who know how to learn and think, anticipate and adapt, are resources.

Making your own communications tools enables a deeper understanding of your thinking and composing processes while providing the opportunity to rethink writing. So if you're hungry now, get in line at The Fish & Chips Truck; set up a WordPress site if you haven't already got one. But if you're thinking ahead, consider how much healthier and less expensive learning to cook will be. If you want to live an independent life, consider learning how to source and grow your own ingredients. You never know, you might invent the rhetorical practice that replaces Facebook or Elsevier or Omeka.

Writing and coding are analogous intellectual processes that can reinforce each other

For writers, learning to code isn't the stretch it might seem. Ultimately, writing and coding are about using symbols and patterns to solve problems for people. How

8. The first word processors were printers with keyboards attached. They were software-enhanced typewriters. The new word processor software is infinitely more appropriate for online writing, but most people still use it as if they were using a typewriter, even people who have never seen a typewriter.

can I write a program that will help someone do common tasks more efficiently or enable new insights? How can I write a document such that the difference between what I wrote, what I meant, and what they understand will be as close to zero as possible given the subject, the audience, the genre, the context of reception, etc.? In other words, **writing and coding foster critical thinking, abstraction, anticipation, reflection, precision, and problem solving.** Given enough practice and feedback, both programmers and writers will internalize the process of error tracking, logic testing, and reality testing, and thus come to accomplish more and more with less and less external feedback.

Because both programming and writing are about problem solving and critical thinking, one can facilitate the other. Because both strive for efficiency and elegance, and both require abstraction, concentration, and practice, they reinforce the same intellectual values. It's a shame that for whatever reasons, we tend to voluntarily <metaphor>divide ourselves into two camps</metaphor>: communication people on one side and computation people on the other. Everyone has both capacities in some measure. We just tend to play to our strengths and are therefore weaker.

Learning to program, even at the basic level web-based communication requires, will help you become a more effective writer because it will help you become a more precise thinker and therefore a better communicator. One of the greatest sources of miscommunication is assuming what you mean is clear when in fact it's ambiguous or actually misleading. We miscommunicate this way frequently because most of the time, the people we talk and write to are okay with their own interpretations and unharmed by their misinterpretations, <irony>if you know what I mean</irony>. Computers are absolutely literal. They can't interpret your intentions and therefore you cannot assume they know what you mean, which means that you need to learn to ask for exactly what you want. To write code you need to become explicit and precise. Thus, you'll become a better writer, and a better proofreader too.

Learning basic programming will also enable you to create the environments that best meet *your* specific communication needs, even as those needs change fundamentally over time. Learning to code your own communication environments and design your own interfaces will free you from the tyranny of the software providers and app developers. You can make your own digital world rather than having to confine your existence to theirs. You'll also learn to think in ways more compatible with digital media and overcome the physical constraints that paper media impose.

And finally, coding is fun. It's immersive. It's a deep flow, lost in the zone experience like rough drafting on a good writing day. You can spend the briefest hours puzzling and pondering and testing and tinkering with code. Best of all, when you finally get it right, Ding!

[[Search: life hacker, what it takes to be a programmer]]

[[Search: Paul Ford, "What Is Code"]]

1

HELLO WORLD[1]

For what you're about to learn, you don't need much in the way of equipment, but you'll need an Internet-connected computer. For software all you need is a browser and a plain text editor. By plain text I mean a word processor that doesn't invisibly embed layout commands, neither MS Word nor Pages, in other words, but Notepad or TextEdit. There are dozens of inexpensive plain text editors designed specifically for writing online. Two I think worth investigating are EditPlus ($35) for Windows and Coda ($99) for Mac. There are free options as well.

If you want the world to see your work, you'll need to spend around $10 dollars a year for a domain name and roughly $10 a month ($120 annually) for a web-hosting service, both explained in detail below. You don't have to put what you're learning here online, but you'll probably want to, or else how will the world know you can write online? See the section on getting a web-hosting account for details.

While creating and maintaining your-online-self.com won't cost you much money, it will take time to learn what you need to know, and once you get going you'll want to keep learning. You need to find time every day. Since your day is already packed, getting up earlier or staying up later might be a good way to find more time. You don't need long stretches. Thirty minutes to an hour regularly will be enough. Whatever time you find should be as distraction free as possible. Concentration is a key part of learning new ways to think.[2] Distractions like phones and Twitter feeds and audio streams impede learning. True multitasking, doing two things simultaneously, isn't humanly possible, even if switching from one task to another is. Each time you switch tasks you have to

---

1. By convention, the first thing you learn when you learn a new computer language is how to print "Hello world" to the screen. By the end of this chapter, your-online-self.com will be well underway.

2. I've met people who think that one of the rhetorical consequences of digital existence will be the irrelevance of concentration to learning, that the digitally literate will be true multitaskers living forever on the surface of consciousness. Speculation is irresistible, but I don't think we liminal literates will ever know the fate of concentration. For oral rhetors, focus might have been more useful than concentration because they had to function in real time, without the benefit of hindsight or reflection that one benefits from when writing. Perhaps concentration is a literate and therefore terminal phenomenon.

spend a bit of time refocusing your attention, remembering the context and the original objectives. No matter how small any given bit of time is, they add up. The more often you switch, the shallower your level of concentration on each task. Deep learning requires emersion. So find regular times and places where you can run silent and deep, even if all you can manage is thirty minutes a day. A few hours a week adds up pretty quickly over time, as long as you stick with it.

Okay, let's get ready to announce your-online-self.com's arrival to the world. We're going to make a landing screen for your website. First, however, we need to get some basic terminology in place.

The path to success

A path is, of course, a way to get from one place to another, and on the computer a path is the route you take to get to the file you're looking for. On most computers the path is a hierarchically arranged collection of directories (the more familiar word "folder" is a metaphor from the literate era of file cabinets and paper; I use directory and folder interchangeably), starting with what's called the root directory and working down among the subdirectories from there. Most computer users focus on the documents folder and put all other folders below it. Actually, a lot of us throw everything on the desktop because we can see it without using the file manager. A lot of us have crap all over our actual desks too.

[[INSERT IMAGE HERE.]] Were you reading this online, you'd see a photograph of my actual desktop, covered as it always is with papers and Post-It notes and coffee cups, a microphone for podcasting, two keyboards, two monitors, a laptop, and a cell phone, on a glass table 48 in. × 32 in. Images are expensive to print, which makes the visual pun about "crap all over our virtual/actual desktops" impractical in this medium.

You can put a file anywhere. What matters is being able to find it again. Search boxes can help, but being systematic and thus knowing where you put things is faster and more reliable.[3]

A typical path on any computer might look something like this:

```
User/documents/myfle.docx
```

Your first HTML file

Let's say for the sake of getting on with it that **a website is a collection of files containing information encoded for structure and other files designed to make that information human usable (a.k.a. dependencies).**

---

3. As with all enablers, search boxes are both helpful and inevitably destructive. Anything that saves you the trouble of learning something keeps you from improving in exactly that way. Just as chairs make working for hours easier, they also ruin our spines.

Typically, a website consists of multiple HTML files linked together by a navigation scheme that lets a user find quickly what he or she is looking for while providing immediate access to everything available. This is no small rhetorical task: Here's what you were looking for and here's everything directly related, over there are some further steps, and over there some completely different things you'll want to come back for. Have a nice day.

Making a website means typing plain text (no formatting code) files and then marking up the content using HTML and then linking the files in useful ways. If you want anyone who isn't looking directly at your computer to see the files, you'll need to store them on a webserver, which is a computer-running software (typically a program named Apache) that can display files to the world. We're going to start with a very simple and local example, local in the sense that what you make will function like a website but it won't be visible to anyone but you because it will be on your computer rather than on a webserver. Later, once you have a web-hosting account, you can reveal it, or a more sophisticated descendent, to the world.

Inside your documents folder, make a new folder and call it public_html. If you don't know how to make a folder because you're using a new operating system or you never really thought about organizing your files before, do a Google search for "making a new file using . . ." and plug in whatever operating system your computer uses.

You'll keep all the files you make for your-online-self.com in this public_html folder. The public_html folder is a standard convention on webservers. It has its permissions set so that anyone with an Internet-connected web browser can see its contents. Because the folder you just made is on your computer, and not on a server yet, you already have permission to view it so don't worry about permissions right now. And since no one other than you can see what you make, don't worry about making a mess.

My default browser is currently Google Chrome. On the rare occasions when I give you specific do-this-do-that kinds of instructions, like I'm about to, I'll be assuming you're using Google Chrome as well. So if you don't have it installed on your computer, you might want to go ahead and install it. You can find alternative ways to do what I tell you to do, you'll just have to think a bit more and translate from the digital environment I'm assuming to the one you want to work in. That might be a good thing to practice, but it might be a bit much to start with.

Anyway, open the Google Chrome browser and type `file:///` into the place where you'd type in a URL to go to a webpage. You'll see a list of all your folders. Keep clicking until you find the public_html folder you made a minute ago. Now you know the path to all the files you're going to be making. You might want to bookmark that path. You might want to write it on a Post-It note (or the digital equivalent). You might want to memorize it. Do whatever it takes to keep you from having to look for that folder over and over again.

Now inside public_html make the following folders: img, css, javascript.

At this point you should have the following paths:

- User/documents/public_html
- User/documents/public_html/img
- User/documents/public_html/css
- User/documents/public_html/javascript

Now, open a plain text editor like Notepad or TextEdit or whatever is on your computer and **make a new file called index.html and save it into the public_html** directory. The index.html file is the default file to be shown whenever a browser points to a directory. If no file called index.html is there, then either a list of all files in the directory will be shown or a file not found (often a file called 404.html on a web-hosted account) will be shown instead of a list of files, for security purposes.

File extensions

A few words about file extensions. The file extension is typically the three (or four) characters after the dot in a filename. You're no doubt familiar with .doc or .docx and others like .pdf and so on. The extension tells the computer what program to open to display a given file. If the extension is .doc, it will open MS Word or whatever your machine "thinks" such files should be opened with (you can change the defaults). The .html extension tells the computer to open the file in the default browser. Confusingly, .htm also tells the computer to open a file in the browser. **The extensions.htm and.html are not interchangeable.** If you have a file called file.htm and you type file.html into your browser, you'll get a file not found error or a blank screen. For all of the project files you make, pick .htm or .html and remain consistent. Inconsistency wastes time. If your naming practices are inconsistent, then at some point, I promise you, you'll be editing file.htm and looking at file.html and you'll lose your cheerful disposition.

So now you have an empty file called index.html in your public_html directory, along with folders called img (for images), css (for Cascading Style Sheets), and javascript (for JavaScript files). Open index.html in your plain text editor if it isn't already open, type the following line, and then save the file.

```
<img src="img/pic.png">
```

You've just used the HTML coding for "display the file named pic.png that you'll find in the folder called img." Of course, since you don't have a file called pic.png in your img directory, when you open index.html in your browser you'll see the icon for a broken image. Excellent. That icon is an important piece of feedback, and you need to get used to using this kind of feedback to diagnose and solve problems. I've already given you the solution because I've told you that your img folder is empty (I was assuming it was). Now put a picture file in your img folder and reload your index.html page. What happened? Why?

Here's how to think through the answer to why. Computers are literal-minded machines. They do exactly what you ask them to do, and if you don't get what you expected, it's because you didn't ask correctly. **Don't blame the machine—it isn't broken.** You just haven't yet figured out how it works. As you start to make more complex assets, you'll inevitably come across moments when you're convinced the machine is broken. It almost certainly isn't. Anomalies are almost always the result of user/designer error.

[[Search: RTFM]]

So, if you got a broken image source icon even after you put a picture in the img directory and you know that computers do *exactly* what you tell them to do, how might your instruction have been flawed? What's the name of the picture file? Is it in the img directory? Did you rewrite `src=` to be the name of the picture file you put in the img directory? Is the name of the file identical to the name of the file `src=` is looking for? Remember that file.PNG is not identical with file.png. Did you forget the = or leave a quotation mark out?

Trivial though it may seem, the troubleshooting thought process you just performed is the essence of how to make computers do what you want them to do. **Computers follow instructions exactly; if you don't get the expected result, then you didn't write the instruction correctly.**

At this point you've got a folder in which to make a website. Because public_ html is on your computer and not on a server (assuming you've not set your computer up to serve pages, a very reasonable assumption), what you have now is a test bed. You can see what you're making but no one else can. For the world to see what you're making, you'll need to put your public_html directory on a webserver, and for that you'll need a web-hosting account. Before we get there, however, let's make something a little more interesting to look at that will give you a chance to think some more about the idea of a path.

Designing your landing screen (index.html)

A landing screen is typically a photograph with a handful of words describing the purpose of a website, sometimes with a login feature, almost always with links into the main site.

[[Search: Google Images landing screen]]

The majority of the rhetorical work is done by the picture. If you go to www .digital-rhetor.com you'll see our website's landing screen. The landing screen examples I've given you under Designs are pretty easy to replicate. Go to Designs/Landing Screens+/Centered and view the source code. Now copy and paste the entirety (command or cntrl a, command or cntrl c, command or cntrl v); save it to your computer's public_html directory, call it centered_screen.html, and browse to it. What do you see? Why does it look different on your computer than it looked on my server?

If you look at the code, you'll see this directly under the `<style>` tag:

```
html {
    background: url('Optimized-Atl.jpg') no-
repeat center center fixed;
```

The problem is that your computer doesn't have the file Optimized-Atl.jpg. If you revise `'Optimized-Atl.jpg'` to read `'http://www.digital -rhetor.gpullman.com/css examples/Optimized-Atl.jpg'`, what happens? An alternative solution is to right-click on my picture and save it to your computer, in the same directory as centered_screen.html. Then you wouldn't need to change the style sheet. But you'd be taking my file. You can right-click and save nearly any image you find online, but you shouldn't unless permission is granted. I grant you permission.

[[Search: Creative Commons]]

Can you make Designs/Landing Screens+/Left Justified work? If you figured out that because you found Optimized-Atl.jpg in the same directory as the file called Centered that you might find Hong-Kong.jpg there too, on the grounds that both files had an expression that looked like url(file.jpg), then you've discovered something about how to read a path on a webserver. The next section gives you some more information about reading a path on a server, but before you read that, see if you can make a landing screen with one of your own photographs. Remember the image file needs to be in the same directory as the html file that's asking for it, or else you need to provide the path, perhaps url ('img/mypic.jpg'). You want an image that looks good full screen and isn't so high resolution that it loads slowly.

[[Search: image optimization for the web]]

When you get a landing screen you like, call it index.html and put it in your public_html directory. If you do that, when a user goes to

```
User/documents/public_html
```

they'll see your landing screen. They don't have to type out the index.html part. That's the default for all directories (actually on some servers the default is default. html and on others it's home.html, but for most it's index.html).

How to read a URL

HTTP stands for HyperText Transfer Protocol and it tells the browser how to get and what to do with whatever is being asked for. The URL tells the machine on which computer and in what directory and in which file to find what you've asked for. WWW stands for World Wide Web. What follows that up until the next / (pronounced forward slash) if there is one is the domain name, the computer, essentially, on which the relevant files are saved. All subsequent slashes (/) indicate a directory. The last item in the URL is a filename, and sometimes a request for a part of a file or for the file to be displayed in some specific way. If there's no filename specified (e.g., www.gpullman.com), then the default file is displayed and the default is whatever is named index.html (or index.php if the file contains PHP code). If there's no index file in any given directory, then you might see a list of the files in that directory.

Go to www.digital-rhetor.com/css_examples to see what I mean. If you go to the end of a URL and backspace to the next / you can work your way up the file structure. Most sites secure directories (i.e., hide the files) by substituting a file not found (404.html) screen for the directory listing in a directory that has no index. html file. But learning how to follow a path can be useful.

Getting a domain name

People get to websites by entering a domain name into a browser. Gpullman
.com is a domain name (they're not case sensitive). You can get a domain name
by registering one that isn't already registered. They currently cost around $10 a
year, but read to the end of this section before you run off to buy one. If you want
some more background on the concept of a domain name, search Wikipedia for
"whois." Or go to ICANN WHOIS, the parent organization for domain registrations (http://whois.icann.org/en/about-whois).

　　What name do you choose? Well if your own name is relatively uncommon,
you should think about using it. If you're Jennifer Lawrence or John Hall, you'll
need to be creative. I advise against getting either too cute or too arcane. How
will you feel about this name five years from now? Can anyone remember how it's
spelled and figure out what it means just by looking at it? Is it short enough to type
in comfortably and fit on a business card? Getting a good domain name may take
some time and thought. There are companies that have registered thousands of
domain names with the hope that someone will want one of those badly enough
to buy it from them, and there are millions of already registered domain names.
So you'll likely have to work to find an effective, memorable domain name. Once
you find an available name you should only have to pay around $10 a year to
keep it. Be careful. Some companies offer free domain registration, but inevitably
there's a catch.

　　Domain names are typically paid for annually. Some web-hosting service providers (you'll need one of those too and the next section deals with that) offer free
registration of a domain name for one year when you sign up for their server service. That's a decent deal, and one that will save you the step of having to "point"
your domain name to your web host, but make sure that they won't subsequently
charge you more than the going rate after the first free year, and also make sure
they aren't going to automatically rollover your annual charge. They should send
an email notification before charging your account.

　　Also, when you register a domain name the company may try to add on
other services. *Domain privacy* is a common offer. By default, owner information (name, address, etc.) regarding a registered domain is publicly available at
ICANN. A company may charge you an annual fee to keep that information
private. Do you care? I don't personally, but I know from experience that right
after I register a domain name I get cold calls on my cell phone (irritating but I
never talk on my phone so easy to ignore) and spamish emails from companies
offering to build a website for me. There are other boxes ticked by default that
you might want to untick before you press Submit. **Pay attention or pay
money.**

　　Getting a domain name doesn't give you a website. It just reserves
a URL for you. To get a website up you need a web-hosting account, which is
basically a virtual computer that you can keep publicly viewable files and run
programs on. The next section walks you through how to think about how to get
a web-hosting account.

Getting a web-hosting account

I'm not going to provide URLs to potential web-hosting providers because no one is paying me to drive traffic their way and, more importantly, you need to **learn how to make software service decisions for yourself.** I'll give you a few ideas about how to select a provider. Along the way I'm going to teach you something about creating tables using HTML. Tables are much more important online then they have tended to be on paper, at least for us discursive writers. Laying out information in tabular form makes it easier to arrive at a conclusion without reading what's there, and deciding without reading is something people engaged with screens prefer.

[[Search: web hosting]]

The categories for comparison will likely be: cost to register a domain name (free *might* be good); monthly fee for server space and bandwidth; the services provided (languages supported, auto software installers such as Fantastico, databases, and so on); the amount of online help available; and the possibility of hidden fees, termination fees, and escalating fees (one month free if you buy a whole year's worth is just a discount, not a freebie). You also need to determine how much product you're getting for your money, but here you'll find a bit of a shell game in that gigabits and throughput speeds are not very meaningful for the average user. Don't buy the high end first. You can always upgrade later if you get into e-commerce or become such a popular site that the volume of users overwhelms the initial pipeline. At the same time, beware of "free" hosting. As with everything in life, there's no free. You'll pay or they'll go out of business.

Another important consideration is whether or not you were able to get a human being on the phone quickly when you called sales. It's even more important to get a person on the phone when you call support, of course, since the sales people get paid to acquire new customers and therefore are responsive and cordial. Help people need to have the same pleased-to-meet-you-happy-to-help attitude but don't always. Most of these server providers are set up to run without much in the way of direct human support, and as someone becoming highly digitally literate, you should be getting more comfortable with learning from web-based materials, without direct human interaction. However, you're purchasing a service and, whenever your money is on the line, you need to know you can find a real company representative if you need one. Finally, look for reviews from customers and former customers if you can find the latter.

It doesn't matter whether you choose a Linux or Windows server for the purposes of this book. What code I offer should work on either.

A good way to keep track of all the data you've generated by searching for a web-hosting service provider would be to write it down in a table so you can see it all at once and make comparisons across different categories. Actually, given only a handful of alterative providers, a table might be overkill for self-deliberation. A table would be more useful if you were summarizing the information for someone else. And, of course, a pseudo table might make a great advertising tool.

On paper (and on a screen) such a table would look something like this:

Host	Features	Fees	Help	Reviews	Cancelation
bluehost					
DreamHost					
GoDaddy					
HostGator					
HostMonster					
InMotion					

I haven't included any data here because live information changes while the printed representation of information doesn't. Also, the hosts I've listed are actual hosts and I don't want to misrepresent them. Neither am I recommending these nor not recommending others. **You need to figure out what host will best serve you.** So, design your selection criteria in a table like the one above (you need more columns). Add in all of the web-hosting service providers you can find (you need more rows), and then do your due diligence. Check the options. Compare the prices. Read customer reviews. Don't pay for a whole year upfront unless you're absolutely certain of your decision and the discount is worthwhile. Make sure that the cancelation process is straightforward. Also, beware of official-looking ranking sites that might be shills for hosting providers (e.g., the first two or three listed in a Google search). A single person could offer multiple brands all running in pseudo competition with each other because setting up a reseller hosting site is easy. In the end, the product you're buying is really just customer service. The computers that function as servers are all pretty much the same and in some cases really are the same, just with different companies selling access to the same product.

For the exercise that follows, I'm assuming you have some data as a result of your decision about what web-hosting provider to go with. The HTML code for a hosting provider comparison table would look something like this:

```
<table>
  <tr>
    <th>Host</th>
    <th>Features</th>
    <th>Fees</th>
    <th>Help</th>
    <th>Reviews</th>
    <th>Cancelation</th>
  </tr>
  <tr>
    <td>bluehost</td>
    <td></td>
    <td></td>
    <td></td>
    <td></td>
```

```
      <td></td>
    </tr>
    <tr>
      <td>DreamHost</td>
      <td></td>
      <td></td>
      <td></td>
      <td></td>
      <td></td>
    </tr>
    <tr>
      <td>GoDaddy</td>
      <td></td>
      <td></td>
      <td></td>
      <td></td>
      <td></td>
    </tr>
    <tr>
      <td>HostGator</td>
      <td></td>
      <td></td>
      <td></td>
      <td></td>
      <td></td>
    </tr>
    </table>
```

What's missing, of course, is the data for comparison. You need to put what you found while researching hosts into the table. Putting the data into this table is worthwhile because it will give you a chance to think structurally rather than visually. The first time you saw a table on a screen or in a book you had to figure out how to read a coordinate system. That happened so long ago that you don't think about how you do it when you do it now. Reproducing a table using HTML forces you to think about how **seeing is a kind of thinking.** The code makes you focus on the structure, and understanding the structure of information is a key capacity for writing effectively online. What you see is at best only a visual representation of what you get and the visualization may be completely erroneous or misleading. **Data isn't the same thing as the visualization of that data.** Algorithms are to data what "mere rhetoric" was to philosophy when Socrates was alive.

Being able to design and populate a table with data will be a useful skill because helping people make decisions based on a comparison of features is a common website practice (although much of what you see along these lines, on product websites especially, are apples-to-prunes comparisons). There are free tools online for making tables quickly. But learning how to read the code is a critically important skill because you'll be making things that are filled with code and so **you need to get used to seeing tags and knowing what they do and when they're correctly and incorrectly formed.** If you're in the habit of just skipping over them, you won't be able to function effectively in a non-WYSIWYG environment.

[[Search: table generator]]

Remember, **HTML is about the structure of information rather than the appearance of information.**

Even when the HTML has been interpreted by the browser and the code is conveniently hidden from the user, tables can be hard to read. Some of the usability limitations can be reduced by alternating row colors (zebra stripes) and/or changing a row's color when a user hovers the mouse over it (change on hover).

Want zebra stripes?
[[Search: CSS table alternating colors]]

Want to change color on hover?
[[Search: CSS table highlight on hover]]

Bored?
[[Search: HTML table header sort on click]]

Years ago, before CSS was widely supported, ingenious web designers created elaborate images in Photoshop and then "sliced" them up into tables to make them screen ready. This infuriated the semantic markup purists who believed that table declarations should be reserved exclusively for tabular data. The controversy died off as CSS became more robust and more widely supported by the browsers and using tables for positioning elements on a screen was no longer a convenient hack. **Writing online is about finding workarounds for design constraints imposed by software and hardware.** These constraints are constantly changing and so workarounds come in and go out of fashion rapidly. If you can't do something directly, consider an indirect solution. But you should also keep in mind that a hard-won solution may provide a few months of glory (and criticism) only to fade quickly from the scene because the need for it has gone away. Web assets can be ephemeral. You have to keep moving. Think around. Think ahead. Let go. Move on.

Cloud hosting

There are alternatives to traditional hosting providers in the form of cloud services. Amazon Web Services, Microsoft's Azure, and RackSpace are three well-known options. In each case you can "spin up" a virtual server, initially for free, and build your digital existence from there. Cloud-based web services are extremely powerful, scalable, and flexible. You can do more things and pay only for what you use. You have more control over a cloud solution than you do with a traditional web-hosting provider, and many of the traditional providers are starting to offer their own cloud services. I haven't yet made the switch to the cloud and some of what I'm going to show you assumes a more traditional server setup, specifically the existence of an overarching piece of software called CPanel. If whatever you use doesn't have a CPanel, it will have something like it called something else. No worries.

From your desktop to the world

The files you've written so far are living on your desktop or laptop. For the world to see them you need to get them onto your server. To move a file from your machine to your server you'll need a File Transfer Protocol (FTP) program. Most web-hosting accounts come with one. If your server has a CPanel it will be listed there. Both Coda and EditPlus have built-in FTP capacity. Because I don't know what your particular setup is, I can't walk you through the process in any detail. Basically, you make a connection between your local machine and the server, and then you upload your HTML file(s) and any dependent files (e.g., pictures) into the public_html directory on your server.

If you don't want to mess with moving files from your local machine to the server, you can create and edit files directly on your server, using whatever software your hosting provider makes available (again likely found on the CPanel). If you write directly on your server, save a backup copy on your local machine or on Dropbox, Google Drive, or OneDrive at the end of each work session. If you're using a reputable host, they'll be keeping backups too but accessing them isn't necessarily a simple matter. If you trash a file online and you have a backup within easy reach, you'll be up and running again much more quickly.

[[Search: uploading files to [your host provider]]]

Markup

Any text that's written for online delivery, any natively digital text, is "marked up." A markup language is a set of tags, typically written like <this></this>, that labels the parts of a document, identifying its structure: heading, paragraph, block quotation, ordered list, unordered list, and so on. Each tag identifies an element in the structure of a document, giving it a handle, as it were. Thus, marking up the content of a document turns text into a kind of data.

HTML is a set of tags originally specified to make academic articles easier to share over the Internet before graphical user interface (GUI) browsers became the norm. HTML tags have no direct effect on the appearance of a document. They just label the parts. So, for example, a typical academic paper when viewed on something other than a graphical browser might look a bit like this:

```
<body>
<h1>Title of my paper: a great idea</h1>
<h2>Introduction</h2>
<p>The problem . . . </p>
```

```
<p>The work of others . . . </p>
<h2>Solution </h2>
<p>Here are the steps to follow . . .</p>
<ol>
<lI> One </lI>
<lI> Two </lI>
<lI> Three </lI>
</ol>
<h2>Conclusion</h2>
<p>Further research . . .   </p>
</body>
```

Notice that every label is first turned on and then turned off. Some of the HTML labels don't have to be turned off (<p>, <li>, <br>), but it's better to get in the habit of using strict markup practices because computers do exactly what you tell them to do and typically they won't stop until you tell them to stop. (When you view the source code on my website you'll <blush>see that I'm not in the habit</blush>.)

HTML is used to label the content. The style is handled by what's known as a Cascading Style Sheet (CSS). Every graphical browser has a default style sheet that it will use if no other sheet is specified, and that's why if you were to transcribe the HTML above into a file, call it, say, file.html, and view it in your browser it would look *like* this:

Title: a great idea

Introduction

The problem . . .

The work of others . . .

Solution

Here are the steps to follow . . .

     1. . . .
     2. . .
     3. . . .

Conclusion

Further research . . .

I wrote that it would look *like* that because your browser might not have those fonts and it might choose to show <h1> as something smaller or larger than what it looks like on this page. It's also possible for a user to impose his or her own style or strip a website's style, so you cannot control the appearance of your text on a screen the way you can on a piece of paper. This means that while layout and design matter—in fact, they matter a great deal—you have to use flexible designs and create documents that can be read on a wide variety of machines, browsers, and screens. If you want to reach a wide audience, less is more.

The main point here, however, is that markup is not style. **Markup identifies the structure of the content. Style (CSS) visually represents the structure.** If you decide, for example, that `<h1></h1>` prints too big and so you wrap the title of your document in `<h2></h2>` tags, you'll have erroneously marked up your document. It's not like you labeled the arsenic "sugar," but it's still an error. In digital settings where strict markup standards are enforced, as with Extensible Markup Language (XML), for example, sloppy coding won't validate—that is, it will be identified as nonconforming and either won't display at all or will be otherwise problematic. We aren't working in a strict environment so you don't need to worry too much about how strict your coding practices are, but it's still a good idea to be consistent. Consistency will at least facilitate tracking down bugs and flaws.

Before we move on we need to circle back for a moment. In the HTML example above, I started with the `<body>` tag. I did that for simplicity. Properly formed HTML documents actually start with some metadata that looks something like this:

```
<!DOCTYPE html PUBLIC "-//W3C//DTD XHTML
1.0 Transitional//EN" "http://www.w3.org/
TR/xhtml1/DTD/xhtml1-transitional.dtd">
<html xmlns="http://www.w3.org/1999/xhtml">
<head>
<meta http-equiv="Content-Type"
content="text/html; charset=UTF-8" />
<title>Document Title</title>
</head>
```

The first line indicates the document type definition (DTD) and where it can be found (the W3C URL).

[[Search: document type definition]]

The second line indicates the location of the XML namespace. (Stay with me. We'll come back to XML in a few pages.) A namespace is a specification for what each label in a collection of labels means. You need a namespace because it's possible for each digital writer to define his or her own tags and this will inevitably lead to a conflict of tags whenever similar files need to cohabitate. Although you need a namespace, you don't actually have to write out the XMLNS line because it's the default for all HTML documents. Writing down HTML implicitly indicates XMLNS. You'll notice if you view the source code of my files on the website that I tend to leave it out. Often I start with just `<html>` and sometimes not even that. Bad form. My excuse is that I want to show you only what's absolutely necessary so you don't flinch so often when you reveal my code.

[[Search: namespace]]

The third line, the `<head>`, turns on what's known as the header information. This information, like everything before it, is not displayed on the user's screen but rather is used by search engines to catalog documents by type, author, organization, and keywords. However, you can also create your own metatags if you have some reason to do it, as a way of identifying the author or versions or drafts of a document, for example. Head tag metadata will also prove useful for people writing in teams or passing files from one writer to another.

Notice also the `charset=UTF-8` line. The character set dictates how characters are displayed on the screen and there are several options here. ASCI, ANSI, and UTF-8 are the most common. Character set UTF-8 gives you a pretty wide set of characters, including letters with accent marks and so on. Just keep in mind that if you use an expression with a diacritical mark (e.g., é) that looks just like that on your screen, a user's default settings might transform it into something unreadable if you don't set the charset.

[[Search: charset]]

Before the `</head>` tag is the `<title>` tag. Its contents aren't displayed on the screen. You can see it in a tab of your browser window. It also appears as the first line in a search engine search. So don't forget to include it and make it meaningful. You might want it to be identical to the content in the `<h1></h1>` tag, or you might want it to be an abbreviated version of the same because there's a limited amount of space on a tab.

After the `</head>` tag comes the `<body>` tag. Don't forget to turn it off with `</body>` at the end of the document. And don't forget the `</html>` as the very last line in your file. The web is more like a scroll in some ways than a binder full of individual sheets of paper. It needs to be known where each document starts and stops. Nothing will happen if you forget this particular requirement, but forgetting leads to errors that might matter and some that absolutely will. Be consistently conscientious.

Semantic markup

While there are standard DTDs and namespaces that are used so that all documents of the same type are structured in the same way, such that they can be cross-browser and cross-platform compatible, it's actually possible to create your own tags—like I've done with `<metaphor>`, `<irony>`, and `<blush>`. **Semantic markup refers to the idea of creating labels with meaningful names,** names that describe the specific parts of a particular type of document. A semantic markup language would have no direct influence over the appearance of a document unless it were related (`rel=`) to a style sheet designed specifically for it, but it would permit either a person or a machine to determine if a given document were properly constructed, and it would enable both people and machines to treat a document as data as well as text.

Given a letter, the semantic markup might be:

```
<date> </date>
<sender>
    <street address></street address>
    <city></city>
    <state></state>
    <zip></zip>
</sender>
<addressee>
    <street address></street address>
    <city></city>
    <state></state>
    <zip></zip>
</addressee>
<salutation></salutation>
<body></body>
<closing></closing>
<signature></signature>
<post script></post script>
<attachments></attachments>
<cc></cc>
```

Each part of the document type letter is labeled. If one used these labels when writing one's letters, then it would be possible to create a simple program that would, say, gather all names and addresses and print them to a separate file, arranged alphabetically—that is, an address book, which is exactly what your email program does. This is a good example of the difference between text and data and another good reason for separating form and content. Given that the letter is an archaic document type, this is no big deal perhaps. But given a more current document type, automation becomes invaluable, and to make use of your computer's computational capacity, you have to design your words correctly.

Don't use your computer as if it were a typewriter

Even though few people under the age of thirty have seen a typewriter and people older than that have been using computers for years, most people continue to process words as though they were embossing paper with ink and tiny iron hammers. When they need a heading, they type the phrase, highlight it with the cursor, and change the font family and the point size and maybe bold it so it stands out better. Maybe they change the color to make it even more impressive looking. If they're systematic, they use the same appearance for every heading, and if they're creating a multisectioned document, they use a smaller variation of the same appearance for subheadings.

If you create headings manually and identify each one's function by its appearance individually, even if they all look the same, you'll have to build a table of contents by hand—painful—and if you change your mind about the size of a second-level heading, you'll have to find all second-level headings and change each one, one at a time: this is inefficient, tedious, and error-prone. You might as well be using a typewriter, so unreconstructed is your writing practice.

Instead, you should make use of your computer's computational capacity by using its heading formatting options and thus its style sheet. You highlight the phrase you want to identify as a heading and then you click the relevant heading button. The style sheet does the formatting and you can alter all instances of a first-level heading even if there are thousands of them merely by changing one element in the style sheet. Better yet, because you've identified the structure and not just altered its appearance, the machine can build your table of contents for you. A computer has no idea what a **This section's heading** is, but it knows what <heading 1>this section's heading</heading 1> is.

As you start to move your writing online, you need to be thinking about how text, words on a page, differ from data, properly structured and separately formatted information chunks.

Consider a bibliography. There are dozens of formats, including APA, MLA, Chicago, and Turabian. Below is a bibliographic entry formatted for the Modern Language Association (MLA):

> Pullman, George. *Persuasion: History, Theory, Practice*. Indianapolis: Hackett, 2013. Print.

Here's the same information formatted for the American Psychological Association (APA):

> Pullman, G. (2013). *Persuasion: History, Theory, Practice*. Indianapolis: Hackett.

Although it's unlikely that a paper written for MLA would ever need to be reformatted for APA, because the two style guides represent different disciplines, the concept is what we're after here. And that concept is efficiency. Imagine if you had to reformat an MLA bibliography for an APA publication. How long would it take to redo each entry by hand, assuming you know the conventional differences well enough to get it right each time? If, on the other hand, you had all of your references in a database, you could have the machine reformat the items instantly. **Separate the format from the content and you have a much more flexible and reusable writing environment.**

A machine-ready marked-up version of the same bibliographic information would look like this:

```
<author>george pullman</author>
<title>persuasion history theory
practice</title>
<format>book</format>
<place>indianapolis</place>
<publisher>hackett</publisher>
<date>2013</date>
```

Notice that there's no punctuation (no capital letters, no italics) and no formatting of any kind. The content and the format are completely separate. The structure of the content, on the other hand, is labeled. Assuming multiple entries are all labeled in the same way, you can format and reformat at the push of a button. And you don't have to learn any formatting conventions.

There are several important conclusions here. Obviously, you should **never type a works cited or bibliography** again. You should be using a database program like EndNote or Zotero or an online app (or an app of your own making). Even more importantly, however, you should be thinking of each bibliographic entry not as a single item, an entry, but as chunks of labeled information out of which can be assembled a bibliographic entry or something completely different, say a list of authors, or a graph of publication frequency for a given author, or a map of places the author has published, or something completely different. Maybe you need to know how current the research is or how far back it goes. Maybe you want to visualize the importance of an author by creating a heat map of citations of her work in a given journal over a specified period of time.

[[Search: heat map data visualization]]

Before you design an electronic <metaphor>document</metaphor>, you should devise the labeling system if there isn't a standard DTD. Then you should make the style sheet.

Avoid inline style

If the style and the content are mixed, you have to change every single instance in every file if you want to change the appearance or the layout, and the harder something is to do, the more resistant to doing it you'll be. If you mix your style and your content, you'll have a much harder time creating dynamic content.

This is what mixing style and content looks like—what's sometimes referred to as *inline style*:

```
<P style='font-size:14px; text-indent:50px;
line-height:20px'>Lorem ipsum dolor sit
amet. </p>
```

Viewed in a browser, that marked up text would look something like:

Lorem ipsum dolor sit amet.

The "Lorem ipsum . . ." is just placeholder text used to see what a layout looks like without getting distracted by the meaning of the words. Most people can't read Latin. Oddly, the technique is called "greeking." Nerdly, the text descends from one of Cicero's letters.

[[Search: Lorem ipsum]]

Anyway, if you had a file that contained a dozen paragraphs and therefore a dozen inline styled <p></p> tags, as you will if you use <wince>MSWord's export to HTML function</wince>, and you decided that the font was too big, you'd need to change every instance of <p></p>. Tedious. Fragile. You could use a find-and-replace function in your text editor, but that might introduce errors. Find-and-replace functions aren't necessarily context sensitive. So find and replace isn't perfectly reliable and can be a major pain if it goes wrong. If you have multiple files, you'd have to change all <p></p> instances in *all* files. **It's better to have all style declarations in a separate file and call that into the head of each relevant HTML file.**

This is what strict separation of style and content looks like:

```
<!DOCTYPE html>
<head>
<link rel="stylesheet" type="text/css"
href="style.css">
</head>
<body>
<p>Lorem ipsum dolor sit amet.</p>
</body>
</html>
```

The link rel= code simply tells the browser to fetch style.css and use it as the style sheet for the HTML file. Change the style.css file, and the appearance but not the content of the HTML file changes. When you reveal the source code on a website, you most likely will see the link rel= line. If you walk up the path to the directory where style.css is, you may well be able to download the style sheet, not to steal, of course, but to learn from and modify—reverse engineer, if you will.

File about.html, version 1.0

Let's make some more progress on your website. As it stands now, you have a landing screen, the first thing users will see when they go to your URL, if you name that file index.html (and upload it to your web-hosting account).

One of the most common elements on websites is a section called "About." Typically, this consists of information about the company and/or principle people, and important contact information, phone numbers, email addresses, mailing addresses, hours of operation, Google Map links, and the like. We're going to make a more textually elaborate about.html file, something more akin to an autobiography, so that there are more sections and therefore more opportunities to practice markup. Eventually, you may want to strip your about.html back down to the bare bones: I'm an X interested in A, B, C who values Y and lives in J.

So, what does your discursive selfie look like? Write a brief autobiography using your plain text editor. Call it about1.0.html and save it in your public_html directory. The file should contain a photo of yourself, your name, contact information, something about your current circumstances, what you're studying and/or where you're working, and then a brief autobiography (three to five paragraphs, 400 words or thereabouts). The goal is just to practice HTML and a little bit of CSS, so put some effort into filling out the dots but don't spend hours (yet) on the words themselves. Here's an example:

```
<!DOCTYPE html>
<head>
<link rel="stylesheet" type="text/css"
href="style.css">
</head>
<body>
<h1>Your Name</h1>
<h2>Contact information</h2>
<h3>Year in school</h3>
<h4>Major</h4>
<img src=img/me.jpg">
<p>Born… </p>
<p>Raised… </p>
<p>Educated… </p>
<p>Planning to … </p>
</body>
</html>
```

View the file in your browser.

At this point, the rel= line is calling a style sheet that doesn't exist and so the request is being ignored and the default style sheet is being used. Let's create a style.css file. Open your plain text editor and create a new file with a .css extension. Then transcribe the following code:

```
h1
{
font-family:sans-serif;
font-size:24px;
color:orange;
}

h2
{
font-family:sans-serif;
font-size:20px;
}

h3
{ font-family:sans-serif;
font-size:16px;
}
h4 { font-family:sans-serif;
font-size:12px;
}

p
{ font-family: serif;
font-size:10px;
```

```
line-height:15px;
color:gray;
}
```

Save this code in your public_html directory as style.css or whatever you want to call it and then go back to index.html and see what it looks like. If you don't see a change in appearance, check that the `rel=` line is calling for precisely the file you just made. It's case sensitive. Also make sure that you put the CSS file in the same directory as the HTML file that's requesting it or that you provide the path: `<link rel-"stylesheet" type="text/css" href="css/about.css">`.

Now that you have a relative style sheet working, edit the style.css file to make about1.0.html look different. Change colors. Change fonts. Change line heights. Then head over to W3Schools.com or anywhere you can find some basics of HTML and CSS and extend your knowledge of the standard tags and style declarations. Then mess around with the appearance of your autobiography: make it bolder; make it shyer; make it flamboyant; button it down; frizz it up. You get the idea. Make it look a few different ways. Now, based on the impression the style.css is trying to invoke, revisit the prose style to see if you can make the two different kinds of style match or at least complement each other. Then try a contrast: bold, audacious phrasing displayed in a tiny, cramped, apologetic CSS. On the website under Sections/Delivery/Fonts you'll see how you can use different fonts on the web.

I called this version about 1.0.html as a way to underscore the fact that you'll want to take your autobiography through multiple drafts. A good autobiography takes a lot of time and thought. Moreover, your autobiography should be tailored for different audiences and settings. You don't disclose the same information on a job interview that you do on a date, obviously, and you don't reveal information at the same rate in different settings either. You want to have a single statement of self that can be automatically fit to the setting in which you know it will appear. So about1.0.html might be part memoir (your past), part journal (ongoing present), part blueprint (your aspirations and goals). Eventually, your about.html may shrink to a contact screen with a few sentences and a great picture of you, the rest of your-online-self.com doing the rest of the work.

[[Search: CSS image float]]

Think data not text

Imagine that somehow you were the first person to observe that timing traffic lights would likely improve traffic flow, reduce traffic congestion, improve air quality, and speed up commerce. And let's imagine that you had this insight while living in a relatively small village in the precomputer era (circa 1972). To test your hypothesis you'd need to convince the powers that be that you should be able to alter the way the lights work, and to convince them you'd need data on how many cars pass each light on each day of the week during a given period of time, how many trucks and other vehicles, peak times, dead times, and where the bottlenecks are. Now in a literate age, predigital, that means you'd need to stand on each street corner for days on end with a pencil and paper counting cars, trucks, and other kinds of vehicles organized by time of day, and then repeat this procedure for each light, and then relate each data set to the others. Quickly you realize that data collection will take many hours so you go to the council and say that you need to hire ten relatively unskilled (cheap/temporary) people to collect data. Now your department of one has become a department of eleven, at least temporarily. Eventually you'll need number crunchers and predictive modelers and a few others perhaps.

Now imagine the same situation in the digital age. Now all you need is a cable or two to run across the intersections sending a data point to a database each time a car goes across, four points for a 16-wheeler, and so on. Now, having laid out the automatic data collectors, you go back to the office to work on other things while the data accumulates like raindrops in a barrel. After however many days, you have all the data you want for your traffic flow study and more data in case another thought occurs to you that might be verified by the existing data—for example, the roads that will need to be rebuilt soonest based on 16-wheeler traffic patterns. Digital thinking is about a different way to allocate resources, often meaning fewer people to perform the same work, although often it's just about replacing less skilled labor with more (or differently) skilled labor. Someone has to design the database and the input device, and someone has to know how to mine data, and someone needs to know how to program traffic lights, and so on. No one, however, needs to stand on a street corner day and night using a pencil to make ticks in a box.

This is the essence of digital rhetoric and this is how you need to teach yourself to think. What processes do I need and how might I write the code to automate these processes? How can I take existing code and make it easier and more efficient for people to use? How can I gather data in such a way that I'll be able to use it to answer questions that haven't even occurred to me yet? How can I avoid having to do the same thing over and over again? What, in other words, can I do to make sure I never again stand on a street corner for twenty-four hours ticking boxes?

File about.html, version 2.0

As you remember from a few pages back, we had a template for an autobiography that consisted of the following:

```
<h1>Your Name</h1>
<h2>Contact information</h2>
<h3>Year in school</h3>
<h4>Major</h4>
<img src="self.jpg">
```

```
<p>Born... </p>
<p>Raised... </p>
<p>Educated... </p>
<p>Planning to ... </p>
```

We were using standard HTML tags and we created a separate style sheet so we could alter the appearance of the same information just by altering the style sheet. Now if we rethink the structure of the content along semantic markup lines, we could relabel our parts to reflect the information in each. We can still apply a CSS sheet for appearance's sake, but we can then also include or exclude a section based on the context in which we're presenting it, using computational ideas to alter the content and not just the appearance of the content. For example:

```
<name>Your Name</name>
<contact>Contact information</contact>
<context>Year in school</context>
<education>Major</educational>
<personal>Born... Raised... </personal>
<educational>Educated... </education>
<professional>Planning to ... </professional>
```

If you structure the content of about2.0.html in this way, then you could pull the educational and profession content into a work-related version and leave that out for a more personal version. If you refined the granularity of `<contact information>` to have `<address><phone>< cell><biz email><home email>` and so on, then you could give only business info to potential business contacts and personal information to potential friends. Or you could offer both at once. **If you correctly mark up your content, you can filter it by using rules to define what gets seen by whom in what situations, and you can mine your content for data, thus discovering new content among the old.**

In subsequent sections we'll go over various techniques for including and excluding information based on user and/or context. But for now, let's pull back and take a broader view of your-online-self.com.

If you rewrote your about1.0.html to contain the semantic tags suggested and saved it as about2.0.html and looked at it in your browser, you didn't see anything very interesting because you don't yet have a custom style sheet and the tags you used are nonstandard HTML. To change that, you need to define the appearance of each tag:

```
.name {font-weight: 600;
color:blue;
font-family: serif;
font-size: 20px;
text-align center; }
```

And so on for each tag. Then in the about2.0.html file you invoke each style like this

```
<div class="name">George Pullman</div>
```

Once you have it working, spend some time rethinking the content of your auto-biography.

In truth, autobiography is an exceptionally difficult genre. We're always narrativizing ourselves, but the stories we tell ourselves aren't always the same as the ones we tell the world. Moreover, we don't always tell our story the same way. To complicate our autobiographies even further, our stories may diverge from our behavior such that other people's stories about us differ greatly from the ones we tell. And then again others may project on to us any number of interpretations that we may or may not identify with. Life is complicated. Stories simplify complication but always at a cost.

So you have to ask yourself, and keep asking, lots of questions. Who are you and where are you going? What makes you different? What value do you add? What character traits do you want your work to exemplify? What characteristics will your work need to speak correctly for you? What do you need to be learning next to get there? Resist the urge to accept other people's telling of your story. But don't mistake the voice in your head for yourself either. You're more than a story, more complicated, less coherent. The self is always both more and less than any representation of self. Dynamic content designs and the strict separation of style and content facilitate understanding the representation of self as dynamic, context variant. Just as you can't be all things to all people, you shouldn't try to be the same person to everyone. That's not to say that you should develop a habit of dissemblance, only that you should filter intentionally. What goes on Facebook doesn't fit as well on LinkedIn. What's on your-online-self.com is different from both.

Managing the digital learning project of your-online-self.com

Your objective is to build a web presence from your domain name up. That digital presence is a representation of your current and your aspirational self, your skills and your daily practices as a sign of your upward trajectory, what you can do, what you're learning, and where you're headed. Your goal, ultimately, is to learn something new every day while documenting your learning, building toward a valuable collection of skills and intellectual habits that will attract the attention of potential employers and other people in your field. You're making a (domain) name for yourself, a digital ethos, a brand, if you prefer the language of marketing.

Obviously your-online-self.com is a complicated, long-term (lifelong, really) project. You have a lot to learn and your learning objectives will change as you learn more. You're putting what you're learning out there for the world to see, but because you're in a state of constant development, you'll want to be able to replace the current with the new regularly without just overwriting your history (we learn best from our own mistakes). So you need to be thinking ahead in a systematic fashion.

In my experience, large projects start out as curiosity about something. I might have a couple curiosities to pursue at a given time, but eventually one seems to "have legs," as the journalists say, and I start focusing on it, putting anything I make toward it somewhere I can readily find it, making notes of possible directions, and keeping references and URLs. Once I have a pretty clear sense of where I think I want to be, I fill out a calendar, placing "Done" on the deadline and a series of mileposts along the way, breaking the mileposts into tasks, preferably measurable tasks like number of pages in the case of documents or number of files or functions in the case of content management systems. This chronograph helps me stay focused. I get derailed from time to time, and go down rabbit holes every once and awhile, but the calendar helps me come back quicker.

Keep a digital calendar

Use Google Calendar or whatever your preferred calendar is to map out version 1.0 of your-online-self.com. If you aren't sure what milepost to place on which date, have a look at the suggested syllabus on the website and decide what "grade" you want to achieve. Place the work required for that grade on the last square of the possible time you've got (the last day of "term") and then figure out what projects will get you there. Once you've got a list of those projects, place each on the intervening spaces between now and the last possible point on your calendar, based on an estimation of how long each project might take (i.e., how much time you'll need to learn to pull it off).

An example calendar aimed at an "A" might look something like this if you were starting in September:

September 5, domain name and hosting setup

September 7, landing_screen.html working

September 14, about1.0.html done

September 20, about2.0.html done

September 25, dir.php working and habit of collecting CSS, JavaScript, and PHP examples formed

October 10, launchpad.html done (a version with a JavaScript dropdown list of your favorite sources of information, insights, inspiration, code, and so on)

October 15, designed a JavaScript interactive multiple-choice test quiz

October 20, designed a digital variant of a paper document

October 30, launchpad.php done (a version that has an RSS/PHP feed working)

November 5, got a user comment form working

November 10, got a web form to email user content from site

November 15, portfolio up and running, in skeletal form at least

November 20, flashcard deck is working

December 15, reading_list.php working

January 15, content management system working

If you're still in school, you're accustomed to having someone else tell you what's due when. **You need to get used to being your own project manager.** You also need to get used to thinking beyond any given semester, thus the January 15 entry. Never stop learning *and* documenting your learning (not with credentials but with direct evidence of ability).

Because I don't know you or anything about the circumstances you're learning in, I can't predict if the schedule I just gave you is ambitious or slack or just right. You have to figure that out for yourself and make adjustments as you gain experience.

Can you put the suggested schedule into an HTML table? Can you find a calendar generator online that will put the right dates in the right boxes and thus save you some time?

Design a rhetoric of self-motivation

A sequence of months stretching into even the near future can be a bit daunting. How do you get from here to the milepost you set down at the end of the month? On the days between each milepost, you should list smaller activities (in say thirty-minute intervals, the kind of time you can devote daily to learning about writing online). You want these brief sessions to be habit forming. So make them entertaining at some level: a treasure hunt. How do I use CSS to make the first letter of the first word of the first paragraph ten times bigger than all the other letters and a different font and color, maybe put a border around it? Once you find a chunk of gold, name the file memorably (e.g., drop_cap.css) and then move on to something else.

If you want to build a healthy habit, repetition is key, but you don't want to be doing the same thing over and over again. You want to be progressing, getting better. And to get better you have to know what "better" is and how to measure it. If you don't have a method for measuring your progress, you can lie to yourself about how well you're doing and you can get lost along the way. In *Writing Online*, the units of measure are the projects. Each project requires more learning than the last, but each project can be accomplished at greater and less levels of sophistication, depending on your propensity for this kind of thinking, your energy, your aspirations, your frustrations, and all of the other elements that go into living a goal-oriented life.

Let's do a sort of cognitive walk-through of the concept of a weekly progress chart. Then we'll write the pseudocode to get a semi-computational sense of the process.

Weekly progress chart

The cognitive walk-through of a weekly progress chart would be something like: Predict the number of hours a week you can spend learning digital rhetoric. Let's say five. Then give yourself a set of potential goals and rewards: learn three CSS declarations (one point); find a JavaScript that might be useful (one point); memorize five Internet acronyms (one point); and locate a design you want to emulate (one point). You could give yourself a point for each goal accomplished or use a sliding scale, like one point for identifying a site you want to emulate and three points for actually writing the style sheet. Maybe you get one point for three CSS declarations but you could go hard at CSS that week and give yourself three points for CSS. You should also have a point target, maybe five points a week. Hit the target, get a bonus point. Maybe you want to set a target that would accommodate good weeks and bad, averaging out to five points a day over the course of a few months.

How do you record and display this data to motivate yourself? You could keep a notebook as hardworking, ambitious people have for centuries. You could accord with a friend to compare notebooks every week over coffee on Fridays, to make use of ambition and competition and shame as motivation to keep yourself going. If your friendly competitor isn't in your city, you could set up an electronic notebook or compare notes via email or text message or video chat. Or you could do a CSS graph or bar chart and then put that chart on your website. You could even set it up so your encouraging competitor could record or report his or her achievements and all of your efforts would be public. Or you could create a dashboard, a real-time graphical representation of the data, and put that on your-online-self.com.

Let's pseudocode a dashboard:

```
1. # of hours spent,
   a. if $ontask >= 5, points = +1
2. # CSS declarations learned,
   b. if $declarations = 3, points = +1;
   c. if $declarations = 6, points =+ 2, etc.
3. # of acronyms,
   d. if $acr = 5, points = +1
4. # of JavaScripts acquired,
   e. if $JS = 1, points = +1
5. # of desirable CSS designs identified,
   f. if $design = 1, points = +1
6. # of CSS designs emulated,
   g. if $designdone, points = +3
7. Total points for the week,
   h. $Total = points+points+points+points
      +points
```

What do you do if you don't meet a given target? No change or penalty points?

The next thing you'd need is a way to represent your progress over time. You could do that just as an accumulating number:

```
Week 1, 3 points
Week 2, 5 points
Week 3, 4 points
RUNNING TOTAL: 12 / 15
```

You could represent the numbers visually, via a progress bar for every given week. You could also create a graph of your numbers week by week and month by month so you can get a perspective of your progress over time.

The journey from pseudocode to actual code could take several different directions at this point. You could just keep a piece of paper containing numbers you alter by hand with a pencil, although sharing that wouldn't be very efficient (upload picture). Alternatively, you could use a Google spreadsheet or Excel. Or you could create a Google Form or an HTML form that pulls the existing numbers from a file and then lets you change them in the form and puts the new numbers back into the file. A slightly more robust project would be to use Google Sheets and Timeline.js to make a timeline of your learning.

[[Search: Timeline.js]]

Create a success dashboard

There are five code projects on our website for developing a self-reporting process, all under Sections/Learning+. The simplest project is composed entirely of a single piece of standard HTML 5 code called <progress> </progress>. You can find it at Digital Learning+/Progress Bar. It's neat and clean and you could put one on each of your other projects to indicate how close to finished each project is. Or if you wrote a table with the days of each month in a box of its own with the milepost project goal on day thirty, then you could put a progress bar in each Friday's square.

The second least complicated project is found at Sections/Learning+/Progress Gauge. It uses the HTML 5 canvas element to draw a circle representing the percentage complete a given project is. This example is more complex than the progress bar, but not too difficult to grasp, I think. If I didn't explain it well, you might find a better learning environment at W3Schools.com.

The third least complicated project is found at Sections/Learning+/Progress Chart. It uses CSS to create a bar graph from handmade data.

There's a more complicated example that uses PHP, which you can find at Sections/Learning+/Progress Chart.

And finally there's the Sections/Learning+/Calendar project, which is a full-on, gold medal challenge. You'll want to put the calendar project off until you've finished the Chapter 5 on digital memory and know how to work a database.

Stay focused

When it comes to learning online in general, staying focused and motivated and regularly on task requires a great deal of continuous effort. You don't have a professor knitting her brow at you or co-present learners shaming you into keeping up. While you can certainly find fellow travelers online, and you should, you should also make a habit of charting your progress for yourself.

For some of you this process of identifying goals and parsing them into tasks assessed weekly will be too intentional. You prefer to wander and play, and you find targets and prescribed tasks confining. If that's an honest assessment of your actual learning self, then wander and play, but document the assets you make along the way. You need something to show for the hours you spend on however you spend your hours. If you have nothing to show, then you've no evidence to support your assertion that you're worth hiring or collaborating with.

[[Search: alternative story forms]]

CSS Practice: Digitizing the MLA style sheet

Imagine this. You go to work and your boss says, "We want to start taking student papers online. Build a form that will take plain text input by a user and turn it into standard MLA format." If you're not familiar with MLA, you could substitute APA or Turabian or any paper-based style guide.

First thought, paper isn't digital; MLA format is inappropriate for the medium of transmission, a mixed metaphor, and an ultimately disappointing idea because you can't do on paper what you can do online. But you're in no hurry to join the unemployed. While your critical-thinking skills have evolved to the point where you can see places where literate rhetoric creates digital interference, your knowledge of rhetoric has also taught you to choose your techno-ideological battles carefully, so you file your disapproval under "later" and dive in.

You're aware that the process of receiving student papers online will require building a form to receive student input, as well as getting them to enter the information correctly (some kind of error-checking process). You also realize that the information has to go somewhere (most likely a database) when the student presses the Save button. But before you go through the input side of things, you decide to make a high-fidelity prototype of the output and get approval for that first. Your high-fidelity prototype will be a sample student essay with a style sheet called mla.css containing nonstandard style declarations for all of the elements of an MLA-style essay.

Game plan for replicating MLA-style student paper

Do the semantic markup:

```
< transmittal>
    < prof></prof>
    <student></student>
    <course></course>
```

```
    <assignment></assignment>
    <date></date>
<essay title></essay title>
<p></p>
<blockquote cite="url of source"> </block-
quote>

<footnote></footnote>

</footnote>

<works cited></works cited>
```

Next you'd need to define the style characteristics for each of the elements required by the MLA specifications. In a pseudo CSS code way that *might* look something like this:

```
    .transmittal {
        line-height: single spaced;
        margin-left:1in;}
.essay_title {

        font-family: sans-serif;
        text-justify: center;}
    p {
        font family: serif
        font size: 12px;
        line-height: double space (24:px)
        margin-left: 1in;
        margin-right:1in;
        first-line indent: .5in;}
    blockquote{
        line-height: single space (12px);
        margin-left:1.5in;
        margin-right: 1.5in;
        margin-top: 24px;
        margin-bottom: 24px;}
    .footnotes{
        .5 in hairline
        line-height: single space (12:px)
        margin-left: 1in;
        margin-right:1in;}
    .works_cited{
        text-indent: .5in;  }
```

Can you turn that pseudo CSS code into real CSS? Remember that you can both style standard HTML elements and create your own HTML elements. The ones you create are called "classes" and each class needs the dot before the name while standard HTML elements like `<blockquote>` and `<p>` don't. The old-world idea of single- and double-spaced lines is handled in CSS by defining the `<p>` font size and then using that definition as the base. So if the font size is 12px (pixels), then double spaced would be line height 24px. You'd want your title to be centered in the middle of the screen. Standard readability advice about fonts is that titles should be sans-serif and body text should be serif. A hairline is a thin line that's used to separate sections in print layouts. There's a standard HTML tag for that, `<hr>`. But MLA footnotes are set off by a hairline that is one inch long, as I recall. So you'd need `hr {width: 1in;}`. You'd also need two blank lines above the hairline and one below it.

Keep going on your own

While I encourage you to go through the exercise of making a MLA.css file (or APA.css or whatever you're most familiar with), I'm not leaving you a working example on the website because the value of this exercise is in visualizing and coding the style sheet itself. Copying and pasting a working example is useless because MLA style comes from the world of printed manuscripts. We're writing online, where there are no margins, no pages, and many possibilities impossible with paper and ink. So a more fruitful approach would be to imagine digital alternatives to paper-based conventions for layout that would accomplish similar communication goals, to provide citations (works cited), to offer further context (footnotes), and so on. As digitally literate people we'll also want to think about new forms of communication enabled by digital media (e.g., reader feedback) and alternative style sheets for people with specific needs like vision issues.

To improve your skill with CSS, make a mental note of the design of every website you encounter, and when you see something you like, try to replicate it. You might also leaf through magazines for inspiration and then see if you can replicate the layouts you admire. Remember in that case, however, that paper pages aren't digital spaces. Digital provides a far greater range of communication options. Remember also that you can't control a user's screen and so what looks beautiful in Chrome on your monitor might look distorted in Firefox or Safari or even Chrome on a monitor different from your own. **Test your designs in all browsers and on as many different displays as you can get your hands on.**

The art of diagnostic thinking

As you set out to make digital assets you'll quickly encounter situations where you do something expecting a specific result and either you don't get that result or something you didn't expect happens. If you turn on an anchor tag, `<a href="file.html">`, and forget to turn it off `</a>`, you'll end up with all subsequent information linked to file.html. If you don't point correctly to an image you want displayed, you'll see the broken image icon instead of the image you wanted. You often hear people say "It's broken," when in fact they just don't understand what's going on. **User error is the most common cause of failure.**

If you get an unintended result, and you don't see why immediately, you can diagnose the situation through experimentation. You can hypothesize, test, verify, and then rehypothesize rapidly if you didn't get what you thought you would. This means that through methodical trial and error you can build up a mental model of how the thing works over time, especially if you supplement that process with reading and examples from the Internet, which will enable you to build new, evermore complex and sophisticated digital assets. Practicing the art of diagnostic thinking in a computer environment, where you can't hurt anything or do much more damage than waste time, in a system that's purely causal and therefore knowable, is a great way to develop your ability to concentrate and think systematically, abilities that have a far wider range of application than just computer programming.

Here's a semi-pseudocode version of diagnostic thinking:

```
Observe a problem (no result, unintended
result)
Is it broken or am I confused? (harder
than it sounds)
        What did I expect it to do?
        What did it do?
            Why?
            If I change X, what happens?
            If I change X back, does it
return to the beginning?
            What happens if I change Y?
And if you change X and Y simultaneously?
                (vigorously apply palm to
forehead)
```

Eventually you get a working model, a sense of how the thing functions such that you can reliably alter what it does. If it's broken, you can fix it. And knowing how to fix it, maybe you can make it even better, either reinforce it so it won't break or make it more efficient or more effective. Maybe you can use it in a different setting to accomplish something completely different. You'll know your model is fully functional when you can accurately predict (not just confidently anticipate) the results of your actions. You'll know you've truly learned something when you realize you can use the model in a different setting for a different purpose.

Sources of diagnostic errors

1. Failing to notice a problem.
2. Seeing it but hoping it will go away or it won't matter or no one will notice (denial).
3. Identifying a problem but failing to identify its cause.

4. **Failure to correctly identify a cause may come from a failure of process (broken) or a failure of model (misunderstood):**

- The process error might be something like making two changes at once, thus failing to see the causal chain correctly. (You have problem C, and you think A causes it, but in changing A, you also notice B and think that too might be the problem so you change B too while you're in there. You run the test again and C is still broken. Did changing A not work? Or did you make the wrong change to A—A was too big but you made it bigger instead of smaller? Or have you now got A right but B has broken C? By changing two variables at once, you now know less than you did before—more questions rather than fewer. The worst possible outcome of changing two variables at once happens when the problem seems to go away. Now you don't know how the thing works and you don't know you don't know how it works. Worse really, you think you know. You've turned a mistake into an apparent truth: blissful ignorance. Not just bad, dangerous.)

- The model error might be something like failing to realize that there are multiple causes. (You'll need to change both A and B to get C right.)

- A more problematic model error occurs when you correctly identify the one true cause but fail to realize that it's interdependent with other variables. In such cases, changing one variable has multiple consequences. If you don't realize that changing one variable will have multiple consequences, you'll be creating new problems in the process of solving an old one. If you're too focused on a consequence, you may fail to identify unintended consequences. (If you think A changes B, and you're correct but fail to realize that A also influences C and actually alters D, then by changing B you aren't so much solving a problem as making a mess.)

- A similar error is in mistaking a correlation for a cause. Just because one thing changes as another changes doesn't necessarily mean that you can improve one merely by improving the other. People have noticed, for example, that there's less crime in communities where there's a high density of educated people. Therefore, they reason incorrectly that education leads to justice. Make everyone go to school. The problem is that school doesn't cause education. You can get an education without going to school and you can go to school without getting an education. You can get a degree without getting an education either. Maybe density of education leads to concentration of wealth and wealth leads to justice or at least a reduction in property crimes. At any rate, the problem of injustice is more complicated than the original observation suggested.

- Mistaking the stochastic for the causal, oversimplifying.

5.   Taking too narrow a view of the problem or the situation (some problems are only sometimes problems, or problems for only some people). Making a permanent solution to a temporary problem is worse, frequently, than enduring the problem. Helping some people may hurt others.
6.   Mistaking a benefit for a bug.

Diagnostic thinking is perhaps the most transferable skill you can develop while learning to code. All linear systems can be better understood via consistent trial, error, hypothesis, and try-again patterns of learning. If you can get in the habit of thinking this way, there's very little in the way of technology that can mystify you for long.

Practice diagnosis

Here's a chunk of HTML code for a table containing radio buttons (on/off switches, essentially). When properly written, clicking one radio button in a set unclicks all of the others in the set. Can you explain why a set with two options clicked would be problematic? The bit below doesn't work correctly because it isn't written correctly. Can you figure out why it doesn't work? You're looking for an inconsistency in a pattern. If you can't find the problem just by looking at the code below, transcribe it into your editor and then click around until you identify the problem. Then see if you can describe the problem. Then see if you can predict what will solve it. If you're too impatient for a front-loaded process, click around until you fix the bug and then explain why the last click solved the problem.

```
<table><tr>
<td align="center">
<input type="radio" name="interpretation"
  value="4">
</td>
<td valign="center" >
<input type="radio" name="interpretation"
value="3">
</td>
  <td valign="center" >
<input type="radio" name="interpretation"
  value="2">
</td>
<td valign="center" >
<input type="radio" name="interpretation"
  value="1">
</td>

<td valign="center" >
<input type="radio" name="interpretation"
  value="0">
</td>
```

```
<td valign="center" >
<input type="radio" name="interpretation"
  value="0">
</td>
</tr>
<td valign="center" >
<input type="radio" name="writing"
  value="4">
</td>
<td valign="center" >
<input type="radio" name="interpretation"
  value="3">
</td>
<td valign="center" >
<input type="radio" name="writing" value="2">
</td>
<td valign="center" >
<input type="radio" name="writing"
  value="1">
</td>
<td valign="center" >
<input type="radio" name="writing"
  value="0">
</td>
<td valign="center" >
<input type="radio" name="writing"
  value="0">
</td>
</tr>
</table>
```

Summary

At this point you've started to rethink composition based on the affordances of digital media. You've learned about pseudocode (a very important concept and practice). You've learned about markup and style sheets (CSS) and you're committed to the practice of separating style from content, placing the relevant `<link rel=stylesheet    type="text/css"   href="style.css">` tag between the head tags of each of your HTML files.

Where you are now

1. You have a domain name.
2. You have a web-hosting account.
3. You're on speaking terms with CSS.

4.   You realize that your style files should be separate from your content files.
5.   You have a landing screen called index.html.
6.   You have an autobiographical about2.0.html. If you haven't already, you might want to add a link from the landing screen to the about 2.0.html screen and then a link on about.html back to index.html.
7.   You have a project plan, perhaps a calendar, perhaps some gauges or progress charts ready.

You're well underway. What follows is a semitheoretical discussion of some of rhetoric's key concepts as digital media transforms them. I wrote "semi" because there will be digital assets to be made along the way. **Theory without practice is noise.**

2

DIGITAL RHETORIC

As I hope you recall, I offered the following definition of rhetoric as a preamble to the chart differentiating the three rhetorical epochs: ***rhetoric* refers to a set of practices and intellectual habits that develop in a person the capacity to think clearly and communicate effectively in the dominant medium, leading to a level of civic engagement and social significance commensurate with a person's aspirations, abilities, and opportunities.**

When the dominant medium changes, an intellectual revolution occurs. The transition from the past to the current medium is difficult for many people, especially those most deeply invested in the old ways. The transition from speaking to writing and listening to reading <understatement>wasn't easy<understatement> Plato left a famous passage about the intellectually deleterious effects of literacy (*Phaedrus*, 274c–277) that reverberates today as we transition again, this time from print to mixed media and the digital interface. I'll quote the relevant passages for you at length.

> Socrates:
> I heard, then, that at Naucratis in Egypt, was one of the ancient gods of that country, the one whose sacred bird is called the Ibis and the name of the god himself was Theuth. He it was who [274d] invented numbers and arithmetic and geometry and astronomy, also draughts and dice, and, most important of all, letters. Now the king of all Egypt at that time was the god Thamus, who lived in the great city of the upper region, which the Greeks call the Egyptian Thebes, and they call the god himself Ammon. To him came Theuth to show his inventions, saying that they ought to be imparted to the other Egyptians. But Thamus asked what use there was in each, and as Theuth enumerated their uses, expressed praise or blame, according as he approved [274e] or disapproved. The story goes that Thamus said many things to Theuth in praise or blame of the various arts, which it would take too long to repeat; but when they came to the letters, "This invention, O king," said Theuth, "will make the Egyptians wiser and will improve their memories; for it

is an elixir of memory and wisdom that I have discovered."
But Thamus replied, "Most ingenious Theuth, one man
has the ability to beget arts, but the ability to judge of their
usefulness or harmfulness to their users belongs to another;
[275a] and now you, who are the father of letters, have been
led by your affection to ascribe to them a power the opposite of that which they really possess. For this invention will
produce forgetfulness in the minds of those who learn to use
it, because they will not practice their memory. Their trust in
writing, produced by external characters which are no part
of themselves, will discourage the use of their own memory
within them. You have invented an elixir not of memory,
but of reminding; and you offer your pupils the appearance
of wisdom, not true wisdom, for they will read many things
without instruction and will therefore seem [275b] to know
many things, when they are for the most part ignorant and
hard to get along with, since they are not wise, but only
appear wise. . . .

"Writing, Phaedrus, has this strange quality, and is very
like painting; for the creatures of painting stand like living
beings, but if one asks them a question, they preserve a sol-
emn silence. And so it's with written words; you might think
they spoke as if they had intelligence, but if you question
them, wishing to know about their sayings, they always say
only one and the same thing. And every word, when [275e]
once it's written, is bandied about, alike among those who
understand and those who have no interest in it, and it knows
not to whom to speak or not to speak; when ill-treated or
unjustly reviled it always needs its father to help it; for it has
no power to protect or help itself . . . [277e] no written discourse, whether in meter or in prose, deserves to be treated
very seriously. . . ."

Plato's wholesale rejection of literacy—"no written discourse, whether in meter
or in prose, deserves to be treated very seriously" (277e)—so disturbed subsequent
(literate) generations that many scholars figured he was being ironic, especially as
Plato was literate. If Plato had had an `<irony></irony>` tag we might not
have wondered so much, although one could argue that such specificity would
ruin the text's scintillating effects. Complexity for some; confusion for others.

At any rate, if we take what he wrote literally, it amounts to something like:
education should consist of conversation between a younger and an older person
both of like minds who seek to understand themselves and the world through
dialectical conversation. **Literacy is anathema to learning.** Try to take that
assertion seriously for a moment. What would a person have to believe about the
nature and purpose of education to believe that reading and writing make people
unteachable?

Even if Plato were being ironic, suspicion of the efficacy of literacy was an opinion that at least one other person also went to the trouble of writing down.[1] Consider Alcidamas' "On the Sophists," which argues that learning to write speeches as a preparation for giving them will impair the would-be orator's performance.

[[Search: Alcidamas, "On the Sophists"]]

Even if the arguments against reading and writing proved true, verifiable by research, they wouldn't have succeeded because literacy enabled changes in commerce that rendered intellectual and social objections to literacy moot.

As we transition again, this time from print to the digital interface, we everywhere hear echoes of the ancient lamentations.

In the 1980s well-intentioned people feared that calculators and word processors would keep children from learning to add and spell. The technologically anxious may have intuited the truth. But that truth, if it were true, doesn't matter because computers are now ubiquitous. One can readily imagine someone complaining in the 1990s that one day we'd have so many gadgets that we'd have to carry backpacks full of them everywhere we went. Now all of those gadgets are apps that fit on one device that fits in a back pocket or on a wrist. It doesn't matter if we can't spell, or do fractions, or speak another language even.[2] The device can do this for us on-the-fly. The cognitive and communicative repercussions of the digital shift are so profound that anxiety among those for whom the old ways of doing things were the foundation of their education is understandable. But **anxiety and nostalgia are maladaptive rhetorical practices.**

Resistance will accelerate disaster

<rant>There's a tragic opinion I've read and heard frequently the last few years that goes something like this:

---

1. Actually, two at least. Lao-tzu is thought to have written that "When the people know writing, their virtue deteriorates." *Wen-tzu: Understanding the Mysteries*, Lao Tzu, Thomas Cleary, Kindle edition, 1614, section 102. The concern there is probably more about the inevitable disappointment caused by intentionality, a Taoist preoccupation, as opposed to the deterioration of presence of mind or memory, a preoccupation of early Greeks. Still, for literate types, rejection of writing is an interesting opinion to ponder and perhaps once again relevant as we move online.

2. For those of you who read footnotes, I'm aware that I have overstated this case. There are cognitive changes that happen as a result of learning new languages, as there are for learning to play music or do math in one's head. And there are social advantages to not having to look up everything on your phone. Ubiquitous GPS may mean someday very few people will have any internal sense of place. Few people memorize much of anything these days and our brains are therefore different from those of our distant ancestors. Your great grandchildren won't think the way you do. My position here is merely pragmatic. Change is inevitable and therefore lifelong learning and the adaptive attitudes it requires are necessary for social advancement from now on. Minds will change no matter how set in our ways we are.

The vast majority of intellectual material is not online. People who restrict their purview to what's online have a deeply flawed and incomplete data set, a truncated world view. You can't just Google and Wikipedia your way to knowledge. As libraries continue to discard undigitized books (and records and posters and microfilm), so our knowledge of the past shrinks.

Agreed. I'll get to the real tragedy in a moment.

There's a variation of this argument that complains that digital forms are inferior to their analogue progenitors (e.g., "iPads, Hotels, and Learning," April 1, 2015, *Inside Higher Ed*), and studies showing that students retain more when reading from books and taking notes with pens and pencils instead of with computers. These two variations of the narrowing worldview opinion are misleading because the error that leads to lesser learning isn't the machine but the way the machine is used.

If you take notes verbatim, as you can if you can type as fast as a person can talk, then you aren't even listening let alone cognitively processing, synthesizing, connecting, or moving the contents of your short-term memory to long-term storage, nor are you practicing the critical cognitive activities that the inefficiency of pencil and paper force you to perform. The error is in thinking that verbatim is preferable to your distillation of the original. <aside>It's not hard to imagine Plato shrieking, "Put your confounded stylus and wax tablet down and answer my question you lazy . . ." (*Phaedrus* 238d)</aside>.[3] You can use a keyboard to facilitate synthesizing and connecting while the machine literally records verbatim in the background, so you can hear the lecture again if you want to. Better yet, listen and ponder as the machine records and then take notes after class. Then replay the recording while you ponder your notes. Active learning is far superior to scribbling like mad while the stooped-shouldered-one drones on.

As for complaining about how unusable a digital interface is as compared to the paper original, that's either a failure on the designer's part or a failure on the irritated user's part to understand the interface. These arguments against design and utility are based on refusal to learn and adapt. Believing an irrelevant truth (only a tiny part of the world's legacy has yet been digitized) will keep a person tied to the past. <aside>When as teachers we hand this belief down to our students, no matter how well backed up by "research" we are, we're merely extending the cultural lag into the next generation. Better at those moments that they really are playing Candy Crush *and* not paying attention to us.</aside>

Lamenting the loss of paper artifacts, and blaming the device for not accommodating our old ways of working, while refusing to learn how to make computers do what we know we need them to do, is tragic. Complaining and lamenting and ranting against the loss of a past era will only ensure its loss. If instead of complaining about the loss of print media every mourner grabbed as many paper documents as they could and started scanning like mad, and designing usable

---

3. `<aside>` is an actual HTML 5 element, unlike `<rant>`, which ought to be.

interfaces for content management systems through which they could share that content with others, our intellectual world would shrink that much less. And if everyone who stubbed their thumbs on a crap interface learned design and usability and stepped into the industry to make sure that at least their designs were human usable, then much more of the larger known would also be knowable. <peroration>There's no point in wailing as a tsunami roles in. Grab your children and run like hell for higher ground. </peroration></rant>

The upside to giving in

The longer we wait the more damage we do both to the legacy traditions we wish to sustain into the future and our relevance to intellectual life. Fortunately, there's more carrot than stick in the transition from print to mixed media if we're willing to retool and relearn.

It's not as though the traditional forms of rhetoric, public speaking, and prose composition are irrelevant today. They remain critically significant, and nothing benefits a career more than the ability to give a great speech (on camera). Prose too still matters, but digital words aren't exactly prose. The new features of rhetoric have to do with interactive and dynamic capacities of digital media that afford opportunities that paper and even face-to-face interactions can't.

Here's an extended example of how a digital reading experience can differ in positive and interesting ways from the print media experience.

Getting Alcidamas to "speak" for himself

Above I referred to Alcidamas and I gave a parenthetical reference to the text I was referring to. In a Works Cited section of a book you'd find a traditional reference of this kind:

> Alcidamas. "On the Sophists." Trans. LaRue Van Hook. *The Classical Weekly*. Vol 12, 1919.

Were you to have learned directly from Alcidamas in the predigital era, you'd have had to have access to an excellent library, which meant of course taking the time and energy to get up and go somewhere. You might have <irony>discovered that your library didn't have a copy of a journal published in 1919</irony>, and so you'd have had to wait for interlibrary loan to mail a photocopy of it to your library, at which point you'd have had to go back there to get it.

I suggested you Google Alcidamas because doing so would give you instant access to the text I was citing. From a writer's perspective, sending readers off to I-don't-know-where might be problematic. You might go. You might not come back. Even if you did come back, there would be a lengthy delay between the time you read Alcidamas and the time you picked *Writing Online* back up where you left off, although nowhere near as long as if you had to interlibrary loan the essay. I'd have no idea if you now knew what I was writing about or not. I'd need to assume you had done the background work if I were to continue, or I could, as I would in a literate rhetorical setting, summarize or paraphrase the text in question so I could make the argument I wanted to make (as I did with *Phaedrus*), while simultaneously increasing the literacy divide between those who have access to sources and those who have to accept the paraphrases of those who have access.

Digital rhetoric enables a completely different, more immediate, more dynamic kind of user–text interaction, or reader experience to use the old language, and therefore some different rhetorical options.

You could **link to the specific text** and thus offer it verbatim, such as

```
<A href="http://www.classicpersuasion.org/
pw/alcidamas/alcsoph1.htm">Alcidamas</a>
```

rather than asking the user to search. That way if I bothered to click the link I'd find what you wanted me to see and not other, perhaps distracting, things. But I'd have left your site and might or might not bother to press the Back button.

Alternatively, you could serve up Alcidamas' text **in a new tab:**

```
<A href="http://www.classicpersuasion.
org/pw/alcidamas/alcsoph1.htm" target="_
blank">Alcidamas</a>
```

The trade-off with this method is that sometimes users don't notice a new tab has opened. They think they did something but nothing has changed in their field of vision, bewildering them. You could make the Alcidamas piece pop up on hover using some CSS coding, but the "speech" is too long to be readable in that setting.

Alternatively, you could use an `<iframe></iframe>`:

```
<iframe src="http://www.classicpersuasion.
org/pw/alcidamas/alcsoph1.htm"></iframe>⁴
```

An `<iframe></iframe>` would allow the user to scroll the text in place, not having to leave your site while still reading the whole text, or at least skimming it some. Given that you know a user will likely skim, you could just offer a few salient quotations inline, in the body of the text you're writing, as you'd do for a paper-based academic article. Or if you aren't inclined to be dictatorial about what your users experience, you could display the entire text in the `<iframe></iframe>` so they can peruse the whole thing or parts of it as they wish. You could even mark that text up using CSS, providing commentary and additional references to supplement the text itself.

[[Search: iframe dimensions]]

There are other techniques for showing marginally relevant content while still retaining your user's attention. You can still use footnotes and endnotes, although since there's no real bottom to a screen and no end to the Internet, they're vestigial practices (in-place popups on hover are digital footnotes). You could reserve an area of the screen down either or both sides for displaying additional content when a user hovers over an annotated section, although again, that won't work

---

4. There's a potential copyright issue with this method. The text you put in an `<iframe></iframe>` needs to be public domain or your own work, else you're leaching someone else's content. That's unethical and libelous.

well for longer texts that require scrolling: Odd that both <metaphor>scrolling</metaphor> and <metaphor>marginalia</metaphor> have returned.

What other techniques can you think of for displaying additional information at the user's request (and otherwise hiding it so the screen remains uncluttered)?

Quizzing users

Even though as a digital writer you can provide me, your user, with everything you want me to experience all in one place, and thus maintain my attention while providing far more than can be found on a page or dozens of pages, the fact remains you don't know if I read or understood what you gave me, unless you interact with me. With some basic coding you can create a compelling facsimile of interaction. Later you'll learn how to actually interact.

Offering a text in an electronic form enables the opportunity for self-paced testing that would let a user know if he or she understands what's necessary before deciding to move on:

```
Which of the following is a deleterious
effect of literacy according to Alcidamas?
a) Ruin your eyesight
b) Dull your wits
c) Introvert you
d) All of the above
```

There's an example of all this on the website, under Sections/Rhetoric+/Reading. There you'll find the code for making a dynamic multiple-choice test with answers. The example is dynamic in the simple sense that the text changes based on what a user does. But it's not dynamic in the more complex sense of getting information from elsewhere and presenting that information to the user based on his or her choices. The script I've given you also isn't truly interactive in the sense that I'll never know what you clicked on or what you did after you clicked. A more sophisticated script could send user action data back to me and I could then offer further instruction or additional information. Even the simple example I'm giving you could be designed to withhold further information until the user clicked on the correct answer.

Dynamic interaction is the essence of what's known as adaptive learning and when coupled with what's called machine learning—the fact that software can draw inferences about thinking patterns from user behavior and thus offer smart hints that guide insight or at least relevant recall—promises a great deal for the future of learning technologies. Adaptive software, however, encourages passivity on the part of the learner and also encourages an impulse to game the system— for example, keep choosing options at random until it gives you the answer.[5] At

5. I'm being intentionally simplistic here. There are ways to keep people from just guessing until the answer is given, by ticking the points awarded down to zero, for example. For my purposes, encouraging you to make your own simple question/ answer machines is plenty. If you're ready to move on, don't let me stand in your way.

any rate, building your own simple question, hint, and answer testing systems is a great way to verify that you know something because it's a highly active learning activity. You not only have to figure out what the answer is, you have to figure out the question and some plausible but incorrect answers as well. In other words, **making the test requires far deeper learning than taking the test.**

Mid-chapter assignment: Practicing digital composition

Head over to the website at this point, if you haven't already (Sections/Rhetoric+/ Reading), and hack about with the Alcidamas example. If you want to go at this hard core, read the Alcidamas piece and then write some good questions in place of my very perfunctory examples. If you don't care for the Alcidamas piece, create a test for something else. What other kinds of digital rhetoric could you accomplish with the hide/show toggle technique?

Finally, I've left a highly CSS- and JavaScript-stylized version of Plato's complaint about writing (*Phaedrus* 274–277) for you on the website, Sections/Rhetoric+/Texts. After looking at the source code for it, find a brief piece of electronic text that you can provide popup marginalia for and see if you can make your own example of digital rhetoric.

[[Search: Trithemius, "In Praise of Scribes"]]

The piece doesn't have to be from the history of rhetoric to qualify. You want something that you can provide some deep background on, something you can <metaphor>footnote</metaphor> thoroughly using glosses, images, links, video, and further elaborations in the form of words.

You could use about2.0.html for this project instead of some other electronic text. Can you make a Google Map pop up when a user hovers over the city or town you were born in? What about pictures of your parents? Maybe that becomes about3.0.html.

Digital citizenship

Determining the reliability of information

Differentiating truth from illusion and identifying bad deals before you make them has never been easy. While the web doesn't worsen that fact of life, it does increase the frequency with which you have to judge the veracity of information and the reliability of the people who seem to be offering that information. The rules of oral and literate rhetoric still apply. **You can trust people who share your interests or will fairly benefit from your benefiting.** The problem for digital citizens is that machines can be mistaken for people and people can hide behind machines. In the predigital world, a shady character who offered inferior goods or inflated prices would be run out of town or at least put out of business soon enough because word would spread like a virus, and since moving from town to town wasn't always an option and in any case required real effort, people might think twice about swindling their neighbors. But on the web you can pack up and move out and set up shop down the road just by clicking a button or two. Anonymity, the absences of a physical location, the low cost of (re)production, and the highly mobile nature of digital existence make it easy for people who have nefarious tendencies to prey on the digitally innocent and difficult for people who get taken advantage of to find justice. **There are no digital neighbors.** Bullying, phishing, spamming, trolling, and scamming—all manner of ill-mannered rhetorical behaviors are greatly enabled by anonymity and the immaterial nature of the web.

Let me give you some rhetorical advice based on those premises. (If you'd like to question those premises, I encourage you to do so. I too have found more than a few helpful, faceless, pseudonymous, avatar-souls online.)

[[Search: crowd sourcing]]

Read online reviews suspiciously. Companies pay people to write positive reviews about them and to trash their competitors. People caught in the grip of fandom will trash their love's competitors for free. People set up websites with the intention of reporting on an industry but end up merely plugging their heroes and castigating their villains. Realize that bots can Tweet, that Astroturf grows faster than grass roots, that algorithms provide advice. Just as you can't judge a person by their smile or a book by its cover, you can't judge a company by its website (unless the company is the website, which is more and more the case these days). As with all facets of uncertainty in life, verify and cross check. Ask around; don't be impressed by logos or digital edifices. **Look for disconfirmation.** Make online purchases with a spending-limited credit card. Use a disposable email address (your-online-self.com comes with as many email addresses as you want) for purchases so your primary inbox doesn't fill up with ads and junk. Use nonsense phrases for passwords instead of single words, no matter how creatively speiied (*sic*). When practical, use two-factor authentication. Use the browse incognito or private browsing function of your web browser. Turn cookies off. Turn remember passwords off. Think twice before enabling location awareness or sharing contacts. Don't use autofill on any mobile computer—any computer that might get stolen or one you might accidentally walk away from. **Consider practicing a little inauthenticity for self-defense.**

[[Search: Astroturfing]]

[[Search: *New York Times*, "The Agency"]]

Social and content marketing

Exposition is prose designed to inform or explain. Exposition is supposed to be objective in the sense of not being biased toward or away from any specific perspective. A sales pitch by contrast is language designed to create desire and belief. It often uses grandiose language, exaggerated claims, and prose designed to disarm and charm its readers. Marketers have known for years that if you can dress a sales pitch in expository language, you can disarm your potential buyers and thus have a better chance of charming them, getting them to accept the promises for health and happiness and popularity that come from using your shampoo, for instance.

Content marketing takes this approach to the next level. By using blogs and infomercials, sometimes in prose form, the appearance of objective reporting is maintained while the buy-this message gets slipped in. You'd expect to find ads for products on a company's website, and you do, but since marketers know this they indirectly market their material by paying other people to write about relevant topics and offer the occasional plug for a product: the more indirect, the subtler, the better. I read a full-page article in a men's fashion magazine recently that offered advice about how to do your laundry, use cold water more often than hot, don't machine wash your jeans, take your suits to the cleaners only a few times a year, the triangle on the label means bleach, and so on. Among the advice was a brief mention of a recently manufactured appliance for steam dry cleaning your clothes. Because I saw this page in a magazine, I assume they were paid to mention the product and that the layout person knew where best to place it. There's currently a very robust industry for content marketing, and if you're good with language and can develop an interesting take on a lucrative market, you can blog your way to a six-figure income without investing more than time. Mind you, for every six-figure winner there are hundreds of thousands of folks who blog diligently away making nothing ever.

Another common form of indirect advertising that you need to be aware of is the paid search. When you search for something you get a list of links in return. Typically there are two or three at the top of the page that comes back and a few down the right side that appear there because the owners of those websites paid to make that happen, using a price for keyword formula. We tend to think that the highest place on the list of links is reserved for the most relevant result, but that's inaccurate. The highest goes to the highest bidder. After that, place goes to relevance determined by algorithms that privilege number of sites that link to a site, the frequency of the search term's use on the screen being linked to, metadata contained on the site, frequency of views, and so on.

[[Search: search engine optimization (SEO)]]

If you're a part of the Googlesphere—that is, if you have a Gmail account and use Chrome and login while you're online—then Google knows what you're searching for. Even if you aren't logged in, Google will offer ads based on what you searched for and your geographical location. If you haven't noticed this technique before, try it. Search for a product of some kind and then count the number of times you see an ad for it as you go about your infotainment business.

Here's an example from the somewhat distant past: on Wednesday, September 19, 2007, I uploaded a picture of our pug into Facebook (the last time I uploaded a picture into Facebook, btw.) Seconds later, this is what my screen looked like.

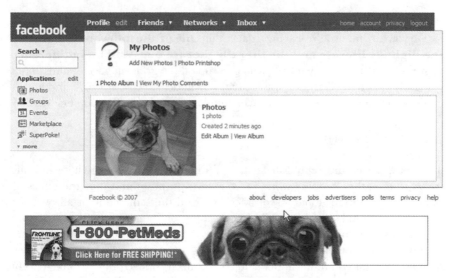

In the past websites used what were called cookies to track users. Typically they simply wrote a small text file to your computer that identified your machine. Then on the server side they were able to track when you were last at the site, where you came from, what you looked at, and how long you stayed. They used this information to tailor their site to user preferences and interest but also to advocate for better deals with advertisers. The more unique visitors and the more frequent each visitor, the more they could charge for their ad spaces. Cookies are being superseded by sophisticated position-tracking tools that work because so many of us are on our phones all the time and have location awareness enabled. Now we can get ads for products on sale in our vicinity, deals at nearby restaurants, sale prices for airfare to places we just searched about, and so on. In return for making ourselves available for such marketing opportunities, we can know how far we are from home and how long given current traffic it will take to get there, and what the weather forecast is, and how our stocks are doing, and pretty much any other real-time information we want, all of which of course goes back to the marketing departments. You can think of your "smart" phone as the ultimate cookie, GPS aware and always checking in with headquarters. Every time you're on any website that you log in to, the same thing is happening: **you're giving your data to corporations with the result that they can target you for specific marketing attempts.** Everything you do online is data someone or something is using to address you rhetorically.

Knowing that your online activities are being recorded, in the aggregate and anonymously for the most part, and stored as data that can be used by corporations and companies and sold or subpoenaed, means knowing that you're never alone online and thus should use a computer (or phone) always as though you're doing so in public. There's no expectation of privacy. There are very few truly personal spaces anymore either. <melodrama>If your phone is on, you're a blinking light on any one of perhaps hundreds of digital maps.</melodrama>

[[Search: virtual private network (VPN)]]

Do you care that you're leaving a data trail? **One of the differences between the digitally literate and the literally literate may well be indifference to privacy.** Perhaps only people who grew up off the grid will have qualms about being always on it. Perhaps "transparency" will dethrown "privacy" and a generation from now no one will know what thinking in isolation from others was like.

The ethics of reuse

The copy, paste, and republish facility of digital rhetoric makes it technically trivial to use other people's work for your own purposes and thus the ethics of reuse is an important topic to consider. You find the same content all over the web, often rebranded and unattributed. As a person intent on crafting a positive digital presence, you don't want to engage in these practices, so you need to find (write) material you can legitimately use. Images are especially important when designing digital communications and so you need to learn how to take decent photographs. You also need to know where to find photographs you can fairly use. There's a dropdown list of such sources on the website (Designs/Launch Pads+/News Stand).

It's tempting to lament the loss of individuality that copy-and-paste rhetoric seems to invite, but it's historically inaccurate to consider the phenomenon of "borrowing" a digital invention, as Earle Havens explains:

> Though the Latin verb *legere* was commonly used in the
> ancient world to denote the act of reading, it also meant to
> single out, select, extract, gather, collect, even to plunder and
> purloin. In the classical sense of the word, reading was by
> no means a passive or receptive act. At its most basic level,
> reading was an inherently active, discriminating, and selective
> exercise. One did not merely encounter a text; one harvested
> it, separating the wheat from the tares in order to glean the
> pith and marrow. The term also signified a kind of rapine,
> even the violent confiscation of the fruit of another man's tree.
> (8) *A History of Manuscripts and Printed Books from Antiquity to the
> Twentieth Century*

At least now we don't have to *cut*-and-paste. We don't have to literally rip pages out of books or take from one person to have for ourselves.

[[Search: Jefferson Bible]]

Copyright is an historical phenomenon, which isn't to say that ownership doesn't matter or that all intellectual property wants to be free. It's just to observe that the rhetoric of an era is a complex of expectations, practices, laws, experiences, and opportunities, ways of being that lead to ways of thinking and not just a set of "rules" one learns to follow or even laws one is punished for breaking. It's merely the ease of replication and reconfiguration that differentiates digital rhetoric from its ancestors in this regard.

When you put a file on a server you're making it public, and if you aren't careful about displaying copyrighted material, you're almost certainly going to get a cease-and-desist order from the owners of the copyright. Using other people's CSS and JavaScript and code is a slightly different case. Unless the author has explicitly forbidden its reuse or hidden or encrypted the code and you weaseled it, you can copy and paste at will. But be kind and responsible. If the code you have your eye on is just another example from many examples, you needn't give credit. But if the code writer offered something unique or explained how it works, you should give credit.

Obviously there's a great deal more to be said about copyright and the Internet. Copy-and-paste culture has created entirely new genres that rely on "borrowed" material, mashups (digital collages), fanzines, sampling, and Photoshop battles. If it's been done it can be redone. There's an element of homage involved in the conscious sampling of others' work, but there's also the potential for theft and abuse of others' ideas, just as if you quote someone out of context you're mistreating them.

You needn't become a copyright lawyer to safely navigate web content creation, but you should make a point of learning the basics.

[[Search: creative commons]]

Anonymity and accountability

Anonymity breeds audacity, cruelty, stupidity, and acquiescence. I've noticed that a number of websites have removed their leave-a-comment feature specifically because keeping up with the trolls and the nutters is more trouble than it's worth. Such write-to-the-site features are also security threats as infectious scripts can attack servers. Still, the collaborative spirit of interactive communication that the web enables shouldn't be entirely stifled. Some reviews are helpful, which is of course why you can rate reviews on sites that sell products, since reviews of reviews enable a kind of informal, community-based policing. If you've got something truly insightful *and* useful to say, say it quickly and move on. Better yet, contribute to the conversation openly and directly through your-online-self.com, and thus hold yourself publically accountable.

By far the most significant difference between digital rhetoric and its predecessors is the fact that the camera is always rolling and nothing is ever forgotten. Everything you do online leaves a trail that's being recorded. With great effort you may be able to cover your tracks but by default, the way most of us use the Internet, everything we do is discoverable. In addition, because the vast majority of files take up very little space and computer memory is cheap, everything is out there forever. **When you delete something, you're really just hiding it.** You can delete (thankfully), but system admins can undelete stuff you'd rather the world forgot about. Predigital, our youthful follies remained in the memories of a handful of people who shared them with us. You'd have to do something really stunningly foolish to land in the paper. Today, as you've heard endlessly, no doubt, every indiscretion recorded online becomes something anyone can learn about you. The Internet is constantly looking for the next meme, the next new thing. **The Internet's attention span is nearly null, but it never forgets.**

Given these premises, there are at least two relevant conclusions regarding etiquette in the digital age: expect to see a great deal of ill-mannered and uneducated nonsense online, and don't get sucked into the vortex. Don't respond immediately to any comment or post that has a visceral effect on you. Don't let people bait you. At the same time, don't let your own enthusiasm take what you say or how you respond over the top. Anything you do online will remain forever. And anything you do in the presence of a digital camera, which is essentially everywhere today, can find its way online and thus live forever. Life on the web is a strange mixture of oceanic anonymity and the possibility of getting picked out by a spotlight. So if you're going to dance like no one's watching, just remember that someday someone might be.

As far as your-online-self.com goes, remember that you're building a professional reputation. This isn't a personal home page or an open letter. This is your digital epicenter, the beacon of your brand, a constant source of proof of your credibility and relevance to the communities you want to join and serve.

[[Search: Wayback machine]]

Digital skepticism

Apart from understanding that everything you do online is data of potential profit to a wide range of industries, NGOs, and governments, and realizing that the world of digital work will continue to have profound effects on how we live, not least of which will be ever-increasing shorter subcontracts at more and more companies, it's important, I think, to develop a skeptical or at least reserved anti-fan attitude to the next disruption, the next big "advance," the next big change, because there's another one coming after that. Industries and therefore ways of life that have existed for decades have been disappearing as quickly as you can say "download music," and the disposable nature of digital, indeed all, products along with the rhetorical emphasis on the ever new means that much of the work we do today is ephemeral. What's written in stone can last millennia. Acid-free paper can last hundreds of years. Theoretically, a digital object could last as long as there are power sources to run a device that can read it, but storage devices come and go and the sheer volume of digital assets devalues the vast majority of all of them to the point where many digital assets won't last much longer than the attention span of the people who made them in the first place, even if these assets float endlessly in the vacuum of digital space.

I'm not being grotesquely pessimistic. I'm just pointing out that riding accelerating rates of change means giving up and giving away as much as it means finding the next thing worth working on and thinking about. **Above all you have to give up the idea that education is a product or commodity, something you buy and then own.** Learning is a way of life. Even credentials stale-date. What did you do last week? Forget about last year. What are you learning this week? What's your exit strategy and where is your next landing pad? These are questions your immediate ancestors faced only once in their early twenties. In the digital world you'll have to answer them constantly anew. So it's a good idea to keep a light touch on each new digital thing. Leasing is the new ownership. It's not just that you can't take it with you when you die. You won't want to pack and ship it when you move. Your grandparents had record collections and libraries. What does it mean that you don't? Certainly not that you're less learned or less socially competent. But you're different because your artifacts are digital. Unless of course you're opting out. (Did you notice the last paragraph contained two sentence fragments? Did that bother you?)

Just because you can't opt out of the digital revolution doesn't mean you have to unthinkingly embrace the next big shiny thing. Ponder it. Take it apart. Put it back together and then think about how to reconfigure it. What are the social *and* technological implications? What are the possibilities? Will it be much better a year from now? What will replace it? How will it change how you work, and will the changes be enhancements or disruptions? Can you afford to keep doing what you've always done?

Digital ethos

Ethos is the art of creating a positive impression. Traditionally (oratorically) ethos is about establishing credibility through good will, good sense, and practical ability, demonstrating with one's words that one's advice is worth taking because it's being offered by a knowledgeable person who has the audience's best interests at heart. The basic model was that of the heroic figure, the slayer of snakes and solver of problems, a deep confident voice, a firm handshake, a quick wit, an unshakable, unblinking determination, either saying what the audience wants to hear or preparing them effectively for unavoidable bad news. It didn't hurt if you were tall and good looking and athletic (and male), characteristics commonly accepted as signs of competence.

In the literate tradition, where the author isn't visible to his or her readers, these same values are operationalized by carefully constructed grammatically correct sentences that address a specific issue relevant to the reader's needs and crafted to conform to their expectations or to exceed them in valued ways. If the author is attractive, then his or her publicist has an easier time using their image to sell books. Charisma and the cult of personality would still apply in many cases. But the author's appearance and personal mythology is less important than in oral cultures. The chief difference between oral and literate ethos is that oral ethos is performed live in a shared context while literate ethos has to somehow either transcend a local context or create a context that readers are willing to accept. If a book is addressed to old people who have suffered much in life, young people will have a hard time caring or perhaps fully understanding. Perhaps a few with an "old soul's" sensibility would get it, but only that select few. If a video game captures the imaginations and attentions of the young and the youthful, it might well leave a few olds clucking.

Digital ethos shares qualities from both the literate and the oral traditions. Beautiful spokespeople can make great advocates on a website.

[[Search: good girl Gina]]

A short video can create a vivid impression much quicker than many carefully crafted sentences because of the charismatic affordances video supplies. If video is impractical, photographs carry a similar level of impact, while a slideshow over music might make an even greater impact. Prose alone can carry the day only if the users are readerly types, people who prefer to get their information from words and are literate in the language you're using. The fact that a digital user might come from any community, speaking and reading any language, makes crafting a content management system (to say nothing of a static website) that reaches all people equally well a very difficult thing to accomplish. **The more you say, the harder it is for any of it to be heard.** Huge corporations can hire many people to run websites designed for each nation they do business with, but most organizations can't take a coverage approach. So for most, the best approach is to say only what's necessary and let your users infer everything else.

[[Search: TL;DR]]

Digital ethos takes this minimalistic approach beyond prose style to navigation and design. People tend to be impatient when reading from screens, even the most current high-resolution ones. If they aren't just killing time by flitting from this to that and checking on what their friends, acquaintances, and rivals are up to, they're seeking information to do something. In such information-focused cases, there are almost always thousands of alternatives just a click away. Given this need for task-oriented efficiency, **the default digital ethos emphasizes clarity, brevity, currency, and usability** (no meta language, no self-reflection, no self-consciousness, no anecdotes, no editorializing, no ego-involvement, nothing that will tax a user's working memory). Basically, you should organize and present your information so a user can find what he or she wants within a second of landing on your site, which means anticipating their needs and designing such that reading isn't necessary for more than a few sentences or phrases at a time: think lists, not paragraphs.

High-level example of an effective digital ethos

If a user comes to a DMV site, for example, and has to read political position papers before finding the form she needs to fill out to renew her license, she will figure the DMV is a lousy organization, not just that their website is a mess but that the organization itself is a mess. The DMV's ethos will be ruined no matter how well written the political position papers are or how in line with the user those opinions might be. The best possible site in the DMV case would accelerate the old-world experience of going to the DMV and interacting with a person.

In the past you'd drive or take the bus to the DMV, take a number, wait in line, and when your turn came, you'd tell a person, "I want to renew my driver's license," and they'd hand you the relevant form. A great website would offer the same result without requiring you to go to the place or wait in line or interact with a person. You would see the words, "What may we do for you?" printed on a screen next to a dropdown selection box with all of the possible functions listed in alphabetical order. You identify your need and the machine provides what's necessary, a form more than likely. If a person needs to know something or to have other documents ready before he or she can fill out the form, then there should be some kind of interactive preface to the form, tick each box that applies, okay, here's your form, or sorry, but you need X and Y before you can proceed. **A well-designed screen contains the least number of words necessary to make a relevant statement unambiguously.**

Your digital ethos?

For your-online-self.com you might want to be slightly less information-centric and slightly more self-centric, letting your personality show. This is your-online-self.com after all. But you need to think about how you want the world to perceive you because how you're perceived directly affects what people will think you can do, which has a direct impact on the opportunities you get. A great place to start might be by offering information your intended field will find useful. Ideally, people should be able to infer your competence and energy and ability to contribute value from what you say and how efficiently you say it. Asserting those qualities of yourself is counterproductive. **Saying "I'm a hard worker" is far less convincing than listing your many valuable accomplishments.**

The highest goal for your-online-self.com will be to have something worth knowing that no one else is offering, a service, or an insight or a uniquely valuable perspective, or a piece of quickly appreciated digital creativity. Most of your real networking will take place in social media sites like LinkedIn, Tumblr, Instagram, Pinterest, and Facebook, where millions of people are already standing by. Your-online-self.com is more like a homestead, a digital space you plan to build your brand on over time. You could make it essentially a blog site, with daily or weekly posts, but that means writing something daily or weekly and that gets old quickly. It's just hard to write anything worth reading with that kind of frequency. I started keeping a blog in 2004, after writing the code for it. The last entry was April 2011, hardly a record but not a bad run. I realized very quickly, however, that trying to sustain an ethos and develop a following was way beyond the nature of my real work, and so within a year or so, my blog became basically a digital notebook organized chronologically for the most part (because I was keeping it in blog software, not because the nature of the material made best sense that way) but by subject as well. I wasn't writing for others even though I left what I was doing open for the world to see.

So if you don't have the necessary enthusiasm (and content) for daily writing, design a system that offers regular links to interesting things other people have written and reserve your regular content for much shorter summaries. Aggregate the field's news for other members of the field. Even if you end up mostly aggregating for yourself, anyone who finds what you've been doing will be impressed by your industry and, if nothing else, you'll have a great resource for your own purposes.

Ethos and social networking

While traditionally ethos has always been about representation of character through words and forms of expression, from the beginning the concept has been extended to reputation, as people who have earned a reputation often deserve it. So the more you can accomplish the more opportunities you'll have to achieve because people will increasingly trust you. In a digital context ethos thus includes the practice of maintaining your social networks through whatever tools you choose to use. The most common ones—LinkedIn, Facebook, Twitter, Pinterest, Instagram, and so on—all contribute to what shows up when someone looks for you online, and thus having a strategy (which might include opting out or minimal participation) is an important part of being digitally literate.

As with most things, starting out doing some research about how best to use each of the available tools is important. You might also want to consider developing a K score. Klout.com is a social networking tool that offers an assessment of your social networking influence by aggregating data from all of your social network tools. You receive a score from 0, a nonentity, to 100, a person with Taylor Swiftian levels of social influence. While tweaking elements to achieve a desired score (i.e., gaming a system) strikes me as a waste of time, you might learn a coherent strategy from figuring out how K scores work.

Whether you choose to use Klout.com as your strategy or some other means, your digital ethos is ultimately about Googling well, to put it in the most general terms. For what it's worth, to me the correct approach is to let your work precede your reputation. Let concrete evidence of your abilities drive the buzz.

Digital <metaphor>audience</metaphor>

Traditionally (oratorically), an audience consists of every voting member of a community present when a decision has to be made or those gathered to appreciate an artistic performance. This is Aristotle's explicit understanding in *Rhetoric*. The chief characteristics of an audience are copresence and codependence; each individual is an equal member of the community who succeeds or fails as the community does, ideally at least. While the jurors in a trial are part of the audience, because they have the communal weight of decision on their hands, the accused is not a member of the audience, since his fate hangs in the balance. If acquitted he returns to the status of one who might once again join an audience, but if convicted, he may never regain the status of citizen and so never be a member of that audience again, even were he to somehow be standing in the crowd of onlookers.

When the world became literate, traditional audiences remained important, as did the rhetoric that informs how to work with them, but a distributed audience became relevant to writers. The audience thus became readers. The number of people who might become a member of a writer's readership includes people not present, not voting, and potentially as yet unconceived. The chief difference between oral and literate rhetoric is that while speakers had to infer context from the situation and anticipate how the moment might morph as words were spoken, authors needed to create context, set the scene from which readers were expected to draw inferences about what was happening, to construct a virtual audience out of a conceptual readership. For this to work, a reader, for the most part at least, needed organized schooling, so that one could learn the orthodox methods of interpretation and composition.

Digital audiences share qualities of both the oratorical and the literate audiences. Because it's possible for the world to see a digital performance the moment it's posted online, there's a chance that millions of people might see the same digital act simultaneously.

[[Search: smart mobs]]

Such a coalescence of people in different parts of the world, speaking different languages, inhabiting different contexts, and leading very different kinds of lives with different unrelated needs, wouldn't vote directly, so no such governing body exists (yet), but they might draw sufficient attention to a happening to forge a globally dominant opinion or cause such a stir online that local authorities would respond as if to a virtual vote. This kind of **digital audience is more like a swarm than a congregation or a jury.** They're powerful but ephemeral. They're there for a moment and then they are gone forever, leaving little to no trace of having been, more often than not. The Arab Spring has long since faded.

The more common digital <metaphor>audience</metaphor>, however, shares characteristics with a literate readership. They encounter the digital message not just in different places but also at different times. A chief difference, however, is that many of the people engaging with digital information are looking for information to perform a task, fix a problem, or explain a phenomenon—to do something. Users are focused on a task that isn't reading or watching but requires reading or watching. They want the source of information to be simple, fast, efficient, and effective. They don't want to admire the interface or ponder the complexity of their task. The author is decentered. The prose is transparent, as is the interface.

Now it's true that people enjoy immersive experiences online: movies, games, graphic novels, and animations, even novels and poems. If deep creative content is your-online-self.com's goal, file the task-oriented orientation of my advice under for what it's worth. Most of the people I know would rather read a novel in book form than read a digital variant. Current sales figures seem to indicate a plateau for e-book sales. The important thing here is that the novel is a paper genre, arguably one that has already been replaced by the serial video drama in the public's imagination. The 19th century had the serial novel (e.g., Dickens). The 20th century had the sitcom (e.g., "All in the Family"). We have The Wire.[6]

6. Feel free to swap out my examples for your own. If you were going to replace the last four sentences with an online asset, how might you swap the content of the examples dynamically?

[[Search: digital book sales flattening]]

Another characteristic of the digital audience that we need to keep in mind is that they can, if we enable them, offer feedback in the form of comments or ratings.

We can consult them like beta testers (even without their awareness) and so constantly change and refine a digital project based on data about successes and failures. Any digital object that's maintained remains in a constant state of change. Usually the changes are made with an eye toward improvement but objects also bloat and morph. Not every release is an incremental improvement. This is because of the flow of feedback. Digital users are far more promiscuous than either the literate readers or the oratorical audiences. You don't even need to know how to read to learn from digital objects. Digital audiences are neither invited nor qualified. They just show up, often anonymously, and then just as quickly disappear.

If you have a signup feature, you can track specific user actions and perhaps develop a sense of community, people working together for individual gains that benefit the group. But often a signup requirement will turn people off. This is why we see so many freemium deals on the web, try before you buy, and so many services that let you watch others for free but require you to sign up to participate. **Building a virtual community thus becomes a primary goal of the digital rhetor.** Whereas orators spoke directly to the people with whom they lived and so were born into an audience for the most part, and authors wrote for a universal audience or an abstract "dear reader," and therefore had to create a conceptual audience out of what they knew about educated (literate) people, concrete representatives of which groups they'd have from their days in school and their experiences with contemporary literary and literate people, the digital rhetor has the potential to create a community in the digital space he or she is designing that might consist of a hugely diverse population of people from anywhere at all, with nearly any background and education, anyone of whom might offer feedback or even contribute content if so enabled, but only in very rare circumstances would they "vote" in any real sense. Liking and disliking come about as close to a vote as there is.

Given the capacity for websites to translate the language they're written in, a digital rhetor might even be interacting with people of differing languages. He might attract repeat visitors, some of whom might contribute content directly or offer constructive feedback that enables him to refine his messages and tailor the experience he provides so that eventually he has a digital audience, people who share an experience, a goal or a set of goals, and who return regularly. Such a digital community might eventually exist as a contact list or an email list, enabling the digital rhetor to incorporate them into a new project, thus building a digital community that might transcend the current context and allow for mutual involvement over time.

User comments

One way to build community is to give users an opportunity to interact with your content and each other through your content. The most common way is to invite users to leave a comment on a given article. Head over to Sections/Rhetoric+/ Audience+/User Comments and see if you can **write a form that will take content from the web and print it to a file.** Once you've got it working, think from a technical perspective about how you might incorporate user comments into your-online-self.com.

Letting people write to your server is dangerous in several different ways. A leave-a-comment feature offers an opportunity for trolls, bots, haters, and the rest of the Internet's menagerie of mal and discontents, to deface your efforts, to say nothing of hacker attacks. So once you've learned how to enable commenting, think carefully about whether or not you want to use what you've learned how to do. **Just because you can doesn't mean you should.** At the very least you're going to have to vet what your users offer as content, distinguish the graffiti from the scams, the kudos from the come-ons and the farq-ues.

There are several things beyond safety to consider here. For one thing, if you have a number of users leaving comments, you'll have to accommodate an ever-lengthening section of user-generated content. Do you want to put the comments at the bottom, as is customary? Or would putting them on the side offer some kind of benefit? What about attaching a comment box to a part of a larger screen, say as part of a column in a multicolumn layout? If you're inviting input from users after the fashion of comments in the margins, perhaps you want to tie a comment box to each paragraph or at least each section. That would get complicated quickly, of course, but **you can do it.**

If you head over to the website now to see if you can get user-generated content working, it may be a few hours (or days) before you come back to this part of the book. That's fine—good even. Writing from the web to a file is a very valuable piece of digital rhetoric and one worth struggling with. What I've left for you online will get you started, but you should take more time with it than simply copying and pasting.

Password protection

If you're going to allow comments, then you need to take some safety precautions. One way to keep spammers, scammers, and trolls out is to password protect the part of the site that allows comments. You could require users to ask permission to participate and then when you've checked them out, email (or text) them the password. There are more secure authentication methods than what I'm offering below, but this will get you started:

```
<?

$username = "username"; // whatever you
want
$password = "password"; // whatever you
want

if (!isset($_SERVER['PHP_AUTH_USER'])) {
// show login
```

```
header('WWW-Authenticate: Basic
realm="your-online-self"');
header('HTTP/1.0 401 Unauthorized');
echo 'Text to send if user presses Cancel
button';
exit();

} else {
if (($_SERVER['PHP_AUTH_USER'] ==
$username) && ($_SERVER['PHP_AUTH_PW'] ==
$password)) { // verify
echo " Welcome message";
} else {

echo "The username and/or password you
have entered is incorrect!"; // feedback
on failure
exit();      // stop if fail
}
}
?>
```

[[Search: CAPTCHA]]

There are several different ways to password protect a file or a directory of files. This one isn't very sophisticated. For one thing, because everyone logs in with the same login and password there's no way to track who is doing what. Because everyone has the same identity, you can't provide different content to different levels of user. Also, because the password is the same, anyone can give it to anyone else and you have no control over that. You could at least change the login and password periodically and then your users would have to touch base with you to continue their access.

[[Search: .access]]

You can find a working example under Sections/Communications/Audience/User Passwords. In Chapter 5 on digital memory there's another technique that uses a database for user authentication.

Location awareness

Here's another relatively simple example of how digital information can be tailored for different users. Websites can know where you're looking at them from, which means they can target their advertisements for you and even make use of current events to tailor messages based on the city or region you live in. On the website, under Sections/ Audience+/User Awareness you'll find the following PHP code:

```
<?
$ip = $_SERVER['REMOTE_ADDR'];
$details = json_decode(file_get_
contents("http://ipinfo.io/{$ip}/json"));
```

```
echo "You're in ".$details->city;<br>
echo "<br>Your browser is: ".$_
SERVER['HTTP_USER_AGENT']."<br>";
echo "<br>Your language is: ".$lang = substr
($_SERVER['HTTP_ACCEPT_LANGUAGE'], 0, 2);
echo "<br>You came from: ".$_SERVER['HTTP_
REFERER'];
?>
```

If you copy and paste that code from the website, name it anything with the .php extension, when you browse to that URL you'll see what city you're in, what language your computer is using, which browser you're using, and the URL you were at before arriving on the page.

[[Search: $_SERVER]]

As written here, the information stays on the user's side. But you could rewrite this script to send you the information. Or use it to alter what a given user sees.

Because I can know what city you're viewing my website from, I can tailor my message to you that much more closely. Because I can know what browser you're using, I can offer a style sheet that fits it exactly. Because I know what language you're using I can respond accordingly.[7]

In the digital epoch you no longer need to spend time with people directly to influence them directly, nor do you need to be addressing people who are fundamentally or at least educationally like you. You can know people you've never met. You can influence them without them even knowing you exist. You don't even need to speak their language or share their education or their values. You don't even need to be a human being. The idea of the universal literati, that all readers are fundamentally the same, ignores the profound regulatory effect education has on people. If there ever were a universal reader it was because there was a universal method of education. To be literate was to share a set of interpretive practices, expectations, values, and attitudes. Part of learning to read is learning to pretend to be a certain kind of person until one actually becomes that kind of person. **Digital rhetoric makes it possible to replace the fiction of the universal reader with real, and real-time, knowledge of who is out there based on where they are, what they're doing, what they're liking and disliking, whom they friend, whom they LinkedIn with, and so on.**

Your online self is more transparent than you might think

If you've ever been offered something in return for your email address, and you entered your actual email address, you've revealed your identity, of course. But have you ever been to a website that asked for your birthday? What about your zip code? If you offer both of those pieces of information to the same site, the owner of that site is very close to identifying you personally. Give them your gender

---

7. I'm speaking hypothetically here, my website doesn't know any of those things.

and they have you. All of this is explained beautifully at the Electronic Frontier Foundation's "A Primer on Information Theory and Privacy." If you put a form on your website that requests this information and offers some incentive for filling it out, you can assemble a database of actual people without ever meeting any of them (and without their knowledge if they're digitally innocent). The reverse is also true. The apparent anonymity of the web is an illusion easily pierced by anyone who knows even a little bit about digital sleuthing. To get a sense of this, go to https://panopticlick.eff.org/.

[[Search: Digital Advertising Alliance]]

Web forms

A web form is an interface that asks users to enter information that's then stored on the company's servers, typically in a database. Every time you buy something online you fill out a form, unless you're a repeat buyer and gave the company permission to auto-populate the form on your return. Or set your browser up to do that:

```
<form name="creepy" >
<input type = "text" name="zip">
<input type = "text" name="bday">
<input type = "text" name="gender">
</Form>
```

Open your plain text editor. Type the preceding code into a new file and save it as creepy.html. View it. Useless, right? How do you modify that code to make it useable? And how would you need to style it to make it pleasing to look at? And finally, what do you need to make it functional?

To make it useable you need to tell the user what she's looking at and what to do:

```
<form name="creepy">
<input type = "text" name="zip" value =
"Please enter your     zip code">
<input type = "text" name="bday" value =
"Please enter your birthday">
<input type = "text" name="gender" value =
"Please enter your gender">
<input type = "submit" name="submit">
</form>
```

There's a potential problem with this form as written. How do you write your birthday? Does everyone do it that way? If the user input can come in various forms, then you have to have some way to parse what comes to make it machine usable—for a birthday to be meaningful to a machine either all birthdays need to look the same, such as mm/dd/yy, or you have to rationalize whatever you get—that is, turn all birthdays into the same form. Because transforming dd/mm/yyyy into mm/dd/yy is beyond this book at this point, what can you do to improve the chances your users will do the work for you? You could provide a lead and hope the users follow it:

```
<input type = "text" name="bday" value =
"mm/dd/yy">
```

You have the same problem with gender (m for male? f for female?). Because the number of possible responses is relatively small, unlike with birthdays, you could offer a dropdown menu that would force the user to choose and let you determine what the choices look like to the machine. For instance:

```
<select>
<option name = "female" value = "f">
<option name = "male" value = "m">
</select>
```

Alternatively, you could use a checkbox:

```
<Input type = "checkbox" value - "1">
```

If you did that, you could just offer one box with a value set to 1 and let the machine interpret null as 0, but that would look weird to a user. Do you ask them to check m or do you ask them to check f? Either way you'll be puzzling close to half your potential users. **To be digitally literate means being able to think like a computer and a person simultaneously.** In this case you can be pretty sure, I think, that nearly any given user who wasn't an f would be stymied by a single checkbox labeled f with no other option apparent, since he would need to infer blank = m, and that's just not how people think when they're being people.[8] The world of human beings contains more than just m and f, of course, but let's leave this at that.

To make the form pleasing to look at you need to make it stand out from the rest of the screen. The design principle of cohesion dictates that similar things should be visually similar and grouped together, thus isolated in a sense from everything else, so people can clearly see the group as an independent unit. There's some standard HTML for making a form stand out:

```
<form name="creepy" >
<fieldset>
<Legend>Reveal yourself to me:</legend>
</fieldset>
<input type = "text" name="zip" value =
"Please enter your zip code">
<input type = "text" name="bday" value =
"Please enter your birthday">
<input type = "text" name="gender" value =
"Please enter your gender">
<input type = "submit" name="submit">
</form>
```

8. It's a bit like that old joke about the logician who upon announcing her pregnancy and being asked is it a boy or a girl answered, "Yes!"

To make this form functional you'll need to learn how to collect user input. The first thing you need to do is change the first line of the form to look like this:

```
<form name="creepy" action="dosomething.
php">
```

The expression `action="dosomething.php"` tells the form to take the information given by the user and process it through a file called dosomething. php. Typically, dosomething.php would put the form's content into a database or save it to a file or use it to look something up and then do something else.

What kinds of information might you want to gather via a web form? Well, you might ask users to sign up for a newsletter or request notification about significant changes. A really simple form would simply ask the user to give you his or her email address and then it would email you that person's email address. This would be a manageable technique only if you got very few of such interactions. The last thing anyone wants is more email.

An email form would look something like this:

```
<form name="email form"
action="mailto:you@your-online-self.com"
method="POST">
<fieldset>
<Legend>Reveal yourself to me:</legend>
</fieldset>
Name:  <input type="text" size="20"
name="name"><br>
Email: <input type="text" size="20"
name="email"><br>
Subject: <input type="text" size="20"
name="subject"><br>
Content: <textarea cols="20" rows="30"
name="content"></textarea><br>
<input type="submit" value="Send mail">
</form>
```

Technically, you don't need to ask the user for his email address because the email system that the user had on the computer he sent the form from would have that in the From: line of the email it sent you, unless he sent the form from a public computer on which he didn't have his email set up. Putting the name and the email address in the body of the email might make it easier to understand the email when it comes. You could improve this rather simplistic method by including a hidden subject line and then have your email client stash all email with that subject line in a separate folder:

```
<input type="hidden" size="20"
name="subject" value="Prospects">
```

For this to work you'd need to have a folder called Prospects in your email folders and you'd have to give your email client the rule that says put all Subject: Prospects in the Prospects folder. You can [[Search]] that.

Because mail-to forms require an email program, you might prefer a more mobile alternative. You could create a form that processes the user's information using the PHP mail function. That would look something like this:

```
<form name="email form" action="email.php" >
```

If you do it this way, then you need a file called email.php (or whatever) to process the form. If you want to have fewer files on your server, you can make a form that's self-referential—that is, one file that both receives and processes the information. To do that, the first line of your form would look like this:

```
<form name= "email form" action="<? echo
$_SERVER['PHP_SELF']; ?>" >
```

File email.php

Here's what an email.php file might look like. Notice that the form is presented to users after it's processed. In other words, when users first come to email.php, they see the form because they haven't done anything yet, but once they press the Submit button, then their information is processed and they see the thank you feedback information. If you're still thinking in literate, linear ways, then you might be tempted to put the form first and then the processing information. You can make that work, but the "inverted" way shown below is more digitally apt because it's responsive rather than reactive. If you put the form first, then the users see the form even after they press Submit, so the result is user-confusing.

```
<?
//check to see use submitted form
if(isset($_REQUEST['submit'])){

//attach user information to variables for
processing

$name = $_REQUEST['name'];
$email = $_REQUEST['email'];
$subject = $_REQUEST['subject'];
$content = $_REQUEST['content'];
$your_email = 'you@your-online-self.com';

//send email
    mail($your_email, $subject, $content,
"From:" . $email);

//provide user feedback

echo "Thank you for contacting us!";
exit;
  }
 else;
```

```
//if user has not hit submit, show form
print "<form  name='email form' action='".
$_SERVER['PHP_SELF']."' >";
print "Name:  <input type='text' size='20'
name='name'><br> ";
print "Email: <input type='text' size='20'
name='email'><br>";
print "Subject: <input type='text'
size='20' name='subject'><br>";
print "Content: <textarea  name= 'content'
cols = '20' rows='10'><br>";
print "<input type='submit' name = 'submit'
value='Send mail'>";
print "</form>";
?>
```

The website (Sections/Rhetoric+/Communications) offers a slightly more complicated variation of email.php that can send HTML-encoded email.

Email isn't the only way to get user information, of course. The fact is that often you don't need to know who they are personally but do need to know more generally what they want and why they have come to your site and perhaps how they got there. The standard methods for this are known as web analytics. Your web-hosting account (see Chapter 1, section "Getting a web-hosting account") will offer you this as a feature. Learning how to make sense of the data you're given takes time and thought. For us at the moment it's enough that you understand that such data is constantly being logged and that businesses, governments, and nongovernment organizations, as well as individuals are using this data to tailor messages and in some cases track users. In the best possible world such data makes it easier for us to do what we want to do; in a less perfect world such data makes it easier for people to sell us stuff by showing us items for sale that directly relate to a web search we did recently or something we bought last week. In the worst worlds, such data enables surveillance. We live in all of those worlds simultaneously.

[[Search: Google Analytics]]

[[Search: user agent]]

Personas

The data analytic capacity of websites enables the collection of user information from which it's possible to glean nearly anything about one's users, but the raw data isn't always easy to make sense of and there's so much of it that divining your users from it can be difficult. A less data-centric and more traditionally creative technique involves imagining your users as belonging to types that you can identify in detail, not so much from their behavior online but from the nature of the content you're providing and your direct interactions with people who use the kind of content you offer. You can use this knowledge to create a better experience for your users.

Persona refers, in this context, to **a fictional user composed out of generalized information about real users.** This fictional user is given a name, specific personal traits, attitudes, possessions, and activities. He or she is not an archetype in that most sites have several personas that they use to visualize and concretize an audience, but he or she is representative of an audience segment.

The practice is both straightforward and complex. You come up with a series of questions the answers to which will give you a clear and specific image of a segment of your intended users or user groups. You obtain the answers either by mining the user data (using tools like Google Analytics), by user surveys or user site visits, or by simply imagining what the plausible answers would be. This last approach, while obviously data poor, is also obviously the easiest to perform, as long as you're good at empathizing and have some sense of how the people you serve work and live.

Once you've got a clear sense of the types of people who are using your site, you get an image that reflects the persona, and you create a document that has both images and Q&As. This document then becomes a "member" of your audience, or a user type. These documents are often printed out and pinned to cork boards or taped to walls. They're a concrete reminder of an abstract idea. They remind you that you're communicating with real people.

Persona design and maintenance isn't all that important for your-online-self. com at this point because you are your initial audience, but personas are a very important part of all digital businesses and knowing about them, how to create them and how to use them, is a portable skill. If you wanted to show a prospective employer that you get it, you could **make a persona and put it with the other digital assets in your portfolio.**

How to make a persona

Get a photograph of a person, head to foot. Then using a graphics program like Skitch, Snaggit, Photoshop, GIMP, or whatever, surround the figure with text boxes containing key features of this persona, content that would help designers and writers make accurate inferences about what's needed to reach the real people this image represents. Below is a list of topics you might use to generate content.

Persona topics to consider

- Age
- Gender
- Location
- Ethnicity
- Marital status
- Children
- Education

- Income
- Occupation; time in position
- Leisure pursuits
- Class or station in life
- How do they dress at work (labels and logos are a bit like tribe or gang insignia)
- How do they dress at home
- Get a photograph of a person who visually reflects a segment of your intended audience that reflects the above decisions and anything else you can imagine might be relevant to imagining who you're addressing. Ideology plays a part in this, as does copyright, and also you need to consider the figure's pose and setting. Since you don't plan to publish your persona for profit, you needn't worry about copyright, but ideology needs to be considered and overgeneralization or stereotyping avoided.
- Where does this persona shop?
    - Target or Walmart (make use of existing market research)
- What does this persona drive? (Or does this persona take public transit?)
- What brands does this persona identify with?
    - Starbucks, Dunkin Donuts, Niche café, instant coffee at work desk
    - Apple or PC
    - Adidas or Puma
    - Coke or Pepsi
- Does this persona drink?
    - Beer, wine, liquor, none; if this persona does drink, what brands?
- Does this persona read, and if so, what?
- Music
- Television
- Catch phrase and or keywords
- Technical expertise
- Computer equipment
- Computer comfort level
- Time on relevant tasks
- Attitude toward your product
- Goals, both long term (life) and immediate (experience)

If you want to make a persona as a digitally native artifact, you could use what's known as a segmented hypergraphic (SHG) technique. This is some scripting that turns sections of an image into hotspots that pop up some additional information on hover. To make the best use of this technique for a persona, you'd need to have enough contextual detail in the figure to make enough hotspots plausible—for example, carrying a bag to represent kinds of ownership (messenger, backpack, Birkin, paper, or plastic), as well as clothing and gear.

[[Search: SHG or segmented hypergraphic]]

If you're in job-seeking mode, you'll want to **make personas of potential employers.** The best way to start this process is to identify a potential company. Locate the people in the division you want to join, and then start following them on Twitter and any other public social media venues you can join them on. Then follow whom they follow. Your goal is to get to know these people's professional interests and practices. You're also in the process of revealing yourself to them, since they can follow you back.

While the persona technique is an outwardly focused audience analysis technique, you might find creating a personal persona an interesting psychological analysis. How do you signal your identity to the world? What do the clothes you wear and the gadgets you carry, the places you shop and the products you consume publically, say to the world about who you are?

You could turn your persona template into a form and offer users an incentive to fill it out, thus capturing real rather than imaginary data about users. Given enough of that and enough similarities you might be able to aggregate a persona or two. Of course, you can't trust the input implicitly. Also, unless you were going to put the data into a database rather than just receiving emails, you'd have a lot of by-hand work to do to get data out of the individual entries.

Scenarios

When people are designing websites or web applications, they think deeply about how what they're making will be used, in what circumstances, for what purposes, and by whom. What will the users know? What won't they know? What frame of mind will they be in? What kind of equipment will they be using in what kind of setting? How much time will they have? How much patience and interest? Keyboard or stylus or finger? And so on. Often these scenarios are worked out in detail and several might be worked up, one for each different persona perhaps or for different use cases. Your goal should be to reduce the number of steps required to accomplish the required task. One is optimal, but difficult to achieve. To get to one, you need to know the answer to any relevant question in advance of the given user's arrival at the moment when he or she needs to complete the task and you have to somehow attach the task to a single user action.

We'll get a chance to think a bit more deeply about scenarios (a.k.a. workflows) in the following sections. But for now, why don't you put down this book and look through your browser's history. Can you see any patterns? Do you go to the same places every morning? Where do you go most often? What do your paths tend to look like?

Practice thinking digitally: Coffee house scenario

You run a coffee house and you get a terrific rush of customers between six and seven o'clock every morning. Mostly but not always the same orders, which means you can't fill orders in advance. Coffee can't sit long without getting cold anyway.

But let's imagine that even a ten-minute advance notice would keep your café from getting cluttered with people standing around waiting. An electronic ordering system would also yield data about how much of each product you need to keep on hand, and that information would improve your profit margins. So you write an app that your clients can use to preorder coffee. What would the workflow of ordering coffee look like? Obviously you can't say to your customers that they can have coffee with milk or coffee with sugar but not coffee with milk and sugar. Radio buttons alone wouldn't work, but a mixture of checkboxes and radio buttons would solve that problem at least. What other coffee order variables can you think of?

Let's make a paradigmatic case before making the permutations. So, black coffee + sugar + milk or whole milk or cream + cinnamon:

```
<input type = checkbox name = coffee>
<input type = checkbox name = sugar>
<input type = radio button name = milk>
<input type = radio button name = whole
milk>
<input type = checkbox name = cinnamon >
```

What's wrong at this point? Look at your original specifications. What's missing from the above operationalization of the original specs?

Now build a section for lattes, cappuccinos, and other espresso items, plus decaf options. Once you've got the data input form, you need to design it for viewing on a mobile screen. Mobile screens are typically assumed to have dimensions of roughly 320 × 480 pixels. So you can't just put the whole form on the screen at once unless you print everything too small to read. So, you need to offer a branching decision tree. What's your user's first decision and then what subsequent decisions descend from it?

- Coffee
- Decaf
- Espresso
- Latte
- Cappuccino
- Mochachino

Also, do you need all possible condiments for each base kind of coffee? Does anyone put milk or half and half or crème in an espresso? How do you accommodate a preference for artificial sweetener versus sugar? And what about two sugars as opposed to one? Or double crème?

[[Search: HTML form select]]

You could have a condiments bar and just let clients doctor the main brew themselves, thus simplifying your form. But then you wouldn't have the same level of data because you couldn't control how much milk went into any given milked coffee. And they'd still be standing around while they tailored their coffee. How can you design the form so each person has the shortest possible path to their desired drink? What are all the possible combinations?

What about the 10-minute window? Should you include some kind of a clock for a pickup time so clients can order at any time for pick up at a specific time? Or should it just be that the clock starts ticking the minute the client presses the Submit button? Given that you're making a coffee when they press Submit, you might also want them to pay at that moment also, lest you end up making coffee for people who don't show up to get it.

If you started playing along early, building the form before reading the product descriptions thoroughly, you may have encountered an annoying feature of my description. I told you to build the form before I told you to build it for mobile devices. I wasn't being a jerk. I was just trying to underscore the fact that getting the specifications, all of the specifications, down and signed-off on first is an important part of the workflow. Getting the specifications right is very difficult because few people know their workflow step by step. There are technical problems and there are conceptual problems. **Solve the conceptual problems first and then, and only then, start coding.** This discipline will save you from having to rewrite and redo. Troubleshoot the process and you won't have to spend so much time troubleshooting the code, especially as introducing a change in the code may introduce problems elsewhere in the code if a dependent part has already been written.

Once you've got a prototype, you need to test it with real people. See how long it takes them to order the coffee they want. See what they think about the experience. You need both behavior and perception when it comes to usability testing.

Diagnostic thinking works best in truly causal systems because effects have specific causes, but even with noncausal situations, stopping to interrogate your expectations is critical to problem solving. Don't oversimplify, but **don't mistake confusion for complexity** either.

Summary

At this point in the book you've had a chance to think about how digital texts differ from print texts, how to design texts that can both instruct users and learn from those instructed (albeit at a rudimentary level). You've learned how and why to develop a minimalist ethos, clean, efficient, friendly, and open. And how to see yourself as contributing to collective enterprise through your-online-self.com without being certain anyone will notice until someday they do. You've learned, in other words, the fundamentals of digital citizenship and the guiding principles of digital rhetoric.

Where you are now

At this point you should have
1.   A landing screen.
2.   An about2.0.html (or perhaps about3.0.html) file.
3.   A hypertext variant of a traditional piece of rhetoric that demonstrates the use of layers of information.

4. An interactive user quiz.
5. If you have a form that sends user information to your email address, you rock!
6. If you got a leave-a-comment feature working, kudos.
7. If you got your comments feature password protected, more kudos.
8. If you got the location-awareness feature to write to a file and not just print to a screen, do a victory dance. (But remember you're being watched.)

Now it's time to start thinking about content creation in the epoch of digital rhetoric.

3
INVENTION

Invention is the name given to any process designed to generate content. In the days before literacy what was known consisted of what could be remembered, folk wisdom in the form of proverbs, maxims, and fables, momentous events from the grandparents' or maybe their parents' days, and what today we'd call common knowledge and common sense. The world of the known was finite. Judicious selection from the common store was more important than creating entirely new ideas. Better to say what everyone already knows in an interesting way at exactly the right time than to be entirely original. Rarely would an educated person be surprised by the content of a speech. In a way invention was more about execution ("Delivery, delivery, delivery," as Demosthenes said) and less about actually inventing something new to say ("What oft was thought, but never so well expressed," as Alexander Pope said in "Essay on Criticism").

So in an odd way we've returned in the digital age to an old method of invention, the modular, prefabricated redistribution of common knowledge, at least insofar as that what's known is just an Internet search away. And so much of what gets "written" is really just a reposting of something someone else wrote. The web is an echo chamber. This isn't to say that coming up with new knowledge isn't relevant. Real research matters, but you're much more likely to come across the echoes of it than the research itself. Using curated resources like Google Scholar, EbscoHost, Jstor, and the like are a good start. But you still need to think critically about what you're reading, and not just rely on where it came from. For now, though, let's concentrate on making a web app that will enable the habit of daily information seeking, a launch pad, a new home "page" or default screen for your web browser.

Designing your launch pad

Whenever you turn on your browser it automatically opens to its default site. You can change that default. I'd like to suggest you make it default to a site you've created for yourself that consists of links to the places you frequent and dynamic content you've asked for that's being regularly pushed to your screen (an RSS feed, see below). This way every time you open your browser, it opens a window to your digital world.

Your launch pad has two goals: to enable constant learning, and to show the world what you're interested in and what you're doing. You're not just making a habit of constantly looking for new information; you're developing a personal learning network, trying to attract the interest of others in your field or others like you who are trying to enter a field. In a sense you're offering a service (a research launch screen) and thus promoting yourself.

The automated newsstand

There are two methods of information transmission: pull and push. When you use a search engine or go to a specific website looking for something, you're pulling. If you get an email or Google alert or use a news aggregator, whenever information arrives without you requesting it, that's a push transmission.

What you see directly below is an example of a semi-automated pull search (really more like browsing) technique. It's a simple JavaScript that prints a dropdown selection list to the browser window and redirects the user to the website he or she selects. It's an efficient way to get to the places you always go, without having to remember URLs or doing a search. Because it's a dropdown selection list, you can have as many links as you want without taking up much screen real estate.

```
<SELECT onchange=location.href=this.
options[this.selectedIndex].value
NAME='select'>
<option>Magazines</option>
<option value="http://www.theamerican-
scholar.org/">American Scholar</A>
</option>
<option value="http://www.theatlantic.
com/">Atlantic</A></option>
<option value="http://chronicle.
com/">Chronicle of Higher Ed</A></option>
<option  value="http://discovermagazine.
com/">Discover</A></option>
<option value="http://www.dissentmagazine.
org">Dissent</A></option>
</select>
```

Go to the website, Designs/Launch Pads+/ News Stand, reveal the source code, and copy and paste it into your editor. Save it on your local computer as launchpad.html (or home.html or whatever you like), and make it your browser's default page. From there you'll want to start modifying the content to match your interests and goals. My magazines and newspapers may not appeal to you. You may want to keep the dropdown lists for images and code schools (e.g., code academy) intact and add to them over time.

Tailored search boxes

You might also want some tailored search boxes on your launch pad. Google, you have no doubt noticed, offers to limit your search to specific collections: the web, images, and Google Scholar. You can write a search box that will perform that limit for you automatically. Were you to view the code below in a browser, you'd see an input box and a Submit button that says G Scholar. Type a word, phrase, or name into the box and press Submit, and the code goes to Google Scholar and looks up whatever you asked for, printing what it finds back to your screen.

```
<form style="float:right;" method='get'
action='https://scholar.google.com/
scholar'><input type='text' name='q'
size='20' maxlength='255' value='' />
<input type='submit' value='G Scholar'
class='button' /></form>
```

Boxes like this can work for any reference site that accepts get method queries and has uniform search URLs. If you don't know what that means, open a browser window, go to a search engine, and look closely at the URL that's formed when you query the engine.

Having a view box like this one on your launch pad saves you time by entering the URL when looking for answers. If your launch screen is public, for example, then potential employers or collaborators can see your preferred reference sources, suggesting, perhaps, what kind of thinker you are.

If you don't want a search box on your launch pad, you can **hyper link a search keyword** using a very similar technique:

```
<a href='https://www.google.com/
search?q=myfield'>myfield</a>
```

When you click the linked word, a Google search for that word is launched. Not an earth-shattering advance, I admit, but an interesting capacity. I've used it in the digital glossary on the website so that you get the definition plus a direct link to other explanations. If you're writing contents that will contain some significant technical terms and you don't want to define them using footnotes or even a digital variant like popup on hover, perhaps because the content changes over time or simply because there are many better sources available, you can just link the relevant word in this way and your users will be transported to the search universe. If you want to you could also add a title tag, the contents of which would pop up your quick explanation of the term, saving a user the need, perhaps, to look it up, but nevertheless offering a quick way to supplement your own offering.

The same technique will work for Wikipedia, by the way:

```
<a href=https://en.wikipedia.org/wiki/
word_to_look_up>word to wiki</A>
```

Currently your launch pad pulls information. Now let's make it push. We're going to **turn launch_pad.html into launch_pad.php.**

Information channels

A lot of us, myself included, habitually seek information using news aggregator apps like Zite, Feedly, and Flipboard. These apps find current publications on topics we tell them we're interested in and automatically print (push) them to our screens in pretty and handy formats, with a link to the full piece. Often when you click the link you see the full article presented in the context of the feed script itself, thus you stay in their ecosystem while looking at other people's news. What the aggregators are doing is reposting. They don't create content. They, or rather their algorithms, just find it for you. They're more convenient than a Google search because they restrict the number of offerings to a manageable amount, relieving you from the burden of choice. If they're free and they aren't selling content and they don't have any accompanying advertising, how do they stay in business?

For one thing, their overhead is minimal. They don't have to employ writers or researchers because they repurpose other people's content. Much of the work they do is algorithmically generated. So they don't need to maintain a big payroll or footprint. They don't even need physical servers or cool rooms to house them. The whole enterprise can live in the cloud and be run by a handful of people working on laptops from wherever. The product they make money selling is data about user behavior and interests, audience analysis on a level so deep it enables targeted, one-to-one marketing. You tell it what you want to see and you tell it if you like what it shows you (thumb up or down) and it tailors your options based on your past likes and dislikes. Ostensibly this response to your actions improves the product for you because you're teaching it what you want to see and thus customizing it's algorithm for you. The problem, if you consider it one, is that you can't scrutinize or intentionally tweak the algorithm. That means you're ceding control of what you see to the machine. At the same time, you're providing real-time insights into your interests and needs. You're telling the "machine" who you are and what you want.

The other problem is that you're sealing your mind in an information bubble—an echo chamber of likes separating you from the universe of your dislikes: the intellectual equivalent of a gated community with an app in the guard house. Limiting our sources of information to our preferences is intellectually unhealthy. Seek disconfirmation, dissonance, and difference in addition to confirmation, harmony, and familiarity: stretch your brain by widening your range of inputs. As you seek alternative points of view, however, keep in mind that when people encounter ideas that contradict their own, rather than taking them seriously they rant against them, thus further entrenching their prejudices.

You can't consider yourself a critical thinker if you don't regularly entertain ideas that trouble your worldview. If you can't generate a plausible defense of an idea you don't accept, you can at least try to figure out what belief system enables it, starting with the premise that the believers are also human beings.

Regardless of whether you instinctively like or dislike something, you should make a habit of analyzing your evaluation before expressing it. If you notice you have an immediate response to something, positive or negative, ask why. Does it say on your behalf something you want to believe about yourself (that you have style and class or that you eschew all superficial signals)? Do you dislike it because it fails to meet your expectations or are your expectations out of sync with its goals? Do you like it just because it's familiar, dislike it because it isn't (or vice versa)? With what do you associate it and why? Does it challenge or endorse your worldview? Do you think that the algorithm that feeds you information to like can answer these questions for you?

[[Search: personality algorithms]]

Just because an algorithm can evaluate your personality and make decisions for you doesn't necessarily mean you should let it.

Getting outside the information bubble

News aggregators use Really Simple Syndication (RSS) to locate sites for you. RSS is an XML DTD that prints document trees to a screen. If that string of acronyms left you blinking, don't worry about it now. You can look them up in the Glossary or search them online later.[1] You don't need to understand them to follow the small points I'm making here. Nor to make the digital assets I show you how to make below.

Here's an example of RSS taken from the Center for Disease Control's flue feed:

```
<entry>
<id>49122126-aaf6-4434-b6e8-7e008a7a538c</id>
<title type="html">
<![CDATA[ Situation Update: Summary of
Weekly FluView ]]>
</title>
<summary type="html">
<![CDATA[
According to this week's FluView report,
overall seasonal flu activity remains low
across the United States. Increases in flu
activity are expected in the coming weeks.
]]>
</summary>
<published>2015-01-05T18:00:00Z</pub-
lished>
<updated>2015-01-05T18:00:00Z</updated>
```

---

1. Were you reading this online and I had linked XML and DTD, would you have followed the link and thus broken your concentration? Is this footnote doing that to you now?

```
<link rel="alternate" href="http://www.
cdc.gov/flu/weekly/summary.htm"/>
</entry>
```

The XML tags identify the parts of a chunk of information, which begins and ends with an <entry></entry> tag set. Beneath <entry> there's <id>, a unique number that identifies this entry specifically, <title> of the entry </title>, <summary></summary>, the date published and the date updated, a link to the content, and then finally the whole set is closed with </entry>. By marking up the content in this way, every element of each entry has a name and thus every element can be used as data just as each entire entry can be.

Because information presented in this way isn't easy for (digitally illiterate) people to read, we usually see XML files after a style sheet visually interprets the tags for us, often ignoring some tags to make the entry more visually interpretable—machines need the unique identifying number; people don't. A stylized version of the above might look something like this on your screen:

> According to this week's FluView report, overall seasonal flu activity remains low across the United States. Increases in flu activity are expected in the coming weeks.
>
> Published: 2015-01-05 6 p.m.

There are two important points here: **what's on the screen isn't necessarily what's behind it,** and **what's on a screen is** (or should be) **data even when made to look like text.**

RSS feeds provide regularly updated data from various information channels, the Affiliated Press, CNN, Fox, Reuters, the local junior baseball league, all kinds of sources.

If you get your news directly from sources (and you cast your net widely, even indiscriminately), you avoid the filtration and catering effect that all those pretty apps offer you in exchange for you letting them log your online news activities. You also avoid sending a detailed assessment of yourself as a consumer (and citizen) to marketing agencies. So, in addition to the dropdown list of newspapers and magazines that you made in the previous section, you might want to make (or copy, paste, and edit) an RSS feed reader. I will give you two examples, a relatively easy one and a slightly more complicated one. You might put a feed or two on your launch screen or you might make a separate screen exclusively for feeds.

Weather feed

If you want to start with a simple XML project, there's a script on the website that parses XML data from the National Oceanic and Atmospheric Organization (NOA), Sections/ Invention+/Weather Feed. The script is only a few lines long, and the XML data is, I think, fairly straightforward. See if you can change the given script so that it displays the weather where you are (or where you wish you were).

[[Search: NOA weather XML feeds]]

You could modify this script to offer content based on the weather report. In pseudocode that might look something like this:

```
If "$xml->temperature_string" >= 95,
print "Stay indoors."
```

Can you write the real code? (Hint: search PHP if statement)

You could put this bit of dynamic data on your default page. For it to work you'll need to name your launchpad with the .php extension and put it on your web-hosting account. If you do that, then you'll get a weather report every time you open your browser.

RSS PHP example

If you go to the website and look at Sections/Invention+/RSS, you'll see a dropdown selection list that uses CSS and some PHP to print XML news feeds to a screen. I didn't write that script. I modified one I found online. That screen contains a link to the tutorial I used. Follow that link and you can copy and paste that content provider's code onto your server (it needs to be on a server running PHP to work). Here's a bit of an overview about how the script works.

C. Bavota's script displays the content from a single RSS feed using the following code:

```
$rss = new DOMDocument();
$rss->load('http://wordpress.org/news/
feed/');
```

There's way more to the script than that but those two lines determine that the content a user sees comes from the Wordpress news feed. **Change the load statement to any RSS URL and it will push that content to your screen.** So, for example,

```
$rss->load('http://www.aldaily.com/
feed/');
```

will display the Arts and Letters daily feed. Awesome site, by the way.

You'll need to spend time looking for RSS feeds. The method has become less common now that we're all living inside apps, which is a shame bordering on the dangerous, I think. But if you persist you can still find direct access to RSS feeds. Look for the orange RSS logo (a beacon pulse like the wifi symbol, painted orange and rotated 45 degrees to the right) and when you click it, make sure what you see is XML code. If you see XML, then the URL should work when you put it between the ( ) in the $rss->load( ) line.

The original script displays just one RSS feed, which is fine, but I wanted to be able to get lots of content from different sources all to a single screen, so I modified the original at the top of the file so that it would take a variable from a dropdown selection list like the one on page 72. The modification I made looks like this, at the top of the file:

```
$news = $_REQUEST['rss']; // get url from
user selection
if((isset($news))){  // once user selects,
execute request

all the rest of C.Bavota's code and then
turn bracket off

}

//
```

and then at the bottom of the file I have a dropdown
selection list like this:

```
<SELECT onchange=location.href=this.
options[this.selectedIndex].value
NAME='select'>
<option>Feeds</option>
<option value="rss.php?rss=http://www.
alistapart.com/rss.xml"
name="rss">A list apart</option><option
value="rss.php?rss=http://feeds.feedburner.
com/bestdesigntuts
" name="rss">best design tutorials
</option>

<option value="rss.php?rss=http://
tools.cdc.gov/feed.aspx?feedid=21"
name="rss">CDC Flu</option>
</SELECT>
```

Notice that the name= of the option is RSS. That identifies the URL so that the
$_REQUEST['rss'] will work.

If you find my modification confusing, use C. Bavota's as he offers it. In either
case, you need to go looking for XML feeds that interest you and modify the script
to serve your purposes. If you do this, you'll always have fresh information of your
own choosing being pushed to your website. Such fresh content serves at least two
purposes. It gives you new things to think about every day and it shows the world
what you think is interesting, which speaks to your ethos. If a potential colleague
or employer sees that you read interesting stuff on a regular basis, they might more
readily form a positive impression of you.

Something to keep in mind is that when you use an RSS feed, you're presenting other people's information on your site. You need to indicate clearly where the
information is coming from so that your users don't think you're either the writer or
the reporter. But you don't have to worry about copyright because XML feeds are
intended to make sharing information easier. The idea is to make current information available on any machine regardless of the operating system or browser.

To make your own news aggregator, head over to the website, Sections/Inven-
tion+/RSS, and follow the link to the tutorial.

Using date to preprogram alerts on your launch pad

Most professions have recurring events, calls for conference papers that come out the same day or thereabouts every year, for example. If you put your launch pad on your web server, and call it whatever.php, then you could have it compare today's date with a given date and print something to the screen when they match. Here's a very simple example of content dynamically generated by an event. It's dynamic in the sense that it gets the current date and does something based on evaluating that information. Most of the time it does nothing. But when it gets the information it's primed to respond to, it changes the content on the screen.

```
<?
        $today = date(m ."/". d); // set
$today to current month / day

        if($today == "08/17"){        //
evaluates to
                print "Happy Birthday";
        }
?>
```

If date(yy) returns the current year in a four-digit format like 2016, how could you change "Happy Birthday" to "Happy Birthday; today you're X years old, where X is the difference between the year you were born and date(yy)? (Hint: echo $current_year - $birth_year;.)

Google Alerts

You can supplement your regular sources of information by setting up Google Alerts to receive email notifications whenever something you're interested in gets written about, even in publications you don't normally track. Systems like Google Alerts are known as push communications as opposed to pull. Your option select script is a pull technology. When you want something, you go get it. You actively pursue it. Push technologies are passive from the user's point of view. They send you notifications without your direct intervention. Ideally, as with Google Alerts, you made an initial request and you should be able to turn the push off. Email updates, join our newsletter, receive "free" offer setups, are all pseudo pulls. Once you sign up, they just keep targeting your inbox.

[[Search: Google Alerts]]

Data mining, deriving new information from old

Data mining is big news these days. The web generates data at an exponential rate. And because it mines all manner of things, we can learn from it only if we can figure out what's there for what matters. In the following section I'm going to show you a couple of **simple techniques for searching**

and doing something with what's found. If the iceberg is data mining then this isn't even the tip, maybe just the shadow cast by the sun at 1:00 p.m. in August, but it will get you thinking about words in a more computational way.

Of needles and haystacks

An algorithm is a step-by-step procedure or set of unambiguous rules for solving a problem or making a decision, often, in computational situations at least, resulting in a 1 or a 0, which is a definite yes or a definite no. Through inference from that definition, you can gather that an algorithm needs to end. If you've ever done a search and replace using your word processor, you've used an algorithm. If you start such a procedure in the middle of a file, the machine will ask you if you want it to continue when it gets to the end of the file. If you say yes, it will return to the top and keep going until it gets to the place where you turned it on. Then it will stop. An endless procedure is known as an infinite loop, and **you don't want an infinite loop.**

   A common use of algorithms in textual studies is to search lengthy documents (tens of thousands of lines) for a specific feature. Search every sentence from the Shakespeare corpus for similes (all instances of "like" or "as"), for example. You ask the machine to search for each instance and return any line that contains at least one instance. As that example suggests, a reliable algorithm requires careful advanced thinking because if there are any instances that don't exactly fit the case you have in mind—the way "As" is used in this sentence, for example—your procedure will produce flawed results. When writing algorithms your goal should be a reasonable error rate, less than 1% or better in most cases. Obviously the enormity of a potential error influences the acceptable level of error, but a procedure that often gets it wrong might waste more time than doing it by hand would. For an algorithm to produce reliable output it needs to have reliable input. Ever see "The Big Bang Theory" TV episode where the speech-impaired character Barry Kripke disparages Siri? Rhotacism (pronouncing an r as if it were a w— Bawwy Kwipke) is fairly rare, so a speech recognition procedure that accounted for it would produce only a marginal return on a big investment in processing effort.

   [[Search: elevator speech recognition technology]]

   Another common algorithm is the "if this, then that" pattern (IFTT). If Apple falls below 100, buy. If the forecast calls for a 70% chance of rain, take an umbrella. When you're writing code you need to think in terms of decision situations—that is, given a specific condition, do something. If a user enters content in an email address field that doesn't contain the @ symbol, ask him or her to reenter the content. If a user wants to upload a file, identify the file extension first.

   Let's look at that last example in more detail. There are a number of reasons why identifying a file extension might be useful. For one thing, an .exe extension is executable; it's a program that can run and that might be infectiously disastrous. If all we needed was to exclude all .exe files, then we'd write a script that identified .exe and, thus, by implication ignored all other extensions. But let's say we want something more sophisticated than just yes or no .exe. Perhaps you're asking for images to display on the web. Image files with the .tiff extension won't display in a browser, so that's a potential problem. Neither will a .psd. Or maybe you need to know if an MS Word file is compatible with older versions of MS Word, so you'll need to know if you've got a .docx or a .doc file. At any rate, let's just say you want to know what any given file's extension is.

In PHP, that might look like this:

```
<?
$extension = substr("myfile.pdf",
-3);     // returns "pdf"
?>
```

In pseudocode, that amounts to "go to the far right of the expression in quotation marks and count three spaces to the left." The minus sign makes it count from the end instead of the beginning. Cool enough. But what if the input is "myfile. docx"? That would return "OCX" and that would likely be problematic since OCX isn't a file extension and presumably we wanted the machine to do something with the file extensions it finds. We could say, in all cases of OCX, add D to the front, but that would require an extra step and parsimony is a virtue. So, how do we think about this? Well, what do all filenames have in common? The dot, right? So what about asking the machine to return all letters right of the dot? How would you Google that? See if you can write (find) a script that would find everything right of the dot. I'll save you the trouble, but you should at least look up PHP strpos.

```
<?
$haystack = 'myfile.docx';
$needle = substr($haystack, strpos
($haystack, "." + 1);
Echo $needle;
?>
```

Why is + 1 there? (Hint: you want right of dot.)

There are many different ways to identify a file extension. If you asked the question of Google in exactly the right way, you might have turned up the little known fact that PHP has a function for identifying file types: $path_ info[''extension''] :—fewer lines, faster processing. Think as efficiently as possible. When it comes to computational thinking, there's getting it done and then there's getting it done <verbosity>with the fewest number of lines of code possible</verbosity> elegantly.

Algorithmic invention

Earlier on, when I was trying to convince you that you should learn how to code, I made some menacing statements about how we need to broaden our intellectual skill sets because there are now algorithms that can read and write. As you're still reading, I guess I can assume those menaces didn't turn you off.[2] While what you're learning in this book isn't anywhere near what you'd need to write a writing algorithm, I think we have enough to walk through, in a semi-pseudocode kind of way, how a writing algorithm might work.

If every human expression were entirely unique, we'd have a great deal of trouble understanding each other. For the sake of efficiency and community, we tend to rely on patterns and commonly held perceptions and beliefs conveyed in clichés and stereotypes and proverbs, narratives patterns, and so on. This regularity is what enables programs to write prose.

Let's take baseball for our example. Team A scores four runs and team B scores three runs. Given the difference of just one run, it makes sense that the computer would write something like, "In a close game, team A beats team B by just one run." The only direct input the computer gets with which to generate that story is the names of the teams and the scores. The rest of what it says has to be generated based on rules that you the programmer give it. The pseudocode for that might look like this:

```
Score differentials of 1 = close
Differential of 2 - 3 = handily
> 4 < 7 = destroyed
> 8 = avalanche
```

The intensity of adjectives triggered by the numbers would depend on the kind of game. In baseball a score of three to one is a much closer game than three to one in soccer, typically. So your algorithm would have to factor in the kind of sport. It would also generate much better stories if it could interpret the data as the game was generating it rather than just based on the final scores. Thus, if the game is soccer and it's one to one right up until the last five minutes when team A scores a second goal and then, undone, team B loses focus and team A scores again right away, that's very different than if team A scored three times in the first half and team B finally scored in the last minute, too little too late. Those two events should generate different narratives. The more information the computer has about current league standings, past statistics, health of key players, game time weather forecasts, and so on, the more "intelligent" its stories can be. The longer its lists of options are (how many metaphors for "beats" are there arranged by intensity and frequency of use?) in given situations, the more varied and therefore more interesting its stories might be. Add a review loop into the process, say, readers score a story or review by in-house experts, and pretty soon you could get a computer to write stories that pass for the writing of a person. In artificial intelligence circles, a computer program that can pass for an actual human is known as having passed the Turing test.

[[Search: Turing test]]

---

2. Were this book a website, I could observe people leaving when they read the threat from algorithms and thus perhaps remove it or modify it—real-time editing based on actual user behavior rather than belief or expectation. Were it a full-on content management system, we could asynchronously debate the issue.

[[Search: narrative science]]
[[Search: Persado]]
[[Search: algorithms for writing]]
[[Search: Twine]]

Digital revision

If you've been writing for a while then you've likely heard the adage that all writing is rewriting. We learn a great deal about our subjects and ourselves through the process of revising and rethinking and reviewing our work. Indeed, one of the arguments for learning to write at all is because writing improves thinking—writing, like coding, is about invention and not just communication. **The process of revision is generative;** revision helps us come up with new ideas as we go about clarifying our existing ones.

Computer program writing is a similarly iterative process. You make something. You ask people to test it out. You fix the bugs they found and you listen (or don't) to their advice about additional features, and you release the code. Then you watch it in use. You receive bug reports. You get solicited and unsolicited feedback and start revising the code, adding, changing, making it more efficient, more effective, closer to what people want, and so on. Each time you release a new version you offer release notes with it. What bugs were fixed, what's new, what known issues are as of yet unresolved, what's next—that kind of thing. Typically, the slight revisions are identified by a small increment, version 1.3, and the big revisions are identified by a larger increment, version 2.0, for example. You can think of prose composition in the same terms. Indeed **the meta-commentary of the release notes—that is, what's fixed, what's waiting to be fixed, and what's next—is a great way to develop a fuller understanding of what you're doing.** Before you turn in any essay, you should write a meta-commentary of the release notes variety for yourself if the professor hasn't asked for one.

If a standard release note nomenclature involves categories like stability improvements, bug fixes, improved user interface, enhanced workflow, and added features, what might the equivalent release notes look like for more traditional forms of writing? Bug fixes might be corrections of standard spelling, grammar, and formatting issues, errors that get in the way of usability (because they're distracting and ethos impairing) but don't really hamper understanding. The document can be used, just not to its full potential. Stability updates might mean errors leading to confusion or avoidable disagreements, like making unwarranted assertions or saying things that assume more knowledge of your intended audience than you have. These kinds of errors cause instability in the sense that meaning and intention diverge. User design improvements might be things like more and better concrete examples, further citations, and more careful consideration of counterarguments. New features might be things like supplemental charts or videos, new images, new citations, and the like.

The reason you'd go to all this trouble to document a document as you write it, draft by draft, is to get a sense of your workflow, to learn how you work by watching from a meta-perspective. Thus, this kind of careful oversight process is in fact an inventional practice because you're learning about how much you need to say to write a document that can solve the target audience's problems without further releases (subsequent drafts).

One last point about invention: less is more. We think of invention as essentially additive; coming up with things to say (write, do) implies adding to the existing store, expansion, dilation. But because people don't tend to read very carefully from screens, it's very important that you write only what's necessary when writing online. A strategy here is to write as much as you can, go back and add to what's there, and then when you've <metaphor>said</metaphor> all you can, cut what you've got by 30% to 50% without reducing the number of ideas. Use fewer words and shorter examples. Rather than providing elaborations, explanations, and examples on the surface, link to them so the user has the power to decide how much he or she wants to read.

Summary

Invention has always been about coming up with appropriate things to say. Typically the process is to generate everything that can be said, and then using your judgment about the subject, the occasion, the audience (and in the case of users, feedback), the physical setting, and your intended ethos, you select the most appropriate things and eliminate the irrelevant, inappropriate, and problematic things. You aren't typically creating new knowledge with this process so much as using the existing store to contribute to your communities.

Digital rhetoric makes it possible to find new information buried deep in the data of the common store, and you've learned at a superficial level a couple of the ways you might think about doing that, but for the most part at this point you've learned a few techniques for getting information from sources and repurposing it for your own site. You aren't stealing; you're sharing information, attributing credit to its sources, and designing that information to be read on a screen.

As a more digitally literate person, you're now in the habit of looking for new information and ideas—not just memes and viral vids and Reddit chatter (all fine, of course)—you can like and share, but also for digital assets from which you can build new digital objects and ideas. You're also aware that your likes and dislikes, your preferences and beliefs, are being recorded and used by corporations and agencies.

As a burgeoning digital rhetorician you're also starting to get ideas about writing from the design of digital writing environments and you're starting to think about how to build a content-generating machine, one that will show the world what you can do and not just what you know.

Where you are now

If you've been making things while using this book, at this point you have
1.   A landing screen (do you want to revisit it?).
2.   An about2.0.hml or an about3.0 screen (does it need more work?).
3.   A launchpad.html file, with dropdown lists to cool sites.
4.   A tailored Google search box.
5.   If you have a launchpad.php with a weather feed, good on ya!
6.   If you have an RSS feed, kudos!
7.   If you have a weather feed that's location aware, you rock!

4
ARRANGEMENT

Arrangement has always been about optimizing the order of information based on an understanding of the audience's state of mind, intensity and nature of interest, and knowledge of the subject. The standard **traditional pattern is the given/new.** First say what people already know and believe, then link that to what you want them to learn or accept, the new information. In advertising this creates the pattern like: "On a cold, blustery day there's nothing better than soup and there's no better soup than our soup. . . ." Tell them something they understand and believe, then attach the new idea to that. If you want people to eat alligator, tell them it tastes like chicken. If you want them to love it, dry it, and throw some smoke on it, tell them it tastes like bacon.

When it comes to addressing readers as opposed to listeners, you might want to make the connection between the given and the new more logical and less merely associative, as readers can scrutinize the gap between the given and the new in ways that many audience members may not, being distracted as they might be by the appearance of the speaker and the many other things happening at the same time—mmm bacon.

For larger units of thought, the traditional oral methods of arrangement require transitions that connect what was said to what needs to be said next, offering a forecast or advanced organizer in the beginning and a recap or summary at the end, often with a microversion of the same between subsections, especially if the speech is long. In writing you also need such connective text, text that holds the larger units of text together and gives the reader a sense of where they are and where you're taking them: what's happening now, what's about to happen, and what will happen after that. This is the essence of traditional literate arrangement: linearity. You start at the beginning and you work forward a step at a time until you get to the end. Literate people are so accustomed to this form of learning that they find pleasing the fact that as you read a book, the weight of the pages goes from heavy on the right to heavy on the left, for languages read left to right at any rate. With a scroll you could feel the bottom coming too.

While given/new is relevant on the web, **the more common pattern today is question/answer.** The old-world concept of arrangement has been superseded by the concept of navigation or way finding. The change reflects the fact that digital spaces enable multiple paths and dynamic content, content that changes as a result of arriving information, user action, user behavior, or even random events.

Methods of digital arrangement have evolved considerably in just the last twenty years. If you spend some time on The WayBack Machine, you'll notice that early "pages" consisted of lists of links, oddly enough the way CNN Online looks in 2015. The content providers in those days scoured the web for interesting information and arranged what they found into lists of links.

[[Search: your university's site circa 2000]]

Since roughly 2000, most people have used the web via search engines primarily, typing queries into the URL space and having Google or Bing give us a list of links to sites that tell us what we want to know, or at least offer some sites that seem to have the answers. Then we just jump from option to option until we find the answer we're looking for. We don't typically entertain long answers but occasionally we might go on a bit of journey, following a link that looks interesting, following another from there, and from there. But mostly answer found, journey over.

We have moved from elaborate multidimensional maps of entire sites to designs that are essentially flat, where the user comes in exactly where he or she wants to be without having to click around, to designs that anticipate each user's needs based on information about the user, either "volunteered" by the user's past behavior (where he or she was last, the path followed when last on the site, what was searched for, etc.) or inferred based on the user's location or the device he or she is using.

So, how are people going to find what you have to offer on your-online-self. com? Does it matter what order they see which file in? Do they always have to start in the same place? Does the first screen need to remain the same or should it change every time a user returns? Or should the content change daily or weekly? Should the content vary based on user role (for that you'd need a login identification process)? Are there some files that need to be viewed in sequence, some that shouldn't be excluded from others under any circumstances? Do some files lend themselves to being grouped together but don't need to be seen ensemble to be understood? What kind of information have you got, and what are some of the ways a user might want to experience your files? Is there a path that you need a user to take, or are there multiple paths and the user can choose for himself or herself? You have hundreds of files, how do you put them together or rather what are all the different ways you might put them together, and then how might you offer options to your users based on their different needs?

Because you have to answer all of these questions for yourself, I'm going to walk you through **the most common forms of digital navigation (ne arrangement)** and then leave it to you to decide how to use which when. We'll finish this section thinking about your portfolio because in many ways it typifies the rhetorical challenges and opportunities of navigation.

The primary point to keep in mind is that you need to constantly be thinking about organizing and reorganizing your assets and designing everything in the most flexible ways possible, so that inertia won't hold you on course when chang-ing course becomes a better decision.

Navigating within and among files/linking

The simplest way to arrange information is to link related chunks. In a lengthy file (more than a screen's worth of information) the relevant chunks might be sections. In a given directory the chunks might be files or a specific part of a file. You can, of course, also link to other directories and other servers.

Jump-tos

If you have a file so long that a user would need to scroll through it, then for the sake of their convenience you should break it into sections and then provide the digital equivalent of a clickable table of contents so a user doesn't have to read the whole thing if he or she doesn't need to.

    Internal anchors (a.k.a. jump-tos) have two parts, the link and the section linked to. Here's an example of a standard internal link:

```
<a href="#" name="placetojumpto" >Lorim
epsom</a>
<a name = "placetojumpto">
```

The `<a href="#" >` part of the tag makes what follows, what's called the linked text, clickable. The # symbol indicates to the machine that the link is to a place in the same file. The `name=" "` part identifies or names the section of the file to jump to when the user clicks the link text, in this example, Lorim epsom. Once users get there, you might want to offer them a way to jump back, in case they aren't where they want to be or they learned what they wanted to learn and are ready to move on. You can use a bit of JavaScript for that:

```
<a href="javascript:history.go(-1)" >[Go
Back]</a>
```

Linking files on your server

When you want to link one file to another you use the anchor tag as with a jump-to, but in place of the # symbol you put the name of the file you want the user to see, assuming that file is in the same directory as the file linking to it:

```
<a href="anotherfile.html" >find another
file</a>
```

If the needed file is in another directory, then you need to include the path with the filename:

```
<a href="dir/anotherfile.html" >find the file
in another directory</a>
```

You can link from one file to a specific section of another file by using this code:

```
<a href="file.html#placetojumpto">link
text</a>
```

If the requested file is in a directory below the directory that the file with the link is in, then the pattern is /sub/anotherfile.html:

```
<a href="/subdir/anotherfile.html">find the
file in the directory below the one where
this file is</a>
```

If the requested file is one directory up:

```
<a href="./supdir/anotherfile.html">find the
file in the directory above the one where
this file is</a>
```

If the file is in the main or root directory (public_html), then you can link all the way up just by using two dots:

```
<a href="../dir/supdir/anotherfile.html">
find the file in the root directory</a>
```

If you want to link to another website, use the URL:

```
<a href="http://www.whatever.com">
whatever</a>
```

Sometimes you don't want to display a file but rather offer it for download. This would be the case for PHP files, for example, that you want your user to have as PHP rather than the resulting HTML after it has been processed by a browser. You might also want to offer PDFs for download since they don't always display in a browser. In any case it's good practice to indicate what kind of file type is linked, and that's because computers by default try to open some files with specific programs, which can be frustrating for users if clicking a link fires up a program they don't want to use at the moment. A lot of people prefer to read PDFs offline so offering them as downloads can be appreciated:

```
<a href="file.pdf" download>File (PDF)</A>
```

While the standard <a href...> link opens the requested file in the current browser tab, it's possible to make a link open in a new tab. To do so, simply include target ="_blank" after the name of the file:

```
<A href="file.html" target="_blank">file</a>
```

In addition to the path and file, a link should have a title= attribute. The content of the title= attribute is read by a screen-reading software, and it pops up when any user hovers over the link. The added information can help a user decide if he or she wants to bother following the link:

```
<A href="file.html" title="a great site
for getting place holder text" target="_
blank">file</a>
```

Linking to files on other people's servers

If you want to link to a specific file on another server, then the pattern is this:

```
<a href=http://www.whatever.com/direc-
tory/file.html title = "additional
information">whatever</a>
```

Because you're linking to a resource you have no control over, the link may die at any time without warning. Programs like Adobe's DreamWeaver will check for dead links periodically, which is helpful. But you should check your external links the way ranchers check their fences. Sites come and go. External links die.

Link rot

On the website there's a script that will check a link to see if it's still working. It will only check one link at a time and it won't do anything other than tell you if the link works or not, so it's not terribly useful. You can learn as much from just entering the questionable URL into the search box of your browser. But it's nevertheless an interesting bit of code. One of the things it does is color code the results of the query, which is a technique you can use in other settings for other purposes. You can find the link rot script under Sections/Arrangement+/Link Rot.

The technique is pretty easy to get working just by copying and pasting. Making sense of it, however, may be a struggle. I got it from a great site called Stack-Overflow that bills itself as a community of expert programmers and enthusiasts. I'm at best an enthusiast and so find maybe 80% of what I read there beyond me. But I keep going back because I'm thick like that. I encourage you to develop your will to persist. Feeling dumb isn't pleasant, but feeling suddenly smarter is worth every blush and wince.

Links and CSS

Finally, you can change the appearance of your anchors by using CSS. Instead of using the default blue underline, you can make them a different color or highlighted instead of underlined. But be careful of thwarting convention. If you make your links black with no underline, for example, users won't be able to distinguish links from nonlinks. If you make links yellow background highlighted, they may think you're merely calling attention, highlighting, the word or phrase. Just because you can do something doesn't mean you should.

Menus

Before the preference for flat designs came to dominate websites, before we realized that people preferred to use search boxes, we represented the relationships among files using what were called <metaphor>menus</metaphor>, links grouped hierarchically by subject or purpose. Sites that use menus typically layout their files in two dimensions, major topics across the top, with subtopics arranged hierarchically beneath each major topic. The top layer is referred to as the *global navigation*. The vertical column under each global heading is called the *local navigation*.

Designing an effective menu scheme isn't as simple as it might seem. One way to think your way to an effective menu system, before considering how you want it to look, is to write each primary subject heading on a Post-It note with a unique color, and then place the notes horizontally on a wall. Think about what order from left to right seems to make the most sense.

Once you're content with your primary subjects, write the name of each file that belongs under that subject on a separate Post-It note of the same color and arrange them vertically, just one under the other as the files occur to you. Once you have every file in your collection of files in its proper stack, think about how to order the stack. Does alphabetical make sense? What about least to most complex? What about an ordinal arrangement, first, second, third?

Current Projects	Past Work	Course Work	What I'm Reading
Big thing	2014	English	A running list
Smaller thing	2013	Anthro	
Smallest thing	2012	Outside discipline	

Menus tend to be relatively complex files containing both JavaScript and CSS. As CSS becomes more sophisticated and dynamic, it can increasingly do all of the work itself. You're going to want to keep a running list of examples of menus both as a way of learning more coding techniques and so that you can assemble web interfaces more efficiently.

The most popular technique these days is called "the hamburger." It's popular because it takes up very little screen space. It's called the hamburger because it consists of three lines stacked on top of each other. The hamburger icon is easily identified as a stack, think layers, and can sit quietly in the upper left or right corner, taking up very little screen real estate until needed, at which point the user clicks it and the navigation scheme slides out, or down, or both. The hamburger is a very mobile-friendly design. See Menus/Expandable+/Hamburger.

Accordions

Because people don't like to read from screens, you can make a lot of information easier to navigate by not showing it all at once. Rather than offering jump-tos and jump-backs, with all the screen scrolling thus required, you can just offer a list of links that reveal the relevant content on click, hiding it again on reclick—that is, expanding and contracting.

The Q&A pattern is a common use of this show/hide technique:

```
<script>
function toggle(e) {
if (e.style.display == "none") { // ==
means evaluates to
e.style.display = "";
} else {
```

```
e.style.display = "none";
}}
</script>
<span onClick="toggle(document.all.
HideShow1);">Should      I?</span><BR>
<span style="display: none;"
id="HideShow1">Absolutely, and here's
why…..</SPAN>
```

You can save a user even more time by using an on-hover technique instead of an on-click one. When an event is triggered on hover, the initial context is only temporarily hidden. The user isn't transported, and thus he or she can quickly get back to where he or she was.

Among the other menus you'll find examples of on the website is the mobile ubiquitous icon array. This is a collection of small square icons found floating on the left or at the bottom of the screen, each the icon of a social networking tool like Twitter or LinkedIn, and linked to the domain's presence on such sites. These icon arrays are popular because social networking sites are popular, but they're also a very efficient use of space. An icon communicates a great deal in a very small space.

Segmented hypergraphics

If you have an image instead of text and want to provide supplemental informa-tion without cluttering the picture with callouts, you can used what's called a seg-mented hypergraphic or a hotspot (.shg). Hover over a part of an image and some more information pops up. This technique is great for exploded views of multipart objects like cameras or monitors with complex input options or engines. It's also a good way for finding apps and sites.

[[Search: making segmented hypergraphics]]

Interactive maps are perhaps the most common use of popup-on-hover information repositories. Google Developer has an excellent tutorial about how to make such a map using Google Maps. For a different kind of application of the same kind of digital rhetoric, see the website under Sections/Rhetoric+/Reading.

[[Search: from info windows to a database]

Layered design pattern

If you have information of article length—that is, more than a couple hundred words—and you want your users to decide if they want to read all of it or not, you might go for structure that looks something like this:
1.   Headline
2.   Nutshell—the whole story without detail (don't bury the lead)

3.   Link to the whole thing

`Headline`
`dateline`
Lorem ipsum dolor sit amet, consectetur adipiscing elit, sed
do eiusmod tempor incididunt ut labore et dolore magna
aliqua. Ut enim ad minim veniam, quis nostrud exercitation
ullamco laboris nisi ut aliquip ex ea commodo consequat. Duis
aute irure dolor in reprehenderit in voluptate velit esse cillum
dolore eu fugiat nulla >>pariatur. Excepteur sint occaecat
cupidatat non proident, sunt in culpa qui officia deserunt mol-
lit anim id est laborum MORE>>

[[Search: CSS showing and hiding content]]

If you have many stories to offer, a layered pattern like this makes it possible to
display all you have to offer in a relatively small space.

Hooks for headlines

If your goal is to get people to (one)-click in, then you want an interesting headline. Most headlines are hooks; they're short, sharp, barbed statements designed
to pique our curiosity or raise our hopes or whet our appetites—the subject line
of an email, the headline of a news story, the tease of an advertisement, the "stay
tuned" bait before the commercial break, and so on, all need to be click worthy.
Having trouble reading this email? Click here.

Often delivering on the promise is an afterthought. In the time-honored tradition of P. T. Barnum, if you can get them to pay for the promise, no need to
deliver. Just take their money and show them the door. There are, however, more
legitimate communications online that nevertheless need to make a good first
impression if they're going to get the second look they deserve, and so being able
to bait a hook is a useful rhetorical skill even for conscientious, content-rich com-
municators. A more positive way to put this is the old journalist's adage: **don't
bury the lead.** People will read at length if the ideas are interesting, relevant,
and well written. They'll click away fast if the first screen is a densely packed
jumble of words with no obvious reward on offer. And yet, they won't read at all
if the headline answers all their questions.

The best way to learn how to bait a hook is to make a habit of scanning headlines for the way they're constructed rather than the news they promise. You could
copy and paste a few hundred and then run a word frequency count on them,
or run a word cloud program to visualize frequency. Or you could do it the old-
school way of making mental notes. I find the app Zite useful for this because it
will show you twenty headlines at a time. For a parody of the practice of creating
interesting headlines, check out Fark. At any rate, here are some types of hooks
I've observed:

Enumerate: Seven things you can do to X. Numbers seem to
get attention on the web, perhaps because they suggest a finite

amount of information. People don't like to peer into the abyss
that the endless scrolling capacity of a screen entails. They
like to know where the bottom is. This is why listicles are so
common on the web. So you'll often see numbers in headlines.
Curiously offbeat numbers, like seven instead of a nice round
ten, draw interest by seeming precise, but are often just different
and therefore noticeable.

Rank: Top ten whatevers. The rankings hook works
because people want to see if their favorite is listed, to affirm
their prejudices and preferences, and because such a list might
save them the trouble of making up their own minds. What's
popular is good, right? Of course not, but not everyone knows
this and even those who do will still click to see who the win-
ners and the losers are. Rankings, like all lists, suggest a finite
reading experience, a clear sense of where you are and what's
left and how much time the experience will use, information
for which users are grateful.

Solve a mystery: This works especially well if whatever
you'll illuminate is actually something people wonder about,
but sometimes just suggesting there's something mysterious
about a commonplace happening or event might draw people
in. "Underwater monster captured on video for the first time
ever" is one of my favorite examples. It's got everything, a
number *and* a ranking (first), the promise of a video of something you don't see every day, and a lurid object (monster!).
Turns out to be an ugly fish three inches long, but hey, made
you look.

**Use an indirect pronoun in place of the primary
noun:** If the headline contains the whole story, then only
the people interested in the content will bother clicking it. So
you might want a headline that's a bit more alluring. You can
create a little bit of suspense by being pointedly vague—use
this common household object to lose ten pounds in a day, *what*
every banker hopes you never learn, *what* the pros know and
you can too, *this* fruit will make you live longer. The user clicks
to find out what *this* is.

A cherished belief indirectly endorsed: Why drink-
ing is good for you. Often what you get if you click a link like
this is a rehash of the basic, and mostly inconclusive, literature
about the topic. Effective writers can skew data and assemble
the available research in lots of different ways. They can do
this because they don't get lost in the details of the research,
the methods and results, but rather can find the compelling
storylines. The effects of caffeine, the amount of water you
should drink, indeed many dietary matters fit this form. People

are most attracted to what confirms their prior beliefs, so stories that lean that way draw readers in, especially if the initial hooks suggests some tension, hence indirect endorsement.

A myth dispelled: People like to feel smart and like even more to feel smarter than others. So you can hook some people by suggesting that what they believe is true but not universally understood to be so. In other words, you're going to lift the veil on something your audience already believes they can see through, and they'll take great joy and pride in the wide-eyed amazement of the innocent others. Dispelling actual myths, making people abandon their cherished beliefs, takes a great deal of effort and time and generates a great deal of animosity and resentment along the way. So if you use the myth hook, make certain your intended audience doesn't really believe and that the true believers won't set their gun sights on you, unless you want to court controversy, to generate some kind of a click storm for whatever reason. (A lot of "news" articles are intentionally provocative in this way, so that many people feel compelled to comment in the comments and section and thus the number of site "hits" increases. The more hits a site gets, the more ad revenue it can generate.)

A problem solved: How to do something—save time, lose weight, become more confident, write a novel, anything that even a small percentage of the vast sea of people on the Internet might want. A lot of the people on the web at any given moment are looking for the solution to a problem, and so if you have a solution or can design what you do have to look like a solution, then you can draw people in. If the problem is real and the solution truly solves the problem, then as long as the effort is commensurate with the pain relieved, people will use the site. But to hook people, it's often effective to suggest the solution is easy and inexpensive, because that lowers the barriers of resistance. If you tell someone, I can show you how to lose ten pounds, guaranteed, but it will take an entire month of exercising for three hours a day, your site will go unclicked. Even if your exercise regime is effective and safe and otherwise legitimate, you have to sugarcoat it a bit. This is why "the small print" was invented.

A statement phrased as a question: Should you lease? Rather than entertaining both sides of the possible question of the piece, just argue for the one side. Yes you should lease, and here are all the reasons why. Don't listen to those buy-guys. They are nuts. Etc.

A shortcut: Save time, money, increase the speed of your computer, find more time in the day, etc. (appeal to efficiency, wonkishness).

Ten things every member of [your tribe] should know: Appeal to pride, guilt, identification (if you are or wish you were one of these people, you want to click on this).

Audacious prediction: By 2030 everyone will be flying electric cars. If the payoff is actually a bit less audacious, you can replace the actual promise with something vaguer like by 2030 everyone will be doing this (appeal to curiosity).

Issue a challenge: The hardest X you'll ever love (appeal to pride, competitive spirit).

Boldly assert a controversial position: Donald Trump will win, and here's why (appeal to incredulity).

Use a superlative: Best, biggest, fastest, strangest, ultimate, last (an implied challenge, "Is this really the biggest?").

This weird trick: Promise a surprising and quick solution (appeal to curiosity).

Offer a paradox: Three reasons why you shouldn't, and one reason why you must.

Dynamic arrangements

Dynamic can mean a couple of different things in the context of digital rhetoric. In general, dynamic suggests movement, change. A given change might be initiated by a user (dynamic interaction), by an internal event (getting the current date or determining which browser a user is using) or an external event (the arrival of some information, a stock quote or a storm threat), or by random (a rotation among multiple options determined by the machine generating a random number and then doing something with that random number).

We'll look at each of these dynamic arrangement techniques in turn.

Switching

What follows may strike you as esoteric. If the code mystifies you, focus on the pseudocode. If you can figure out how to describe what you want, you'll have a much better chance of searching for an explanation of how to make the computer do it.

In a digitally literate world we can tailor text (or the user experience more generally) for a given user based on his or her input using the computational ideas of switching and branching. You saw this in action in the very first digital example, the decision tree. A switch would be something like, if user chooses "sports," show a soccer metaphor. A branch would be, if user chooses "sports," show range of sports; when user selects a specific "sport," show metaphors related to that specific choice.

Let me show you how to tailor your prose for an audience using switching and branching. Here's an example of the pseudocode that might represent a simple metaphor-switching mechanism:

1. Offer a choice of either soccer or baseball
2. If soccer
3. Print metaphor 1
4. Else
5. Print metaphor

In natural language that might look like, "If a user indicates she likes soccer, offer soccer metaphors whenever metaphors are appropriate. If, on the other hand, she likes baseball, show baseball metaphors." There's a lovely example of this kind of thinking in JavaScript at W3Schools.com.

[[Search: W3Schools switch]]

In their example, the condition is met not by user input but rather by the machine using a get_date request. Go play with their "Try It Yourself" version. While you're at it, think of times when rather than using guesses or assumptions as a way of tailoring prose for a user you could use their direct input.[1]

Here's a slightly different automated switch example written in PHP. Don't worry about the language. Just see if you can kind of make out what's happening. (Hint: the dollar sign makes the word following it a variable—that is, an expression the content of which can be changed—and the equals sign tells the machine what content to start off with.)

```
<?
$season = date('m');   //in English we
would say, get the current month and call
it $season

if ($season >= 1 && $season <= 4){
$season = 'images/snow.jpg';
}//if the current month is 1,2,3, or 4
show the snow picture
elseif ($season >= 5 && $season <= 8){

$season = 'images/summer.jpg';
}

elseif ($season >= 9 && $season <= 12){
$season = 'images/autumn.jpg';
    }
Print "<img src=".$season." >";
?>
```

1. Americans and Canadians are the only people who call football "soccer." So if your users are anywhere else in the world, calling football "soccer" will be confusing. In the digital world, it's possible to get a fairly good idea if a person is from the United States or not by having the machine "sniff" the language in use. You could then offer alternative views: if en-US, soccer; if en-AU, football. [[Search: PHP accept-language header]] On the website see Sections/Rhetoric+/User Awareness.

Did you follow the thinking? It divides the year (twelve months) into three seasons; gets the current month as a number, `$season = date('m')`, and then switches pictures based on how that number compares to a range, 1–4 = snow, 5–8 = summer, 9–12 = autumn. Why three seasons instead of four? I can't remember. I wrote this code ten years ago. Maybe I couldn't find a good spring picture. I also don't remember why I called the winter picture snow instead of winter (I live in Atlanta where snow = apocalypse). The computer, of course, doesn't know or care *why* something has a given name. People using the website likely wouldn't notice that particular idiosyncrasy anyway, although a tendency toward idiosyncrasy may lead to noticeable problems over time. Moreover, if you had to pass your code on to someone else, when they lifted the hood and looked inside, they'd be confused. Snow, spring, autumn requires a person looking at the filenames to perform a metonymic switch as they read (snow = winter = 1–4). That's not difficult. It's as if snow = winter, even if you don't live where it snows in the winter. But why add the extra, risky, interpretive step? I wasn't writing a poem. I should have used a more consistent naming convention. I should have found a photographic icon for spring too. **Think before you code.**

To verify if you understood this script, you'd need to get your own modification of it running on your server. I'll walk you through the thought process here.

Put all four .jpg files in the same folder; your images folder is a likely place. Put the above code into a file, call it switcher.php, and then modify the code so it can show four pictures instead of three. (Hint: divide twelve by four instead of three).

1. How can you avoid waiting all year to see if it actually works? (Hint: replace `date('m')` with a number.)
2. What happens if `$season=5`?
3. How do you get January (m = 1) to display the winter picture? (Hint: seasons are cyclical, numbers are linear, even though January comes after December, and December is 12, so January is 1, not 13.)

If you want to see this digital form of arrangement online, go to Sections/ Arrangement/Passive.

Temporal arrangement

If you're trying to provide content on a regular basis, to drive traffic and increase your visibility, you might also want to develop an editorial calendar where you let the time of year trigger content you've written in advance, so that you don't have to think up new thoughts on the spot. So, in early August, back to school happens and so education and leave taking and learning and all things related to school become relevant. Every holiday and anniversary of significant events affords the same opportunity for prescience. If you put your timely pieces and articles into a database, you can program your site to pull the relevant article when the relevant date rolls around again. (To see a nondatabased way to program a date trigger, see page 105.)

Rather than thinking in terms of months and days as a way to arrange content, you might want to think in terms of minutes or even seconds. It might happen that you want your users to see something briefly. Maybe you want them to answer questions quickly. Maybe you don't want them to think so much as react. Maybe you have a slideshow with a voiceover and rather than having the user press Next, Next, Next, you want to have the machine advance the slides on a timer.

To create a countdown method of arrangement, you need a while loop. While loops are very useful in lots of different settings because they allow something to happen while something else keeps track of time or waits for the arrival of some event. The basic structure of a while loop written in PHP looks like this:

```
<?

$x = 0; // set time to 0
while($x <= 5) { //loop until x == 5, then
stop.

     print "The number is: $x <br>";
@TXT-last:  $x++; // increment time by one
     }

?>
```

Can you predict what that will do? Not terribly interesting, but it prints to the screen, "The number is: 1. The number is: 2," and so on until "The number is: 5" and then it stops. So how can you make use of that?

Let's say you're designing a timed test for a user. You want to show them some information and ask them to do something while looking at a screen, and you want to limit the time available for the task. You could write a PHP file that started a timer using a loop and then executed a meta-refresh link when the virtual sand ran out. The meta-refresh link looks like this:

```
<META http-
equiv="refresh" content="5;URL=http://www.
your-online-self.com/file.php">
```

The content= number tells the browser how long to wait, so you could just set this number to your desired time and be done with it, but for the sake of thinking through a loop, let's set content=0, instantaneous, and then set a timer to tick down and then execute the meta-refresh. Here's the pseudocode:

```
Set time = 0
While t <= 100, show screen
When t == 100, replace screen with
another.
```

And here's the actual code:

```
<?

$t = 0;
while($t <= 100) {
     echo "The number is: $t <br>";
     $t++;
```

```
print "<META http-
equiv='refresh' content='0;URL=http://www.
your-online-self.com/file.php'>";
}
?>
```

Without running that script, can you anticipate what's wrong with it? How does what we were thinking contrast with what we actually asked the machine to do?

We were thinking *count* seconds to 100, but all it's doing is *printing* at its own pace to 100. A modern computer executes way faster than a clock ticks. You could figure out how many times your computer prints the number is: X to the screen in say 100,000 seconds and then use that number as your base to estimate time: 100,000 = 10 seconds, so to get 30 seconds, set X to 100,000 × 3. But that's kind of messy and horribly imprecise. Worse, it's unnecessary because you can just use the meta-refresh code to accomplish your task. Remember that your goal is always to use the least number of lines of code necessary to get the job done.

[[Search: PHP timer]]

File slotmachine.php

While loops are efficient ways to automate repetitive tasks. Under Sections/Arrangement+/Slot Machine you have a program that chooses a number between one and four at random and displays one of four possible pictures depending on what random number turns up. It does the random number selection three times and thus displays three pictures in sequence. If it turns up three images of a kind, it also prints "JACKPOT." The example code on the website doesn't use a while loop. It uses a much less elegant solution. It gives essentially the same instruction three times in a row. Using a while loop, you can give the instruction just once and have it execute three times (or as many times as you like). Much more efficient.

Narrative in the digital age

The chief difference between digital and textual composition is that digital, if properly marked up with metadata, can actually address Plato's complaint about a text only ever saying the same thing no matter how many or what type of questions you ask it, just as an image never changes (*Phaedrus* 275c). In the digital age it's actually possible to compose texts that don't always say the same thing.[2]

[[Search: Kurt Vonnegut narrative arc]]

Stories have what's known as narrative arcs. The characters start out on one plane and move either up or down. Some stories involve a rise in fortune, such as

---

2.   You can argue that books don't always say the same thing because the reader changes and so interprets the book differently. Classical rhetoric tended to underestimate the role of the audience in meaning making. The point here is that digital texts aren't static the way print is fixed.

Horatio Alger stories. Some stories have a descending arc, such as the fall of man. And some have a dual directional arc, a rise and fall story. Some of the best stories provide an arc that seems to trend one way only to change direction. Now imagine a story composed of scenes each with their own micro-arcs. Depending on the order in which the scenes are presented, the overall curve might trend up with a big down, or it might oscillate up and down but trend mostly one way or the other, or it might trend down but go up a little bit at times. Now add the idea that you could identify some scenes not just by the direction of the arc but by its intensity as well, a big high or a big low. Girl meets boy; they fall in love; it turns out he's married. In one version you learn his old-world parents married him off when he was twelve, and he has never met the girl. In another, events suggest he was age of majority but still too young to marry happily, and he's not seen her in years even though they're still technically married. Maybe in another version he only thinks he's married but isn't for some reason. Work out a few more permutations. Now, if you put each of these narrative chunks into a database[3] composed of say a scene field and a trend field, where each scene is a piece of the story that makes a kind of sense on its own, the way Legos snap together, and the trend field is either positive (hopeful) or negative (distressing), then you could organize the scenes based on the trend field, say two positives and a negative and then a positive or the reverse. Or even at random. The story would thus be very different depending on which way it gets printed to the screen.

When you're reading a story for the first time, you have only a close-up view of the trend so you don't know the whole narrative arc until you're done. It's a bit as though you're zoomed in so close that you can only see a single point on a curve, but when you zoom out you see the curve from beginning to end. What looked like a disaster is now just a blip. All curves are straight lines if viewed closely. A downward trajectory doesn't trend down unless you've got at least two points on the line. Given a few more dots, the trajectory may start looking up. If in addition to the positive and negative field you had a field for intensity, say on a scale from one to ten, then any given downer might be only a minor irritation in one telling of the story, whereas it could be a disastrous down turn at that same moment in another telling. In version A, for example, the heroine's bicycle is stolen and so she has to walk to the train station to tell her love how she feels. Will she make it? In version B, she's hit by a car on her way to the station and never sees him off. What might versions C, D, and E be?

You could add other elements to the database as well. Maybe there are a few scenes that contain a character who isn't featured in the others, with the potential for that character to have a big role or a small role or perhaps no role at all if, in a given telling, his or her scenes don't get called. You could also invoke different settings or times of year. Perhaps even different imagery patterns or objects.

---

3. We deal with the mechanics of making databases in the section on memory; you can jump there if you want to know more about what a database is and how to make one. Alternatively, you may want to just keep reading and then jump back here after you've built your first or second content management system.

You could digitize a mystery story in a similar way. The clues could be coded in terms of obscurity, misdirection, and so on, and then offered in different patterns and at different rates, such that one version might give away the mystery upfront and prompt the user to work back through how it happened, while another version might conceal the mystery up until the very end or perhaps reveal a bit and then take an irrelevant, yet interesting, turn before turning back. You have as many options for construction as you have metatag categories and ways they can be configured.

In all cases, this form of digital narrative is supposed to say something different each time one "reads," or rather experiences, the text and depends on each chunk being interesting on its own and not necessarily requiring any other. If one chunk has a significant character who's never heard from again, that would likely be unsatisfying. If a character has old-world parents in one part but then inexplicably new-world parents in another, the laws of continuity would be violated. You need to make sure that the parts can snap together in different ways without creating ridiculous combinations.

Think of multiple threads, any one of which might weave the tale in a different way. Any reading might have several threads or one thread completely missing. The next time through, that missing thread might dominate. Similarly, you could have versions that have slightly different casts of characters or different interpretations of a character caused by the absence or inclusion of different scenes. So a scene that reveals a fatal flaw would tell the story one way, but were it absent, the story would say something else about how character influences destiny.

Our primary focus is information-rich websites rather than narratives, but the digital facilitates multiple paths even in information-rich environments. You could offer a user a prior knowledge test and then, based on how he or she did, you could send the user to a different starting place. If the user knows nothing, start at one. If the user is pretty advanced, start at ten. If the user seems too cocky, start at twenty, and then after he or she has suffered a little bit, put the user gratefully back where he or she belongs. You have as many options as you have ways to know (not just anticipating or assuming, as rhetors and writers of old, but actually knowing based on user behavior) how much the user knows, what he or she needs to know next, and what related topics he or she might like to explore.

The idea of presenting the same narrative in different ways and thus having a book <metaphor>say</metaphor> different things by enabling it to be read in different ways has been explored in the literate world. Julio Cortázar published *Hopscotch* in 1963. The digital age makes the idea of different versions of the same story ubiquitous because all text, if properly marked up, can be data from which any number of different stories may be told. Just as it isn't entirely new, it isn't entirely easy to write, either. The digital component, the database, is itself relatively easy, and we'll get to it. Writing a perfectly modular composition, where the parts can be snapped in and out in myriad ways, is the not-easy part. If you need to know something to understand something else, then a version that omitted the key detail would be at best inscrutable and at worst just annoyingly inept.

If you want to play around with the idea of a dynamic narrative, you don't have to get a database running. You could simply put the scenes on a Post-It note and move them around to see what effects are created. Storyboarding like this is an excellent way to think through arrangement in general. If you don't have any scenes to work with, and don't think you can or have time to make up a branching storyline, have a look at TheToast.net, "How to Tell if You Are in a Korean Drama." It's an amusing meta-perspective on the apparently limited storylines offered by Korean shows and, because each line is presented as a discrete chunk, you might be able to whip up a mix-and-match collection pretty quickly. Just a thought.

Random arrangements

Random is an interesting organizing principle. It's the shuffle option on your music player or the feeling-lucky option on your search page. You just saw random in action with the slot machine example. If you've got a lot of pieces of information that don't hang together well but any one of which is interesting in and of itself, then you might consider simply offering a piece at random. I have a version of this on one of my class websites where a different definition of rhetoric is printed to the screen each time a user goes there:

```
<?
$textfile ="quotes.htm"; // change to the
filename of your file.

$quotes = file("$textfile");
$quote = rand(0, sizeof($quotes)-1);
print  $quotes[$quote];
?>
```

The text file named quotes.htm contains a different definition of rhetoric on each line in the file. The script reads that entire file into working memory and then selects one line at random. That line is then printed to the screen. You can copy and paste the code from Sections/Arrangement/Random.

The Magic 8 Ball

The toy company Mattel made something called the Magic 8 Ball back in the 1950s and you can still buy one today. It's a plastic sphere with a polyhedron suspended in water inside it and a window that lets you see the polyhedron. Ask a question out loud; shake the ball, and when you stop shaking the ball, your answer magically appears in the window. Think you can make a digital version using JavaScript or PHP or something else?

You'd need a list of generic answers: Stop, Go, Run! Whatever. And then you'd need a randomizer. You could do something like this with PHP:

```
<?
$advice = rand(1, 3);
```

```
if ($advice == '1')
{
$advice = "Proceed!";
}
else
if ($advice == '2')
{
$advice = "Caution!";
}
else
$advice = "Stop!";
?>
```

The script works by identifying an arbitrary string called $advice and associating it with the PHP function rand, where the random number generated will be between one and three. Then there's a branching response based on the random number generated. The double equals sign means evaluate (if condition), and the single equals sign means equate (then set).

With only three options the game would get old pretty quickly, but it would be easy to add to the options. You could even dress the thing up to look a bit like the Magic 8 Ball of old using CSS (see Sections/Arrangement/Randomly Generated).

If you have your content in a database, then you can use the MySQL query RAND to pull content randomly.

It may have occurred to you by now, if the dazzling effect of == versus = hasn't made your head hurt, that random was an option in the realm of literate rhetoric too. You simply asked a question and then opened the book of answers "randomly," and there on the page you (or was it fate?) opened was the answer you were looking for. You could spin a globe and then plan your next vacation around the place your finger landed on. You could flip a coin or spin a bottle. I don't know why, but people love random. Put one on your domain and increase your hit count.

Passive arrangements

By passive arrangement I mean selection of content made by the machine rather than by the user. Instead of having a link text that says "click here," allowing the user to decide if he or she wants that content, the machine just takes the user where he or she needs to be. How do you know where your users want to be? Well, you can infer what they need based on their location and browser setup. You saw an example of user awareness in the section on digital audiences in Chapter 2 (see also Sections/ Rhetoric+/Audience+/User Awareness).

You saw another example of passive arrangement in the section on creating switches, where the date triggers a seasonally relevant image (see also Sections/ Arrangement+/Passive).

And you can always ask your user questions, the implication of which isn't apparent to the user but triggers which content gets displayed or how it gets displayed.

Interactive form for tailoring content

Here's a small project for playing with the idea of tailoring content based on user activity but without the user's direct intention (a semi-passive arrangement). We're going to cover your launch_pad.php with a user questionnaire that lets the user in only after he or she has answered some questions. The script then uses those answers to tailor the content.

Because you're the primary user for your launch_pad.php, what follows violates all rules of usability. You'd never want to ask silly questions of your users or stand pointlessly in their way, even if that user is you. This script is for experimental learning purposes only. Once you have it working you'll want to name it launch_pad_funny_version.php and revert to using the serious version on a daily basis. **Save launch_pad.php as launch_pad_funny_version.php before proceeding.**

While this application is silly, the technique is perfectly sound and you might want to make a more sophisticated version of it if you can think of a real use case. (Hint: maybe you want to test a user's prior knowledge as a way of deciding for him or her what he or she needs to encounter next.)

The form asks the following questions:
1.   What is your least favorite day of the week?
2.   What pet name do you use when you need to encourage yourself?
3.   What is your favorite color?

Given the answers, your launch_pad_funny_version.php executes as follows, in semi-pseudocode:

```
1. Get content from form
   // associate user content with vari-
   ables used to change content of launch
   $hatefulday = $_REQUEST['hatefulday']
   $petname = $_REQUEST['petname']
   $favcolor = $_REQUEST['favcolor']
   $encouragingmessage = "<h1>It's $hate-
   fuleday $petname!</h1><br>But you got
   this!!</br>"
2. Get the current day of the week
   a. $today = date(i); // i means Monday,
   Tuesday etc.
   If $today == hatefulday // if current
   day is same as user input
     Print $encourageingmessage;
3. Change background color of launch_pad.
   php to $favcolor
   a. <body bgcolor = "$favcolor"> //
   this is inline style (it's locally
   over riding the CSS) and bad form but
   the whole game's a bit off side
4. Else, enter as normal
```

So, if on a given Monday you fill out the form with "I hate Monday and my pet name is Gorgeous and my favorite color is chartreuse," instead of seeing what you normally see, you'll see:

It's Monday, Gorgeous!

But you got this!!

And the background color of your launch_pad_funny_version.php will instantly be chartreuse (#FFF00—Yes, as a matter of fact <shudder>chartreuse is an HTML color</shudder>). You can find the code for this method of arrangement under Designs/Launch Pads+/Interactive Launch Pad. You can use this method to tailor any PHP file based on user input. Find the code at Sections/Arrangement/User Input.

[[Search: HTML color names]]

Put Google Search on your-online-self.com

Regardless of what other methods of navigation you offer your users, you should seriously consider offering a search option. People are accustomed to finding things via search boxes and get easily frustrated if they can't remember where they saw something or figure out your naming conventions.

[[Search: how to put a Google search box on your website]]

I found http://www.webmonkey.com/2010/02/add_a_google_search_box_to_your_site/ fairly helpful. By the way, notice how the link shows the year and month (I assume that's what the folders 2010/02 refer to). Nice touch. The user has a sense of how old the information is and the designer/writer has a chronological index of past work. I don't know, of course, if that link will still be working by the time you see it, but I reproduced the URL here mostly just to show you the smart directory naming convention they used.

Designing your portfolio

While we tend to think of arrangement as what happens after all of the possible ideas have been invented and the best few selected from the many, there's a sense in which arranging existing material leads to the invention of new material. By looking at what you've done so far and how the pieces relate or fail to relate to each other, you'll come to think of things you need to do next. You'll notice gaps and identify dead-ends that need to be removed or replaced by very different versions. **A portfolio is both a retrospective narrative and a roadmap for the future.**

You can't just give your users a list of files and consider your portfolio done. You have to arrange the exhibits in a meaningful way, one that suggests a purposeful journey, a long-term thought process. You also want to use your portfolio as a source of inspiration and insight. The narrative connects the dots; the analysis indicates which dots are missing. You're not likely to find the missing dots among your past work. You need to create some side projects, pursue ideas outside your dominant field, to show that you can learn independently and have transferable skills, not just disciplinary knowledge. <aside>No one outside the university has better than a passing interest in what philosophers or historians or poets are up to. It's a shame but there it is.</aside>

Because your primary skills are writing and researching (I assume), **the best argument for hiring you is evidence of your ability to ask interesting questions and find valuable answers.** Another way to think about this is to ask, "What kind of rhetorical problem does each piece solve?" What was the problem? For whom was it a problem? What was the solution and why that one instead of others? You also might want to consider a post mortem for each piece. How well did it turn out? What were its strengths and weaknesses? What did you learn that you have applied moving forward? Remember that in all things **you want to look like a conscientious problem solver.**

Creating coherence out of work you did in completely different settings, for different audiences and with different purposes in mind, is difficult. The difficulty stems from several sources.

If you're a freelance writer, chances are your projects are done because you landed the job and your goal was to get paid. Providing evidence of past success is a compelling argument for hiring you again, so each completed example might be useful evidence, but of what exactly? The nature of the work says something, but what you can say about how doing it advanced your craft will be even more important. Over time you may find a profitable niche to mine and that will provide a source of coherence, but you might want to create the illusion of coherence before it emerges by leaving some of the more random jobs out of the story.

If you're a student, you have an analogous portfolio problem. Most term papers are written to accomplish a single goal: get a grade. After that, no one cares. This means that any given essay is only as good as it needed to be and few have any real interest. Because we had to write so many essays at once, often only one or two might get our full attention, and even then only for a few days. Not an optimal composition strategy, except insofar as it accomplished the only job that mattered at the time.

The other reason it's hard to turn any given term paper into a plausible portfolio item is that many essays are a response to a class context, a question the class is expected to answer, and so don't mean much outside that context.

Rather than thinking about the essays you've written for a grade in college as a source of items for display, consider building new projects out of the more interesting ones. It might be possible to **take the work from two or more different classes and build something new out of them.** You should also make an inventory of the kinds of work that people in the industry you're contemplating do and then make a few examples of that kind of work.

A great deal of what used to be called technical writing, for example, is accomplished these days by screen casting instead of words on a screen. You walk users through a process, while narrating what you're doing and explaining what's happening, all while a piece of software captures what's happening on a screen and records what you're saying.

[[Search: screen-casting software]]

Instead of reading, a user watches and listens and then does what you did. Making a good screen cast isn't easy. You not only have to know what to click and in what order, but you have to speak in an interesting and fluid way about what you're doing as you do it. You need a script. You need a clear outcome. And you need to get from blank screen to desired outcome smoothly and engagingly. You'll also likely need to develop some video editing skills because getting a perfect take, even with practice and planning, won't happen very often, even with a three-minute video. Screen casting takes practice and forethought, but it's a marketable skill.

For the same reasons, you might want to include an audio or a video recording of you explaining or describing something. Consider also offering an infographic as well as any other visual representations of data you can come up with. You want to demonstrate that you have analytical skills too. You may be a writer, but you're more than "a wordsmith."

There are three portfolio design examples on the website (Designs/Portfolios+). In the first example (Portfolio 1), the basic idea is to have a narrative stitch the various pieces together. While the design pattern itself is relatively simple to hack, and you might want to use it for other purposes as well, the portfolio's binding narrative will take a great deal of invention, reflection, and planning (drafting, revising, editing: writing, in other words). In the second example (Portfolio 2), the basic idea is to have a single piece front and center, with a video talking a user through the work and a text version of what the talking head is saying in the space below. Alternatively, you could have the sample you're talking about in the space below. Down the left side there's a space for links to your other projects. The third example (the imaginatively named Portfolio 3) is more like a transcript than a portfolio per se. It also has a couple of slick visualization tools that you might want to add to your code warehouse even if you don't want the whole design.

If your work isn't amenable to a narrative because each entry is a discrete piece of work, then you might want to bucket the example found at Designs/Buckets+/Raised. This design consists of three-dimensional cards, each having an image at the top, text below, and a link at the end, presumably to the full project described in the text. You might also want to include the date the project was completed, as a way of showing development over time, perhaps. Because each of these cards is discrete, you don't have to worry about creating a narrative to arrange them into a coherent body of work. However, if the pieces seem to have nothing to do with each other to the point where your interests seem all over the place, almost haphazard, that may not give the effect you're looking for.

Don't think of your portfolio as a retrospective project. Think of your portfolio as an always partially complete project with each part suggesting further projects that may fill in gaps and lead to a more convincing whole. You should **include projects for which you got neither paid nor graded.** Your portfolio is more than the sum of its parts, and your-online-self.com is more than your portfolio. The larger project is your brand or, if you dislike marketing language, your digital ethos—it's an ongoing, evolutionary self that demonstrates a core set of values through the work it displays.

Because a portfolio relies on the existence of a body of more or less completed work, and you're just getting started, you might want to have a section on your domain that highlights work in progress, current and future projects that show where you're headed. This section might be largely aspirational, but you don't want to look like you're just blowing smoke. Be as specific as possible about the purpose and the parameters of each project and include an indication of its level of completion, perhaps using a technique like the one shown at Sections/Rhetoric/Learning/Progress Report or, if the PHP there is daunting, consider the CSS-only variation at Sections/Rhetoric+/ Learning+/Progress Bar.

Summary

Digital arrangement is about providing exactly the right amount of information for a specific user as quickly as possible. This is a very high bar and one that can't be readily achieved without providing multiple paths through the same material. Make sure you enable a search feature on your site. Make sure also that each section has a meaningful label and that all connections among the parts are evident. If you choose to play around with random methods of arrangement, make sure your users are aware of what's happening and are along for the ride. If they ask a specific question and you give a random answer, they'll wrinkle their nose or worse. If you change content around without explanation or apparent logic, your return customers won't return.

Where you are now

At this point, you've learned that the rhetorical canon of arrangement has become navigation in the digital epoch. Specifically, you've learned many different ways to link files. You've learned a few different menu techniques as well. As a result, whatever files you have on your-online-self.com should be linked in some fashion, unless for some reason you don't want your users to see a given file, which might be the case for some of your code snippets or experimental designs.

You've learned several dynamic methods of arrangement, including random methods. You've learned how to use environment variables as triggers for showing or hiding different content (passive arrangement). And you've learned a semi-passive and yet apparently interactive arrangement technique as well, where a user fills out a form and you show content based on what he or she said in the form. You've learned about flat design and how to put a search feature on your-online-self.com.

In addition, at this point, you should also have a beta version of a portfolio. You'll need to let your portfolio evolve as both your work and your understanding of it changes.

5

MEMORY

Memory has always been divided into the natural (what stays with you without conscious effort) and the artificial (memorization and learning). Oral cultures had highly elaborate methods for remembering information, often in quantities that stagger we literate and postliterate types, such as the entirety of Homer's *Odyssey*. The technique the orators used for developing their artificial memories is known as "the memory palace."

There are a number of fine books that explain the practice in far greater detail than we have space here to attempt, especially as we're focused on building digital variants, but basically an orator made a list of the topics he needed to cover in a speech. Then he designed an iconographic image that contained visual cues for each of the things he needed to say on each topic. These images might be actual sketches or they might be imaginary. In either case they'd be high-definition images, with vivid colors and striking (memorable) details. Then he placed (physically or mentally) each image along a well-trod path through a familiar space. Finally, in preparation for the speech, he'd walk the path (actually or imaginarily), stopping in front of each image and reciting the relevant part of the speech.

As he became more and more practiced at giving the speech, he might walk a slightly different path through the images, to think about how best to arrange the material, to think about how the interpretation of the parts might differ depending on when they occurred, and to keep from getting too rigid in his thinking. The goal was to sound spontaneous and natural rather than premeditated and labored. Avoiding a too-studied manner was why Alcidamas warned against writing out a speech verbatim as a preparation for giving it. Over time the really great orators could develop vast mental repositories of speeches, both their own and other people's, out of which they could rapidly assemble new speeches with the appearance of extemporaneity. They were in a sense recycling, building new edifices out of prefabricated parts. By juxtaposing previously unjuxtaposed pieces, they might create something new, but mostly the emphasis was on saying what was appropriate, not saying something entirely new. In a sense, the orators invented the idea of prefabrication.

Cicero was the first to make a habit of transcribing his speeches, that I know of at least, and he wrote them down *after* he gave them, often embellishing and likely correcting what maybe wasn't to his liking in hindsight. His goal was self-promotion rather than learning, although he no doubt learned in the process.

The tradition of the memory palace survived long into the literate era, as public speaking remained an important skill. But because one could write, the "palaces" became larger and more complex and more detailed, morphing ultimately into elaborate notebooks containing hundreds of pages. These collections of ideas, often taken verbatim from what the collector had read, were known as commonplace books, and creating them was a standard part of being a highly literate citizen.

||Search: Florilegium]]

As books became cheaper, highly literate people no longer needed to keep verbatim copies of sections of the books they were able to find in libraries they were lucky enough to visit, and they started to keep libraries of their own. Today we have the idea of digital memory to add to our natural and artificial mnemonic capacities. Digital memory consists of any of the electronic devices, hardware and software, that you might use to create a sharable database of digital assets—text, images, video, anything that can be digital.

A database is a collection of similarly structured information, each piece of information having a unique identifying key. The key enables you to retrieve a specific piece, while the similar structure allows you to sort and organize the entire contents in different ways. A content management system is an interface between the users and the database.

Most of this chapter is devoted to showing you how to create your own content management systems, but before we get deep, here are a couple of lighter-weight projects for digitally enhancing the traditional practice of memorization.

Flashcards

The most common way to memorize new information is to recite it over and over again. An easy way to automate memorization is to use flashcards. There are a number of really smart apps out there that will not only show you what you want to learn, but will also keep track of what you get right and what you get wrong, and using that data change the frequency with which you see your problem areas. Given the existence of these apps, it might seem counterproductive to make your own, but there's some very deep learning involved in the process of designing your own mnemonic devices. If nothing else, you'll get a cool JQuery and CSS technique out of what follows. You can use it to help your users remember important ideas, to create interactive quizzes, and otherwise get them to engage with your content.

JQuery is a library of JavaScript functions that speeds up the process of making JavaScript applications. It's a code repository in a single file, essentially. You don't have to download or install it. Nor do you have to understand it to use it. You just have to provide a link to a permanent version of it running on a Google server or elsewhere. Between the <head></head> tags of a file that will use JQuery you put the following:

```
<script src="https://ajax.googleapis.com/
ajax/libs/jquery/1.11.2/jquery.min.js"></
script>
```

The numbers 1.11.2 refer to the version of JQuery this program requires. New versions come out periodically, and while maintaining backwards compatibility is a goal of all programmers, keep the version number in mind.

In our flashcard example, what JQuery doesn't accomplish is accomplished by CSS. What you wind up with is a series of "cards" with an image on one side that when hovered over will flip to reveal some text. You could have text on both "sides," for vocabulary review, for example. Head to the website, Sections/ Memory/Flashcards CSS, to see what you can make with the technique. Maybe you can make a digital memory palace with an image on one side and what you want to remember when you imagine the image on the other. You might be able to use this technique to practice visualizing and thereby rehearsing a lengthy speech.

The website also has a flashcard example that automatically rotates through a series of <digital>cards</digital>, with a question on one side, followed five seconds later by the answer. If you view the source code at Sections/Memory+/ Flashcards JS, you should be able to make use of the source code, which uses an array.

An array is a data structure. There are associative and indexical arrays. Associative arrays are lists of items with the numerical order implicit in the way they appear in the set. Indexical arrays, on the other hand, have each item's number explicitly stated. The Flashcard JS example uses an indexical array like this:

```
var splashmessage=new Array()  // initializes
array
splashmessage[0]='Who were Corax and
Tisias?' // item 1
splashmessage[1]='The progenitors of rhetoric,
according to tradition.' // item two
```

And so on. All you have to do is add to and edit the splashmessage pieces using even numbers for the questions and odd numbers for the answers. The original version, which I got years ago from DynamicDrive.com, was written as a slideshow to display images. I hacked it up to function like flashcards. You can get it running for yourself with minimal struggle, I think. If you can't get it working, search the Internet for a more intelligible example.

The last flashcard example (Sections/Memory/Flashcards PHP) is written in PHP and MySQL and pulls its content from a database. It's much more complicated than the previous two, but what you need to learn to get applications like it running is explained in detail below.

[[Search: list of mnemonics]]

A digital memory palace

While the memory palace of old is no longer necessary, the idea of keeping a collection of prefabricated parts out of which you can rapidly assemble new projects is digitally relevant. A warehouse of prefabricated parts lets you think on a higher plane about what you're making as you make it because you don't have to redesign and recode each piece as you need it, and thus get stuck in the weeds. Think about how different Legos would be if you had to make each brick before you started putting them together. The more prefabricated parts you have, the quicker you can assemble new assets. So **get in the habit of searching for and keeping collections of cool bits of code.**

Under the Design tab on the website you'll find some snippets of code that may prove useful. The snippets are grouped under 3D Effects, Buckets, Tables, and On Hovers. Copy and paste any you like and tinker around with them to see how they work. Figuring out how the bits work is a critical step in the process of becoming digitally literate because you won't always be able to just plug in a bit. Often you'll need to modify it slightly, and you can't modify what you don't understand.

You should dedicate some time every day to searching the web for code snippets and CSS techniques. Each time you see a design element you like, see if you can replicate it or find a tutorial about how to make it or an example you can just copy and paste. Each time you get something good that works, save it into a directory on your server.

Designing your code warehouse

Over time your warehouse will become a jumble if you don't maintain order. **Name each file in a meaningful way,** so that when you see the name months or even years later you understand immediately what's in there. If you have meaningful names, then to wander among your collection of parts all you need to do is make sure there's no index.html (or index.php) file in the directory. Absent a file called index (or default.html or default.php in some cases), many servers will simply show an alphabetical list of all the files in the directory. Some servers, however, will show a file not found file (404.html) instead of the lists of files, as a security measure. To get around this, you can write a script that displays a list of the files in a directory. See the next section, "Code warehouse." By the way, in most cases you can edit the default 404.html file. If you do that, you can both further personalize your server space and show the world what a geek you are.

Code warehouse

Sorting and organizing your snippets in ways that will remain meaningful over time may take some forethought. Meaningful names are an important first step, but you may also want to make sure that you leave notes in each file. You can write comments that won't print to the screen using < ! -- .... --> in your HTML files and you can comment out PHP using // for PHP files. I've also found it helpful to include an explanation of whatever technique the example I'm keeping does using the example itself.

You can copy and paste the code listed below from the website (Sections/ Memory/Code Warehouse). Can you read it?

```
<?
$dir = "."; // directory where dir.php is
".." would be one directory up from where
dir.php is.

// Open a known directory, and proceed to
read its contents
if (is_dir($dir)) {
    if ($dh = opendir($dir)) {
        while (($file = readdir($dh)) !==
false) {

print "<a href='$file'>" . "$file" . "</
a><br>" . "\r" ;
        // wrap the name of each file in an
achor to make it clickableSorting an
        }
        closedir($dh);
    }
}
?>
```

What would you get if you had a directory full of image files only and you changed <a href= to <img src=?

This script is simplistic. Once you have it working you'll want to search the Internet for something more sophisticated, maybe one that sorts alphabetically. Maybe you want to exclude some kinds of files or display only files of a particular extension. You could also combine the preceding script with the JavaScript you used from the dropdown selection lists on your launch screen, to save screen space.

Although your snippets won't age in the sense of wearing out over time, techniques come in and out of fashion. For a while, four or five years ago as of 2016, boxes with rounded corners were all the rage. CSS had evolved to a point where a curved edge was possible and once a few people figured this out, everyone was replicating the effect. Now rounded corners are kind of passé. Never stop collecting. You needn't throw out any of your digital assets since what little space any given snippet takes is trivial, but think twice before you bring back the dancing baby.

[[Search: dancing baby]]

Content management

Content management refers to the practice of keeping track of digital assets of all kinds—text, images, audio, video. The goal of the practice is to make sure that there is only one version of any given asset, that it is the most current, and that it is designed so that it can be used in different places without being rewritten or redesigned.

Inclusion

A goal of digital rhetoric is to use information as efficiently as possible, to never recreate or rewrite what's already written. This goal is sometimes referred to as the DRY principle. That is, don't repeat yourself.

[[Search: DRY principle]]

There are several reasons for avoiding repeating yourself (or rewriting code). Replication from natural memory leads to errors and inconsistencies. It's also unnecessary in the digital age to remake something because digital objects can be effortlessly replicated. When it comes to documents, the DRY objective is achieved by simply including the repeated text verbatim wherever it's needed. Most documents contain some repetitive content, such as contact information on an email, legal requirements on a memorandum of agreement, attendance policy on a syllabus, privacy policy on a website. If you let everyone reproduce these from memory, then you'll get inconsistencies and errors and everyone will be spending time redoing something already done. Instead, most server-side scripting languages have an include file function. In PHP, for example, if you want to include a file you simply write

```
<? include('name_of_file.html'); ?>
```

assuming the needed file is in the same directory as the file calling it. Inclusion offers an additional efficiency in that if the contents of the included file changes, all files that include it are instantly updated. If historical accuracy matters, then you have to be careful not to update files that are supposed to be written in stone, and so it's a good idea to keep a list of all included files and the files in which they're included.

Versioning

Versioning, keeping each iteration, is a good idea in general. You should keep an historical record of a document's change over time, so that you have a record of progress, a memory of change, and the ability to revert to an earlier version if something goes wrong. Wikipedia has this function built in. Many content management systems, in fact, make it relatively easy to keep versions, replacing "save" with "save as" where the new name is the original filename plus an auto-incremented number. If you're working in an environment that isn't automated in this way, consider keeping not just backups of current work but do a "save as" periodically, say at the end of every day. Such a digital enhancement of your writing process is vitally important when you're working on two machines at once, as you typically are when writing for the web. Usually you have a development site and a public site, and you test things locally and then put them up on the server. If you happen to overwrite the wrong version, pull down the old one or put up a broken one, you can waste many hours of work. (Trust me, I know.) You can avoid this frustration by always moving files only in one direction. But if you work on multiple machines, as people often do, on a desktop usually but on a laptop when traveling, for example, then sloppy practices can kill productivity.

For a website of any significance, you should keep a document of changes and file dependencies, which images are called in which files and when was each file last updated. That kind of meta-information will allow you to keep track of an ever-changing communication stream.

[[Search: GitHub]]

Databases—dynamic content management

If a website is a collection of linked files maintained by a single person (the web-master) on behalf of a group or organization, then a content management system is a website that can receive files from multiple registered users as well as external data sources. Typically, there's a workflow system where someone has to sign off on a file before it finds its way onto the site, although in the case of dynamic data, once a source is trusted its latest output may be allowed simply to appear without scrutiny. Be careful. Typically, each user has a section of the content that they're responsible for, and the permissions and roles are maintained through a signup and login procedure. While your-online-self.com is, for now at least, a single authored site, I'm going to show you some of the primary parts of content man-agement systems, in case you get an idea that will generate a community of users.

There are many tutorials on the web about how to set up and use a database (DB). Many of these were written by people far more expert in these matters than I am. My plan with the next few pages is to start you thinking about the pos-sibilities a database affords, and to convince you that you can learn to make and use databases to create dynamic and interactive content management solutions. What follows will require you to be patient and persistent. This is by far the most horned-rimmed part of the book. But you're ready.

The example database here will provide your-online-self.com with a running list of things you've read with your highlights and notes, assuming of course you enter the data as you read and you read regularly. You can use what follows to make any kind of content management system you like. I've used this same tech-nique for the glossary that's on the website. I'm suggesting a reading list simply because as a lifelong, independent learner, you read a lot, and anyone who reads a great deal needs some way to remember all that information. If your note-taking practice consists of just highlighting, then unless you have your books (or digital texts) with you, you don't have your notes. More importantly, if you don't extract your highlights and make notes, you won't be cognitively processing your read-ing and you won't get as much out of it. Also, if you keep detailed notes of your reading in a database, and you read and record regularly, your-online-self.com can have regularly updated content without your having to create entirely new content from scratch; you can just share your notes and keep going. That kind of content invention is far more efficient than blogging and can be just as valuable, even more so perhaps, if you have good taste in books and know how to write decent gist.

The reading list DB

Here's the to-do list, followed by explanations, followed by code examples to work with:

1. Set up a database on your server with a table named reading_list containing the fields book_id, title, author, summary, published, and date.
2. Create a file called connect_db.php that will connect a web file to the database for data entry and retrieval.
3. Create a file called put.php
4. Create a file called pull.php
5. Create a file called reading_list.php
6. Upload all four files to your server and debug.
7. Once you have reading_list.php running, see if you can add a field or two, maybe subject (history, theory, politics, literature, etc.) and a type of entry (book, article, op-ed, fiction, nonfiction, poem).
8. Finally, see if you can use some CSS to make reading_list.php more useable and more aesthetically appealing. The version I'm giving you is barebones.

All told, this collection of files amounts to a rudimentary content management system. It's basically what Drupal, WordPress, Vibe, and other professional-grade website-in-a-box software tools do. This will be much more rudimentary, of course, but once you know how to DIY, you can take your content management to the next level and any number of levels beyond that you dare to go.

Maybe you want to create a digital archive of photographs with technical notes about how they were taken or with a narrative to accompany each one. Maybe you want dramatize the major historical events of a city by placing old photographs, texts, and audio recordings over maps of the city as it was at different intervals in the past. Another possibility for a CMS is an annotated and illuminated version of a manuscript or a book. Using the techniques you're about to learn, you could also create a dynamic narrative that can be assembled and reassembled, based on user choices, out of entries in the database. You could also set up and keep a dynamic index of all of your PowerPoint or Keynote slides, a kind of supersized slide deck, if you will, independent of any given presentation, one that allows you to generate new presentations on-the-fly without having to open each individual presentation and copy and paste. Maybe you need to keep an extensive DB regarding clients and potential clients, or students in a program, with photos, biographies, accomplishments, and needs. Maybe you want to develop a learning environment for students consisting of test questions and sample answers and feedback repositories. The possibilities are endless. You could of course buy any one of these tools, but making your own provides ultimate control over the work they enable. Designing your own will help you think for yourself.

Before we do the eight items on our content management list, you need to make sure you've got a database setup on your server. How you do that depends on who your hosting provider is. If you have a Cpanel, a screen filled with icons that denote different programs and tools, then you may see among the options something called PHPMyAdmin.[1] This software is a web interface for making and administering databases. Using it simplifies making tables and fields. Tables are collections of fields, and fields are containers for digital objects: words, images, audio files, and videos. You can think of a database as the electronic replacement for a file cabinet or a Rolodex or any other archive of information sorted and displayed for optimal retrieval opportunity.

A database is a memory palace of nearly infinite capacity. And it can be designed in such a way that you can actually get more out of it than you put into it because you can search, resort, and recombine the contents of a database in ways that are otherwise either incredibly inefficient or actually impossible with paper assets like books and documents. Even digital documents on your computer can't do what they can do if you were to put them into a database.

If you don't see anything obvious from your account's administrative panel, search the web for something like setting up a database on [your hosting provider]. Alternatively, you can search directly on your service's FAQ pages. The information you need is bound to be there. During the setup process, you'll be creating a db_username and db_password. Remember these.

Creating a table

Create a table called reading_list. How you do this depends on how your server is set up. I'd use PHPMyAdmin, which will ask you to name the table and then ask how many fields you want. For the reading_list you want five fields.

[[Search: YouTube: creating a table in PHPMyAdmin]]

Once that's done, you'll likely see a screen asking you to name and define the field types. The names are: book_id, author, title, summary, published, date. You should see a dropdown list nearby listing the field types, and there will be quite a few of them. Each field type choice determines what kinds of things you can do with the contents of that particular field, as well as how large those contents can be. For our purposes, the field types are, in order: INT, VARCHAR, VARCHAR, TEXT, INT, DATE.

INT stands for integer, any whole number. **Every entry in a DB needs to be unique** for it to function correctly, and so you'll see that tables almost always contain an ID field that is auto-incremented, meaning it goes up by one automatically each time a new entry is added. Typically, on the right side of the line where you entered book_id and selected INT, you'll see another dropdown list from which **auto-increment is an option. Select that.** VARCHAR means any string of alphanumerical characters (e.g., words!@#2), typically no longer than 255 characters. How long is the title of any given book you've ever read? Current versions of MySQL have some ways to enable a longer string, but 255 should work just fine. So put 255 in the field next to the name title. VARCHAR

1. Check now to make sure your server has MySQL and PHP running. Check also for PHPMyAdmin. There are alternative tools, but everything I'm saying in the next pages depends on these here.

will work for author as well. Because your summary might be longer than 255 characters (not words but characters), use TEXT, which will give you room for 21,448 characters. What's that in words? About 3,000 if your words average seven characters in length. That should do it for a summary of a book. If you're verbose, read the section on style. You don't need to add a number to the field length when you use TEXT. Published is the date of publication; using INT here will allow you to key-in any date you choose. Date is the date you made the entry. The DATE field type declaration will automatically log the date the entry was submitted for you using the script I'm giving you, generated by a bit of PHP.

File db_connect.php

To get a website to talk to a database, you have to establish a connection. You can do this with a bit of code that can either be written in every file that needs the database (inefficient), or by creating a separate file that makes the connection and then include that file for every other file that needs the database (much better).

File db_connect.php looks like this:

```
<?
$link = mysql_connect("localhost","db_
username ","db_password");
mysql_select_db("db_username", $link);
?>
```

Instead of localhost you may need www.your-online-self.com for the db username and the db_password, those you set up when you set up the database. Save all that as db_connect.php and then point your browser to it. If you got it right, you'll see a blank screen. If some of the information isn't right, you'll see an error message on the screen. Getting this little bit of code running is crucial, and it may take some mucking about. Be patient if you don't get it right immediately. If you're struggling, you should do a search for "connect to a database on [your host provider]." Once you've got it right, you'll be able to reuse db_connect.php.

File put.php

The next step in the process is to write a form that will take content from a user and put it into the database. So you need a file that has an HTML form in it and the PHP code needed to get the content from each field in the form and put it in the correct field in the database.

File put.php looks something like this:

```
<?
//each of the lines below puts the con-
tents of each line of your form into a
variable so that it can be used, stored or
modified
```

```
$add = $_REQUEST['add'];
$author = $_REQUEST['author'];
$title = addslashes($_REQUEST['title']);
$summary = addslashes($_
REQUEST['summary']);
$published = $_REQUEST['published'];

$date = date('Y-m-d'); // this gets the
current date from the server represented
as 2015-05-06, for example
if (isset($add)) { //check to see if user
hit submit button
// process form
include "db_connect.php";  // connect to
the database
// the line below puts the content from
the form into the database, each field
being filled by relevant part of the form.
The contents from the author field on the
form goes into the author field in the
database. Make sure the form names and db
fields are identical. Author is not the
same as author.
$insertresult = mysql_query ("INSERT INTO
reading_list
        (book_id,author,title,summary,pub
lished,date)
  VALUES ('$book_id','$author','$title','$s
ummary','$published','$date')
   ");
if (!$insertresult)      //if the insert
was unsuccessful
{
     printf ("Error creating database:
%s\n", mysql_error ());
     }
mysql_close($link); // close the database
}
print "DONE!"; // provide user with feed-
back

print "<a href='reading_list'>Back</A>";
// provide use with whatever they need to
do the next thing.
exit;
```

```
?>
<html>
<body>
<h1>Add to Reading List</h1>
<FORM METHOD="POST" action="<?php echo
$PHP_SELF; ?>">
<input type="text" name="title" size="50"
value="title"></br>
<input type="text" name="author" size="50"
value="author"></br>
<input type="text" name="published"
value="date of publication" size="50">
</br>
<textarea name="summary" cols="50"
rows="15"></textarea></BR>

<INPUT TYPE="submit" value = "add"
name="add">
</form>
</body>
</html>
```

If you got all of that right, you should see a web form when you go to your-online-self.com/put.php. If the screen is blank, then you've likely left a semicolon or a pointy bracket out somewhere. Once you can see the form, put some content in the fields and press Submit. Then go to PHPMyAdmin and click the browse link. You should see the content you entered in the form there. If there's no data, then there's something wrong with your INSERT statement. **You need to make sure the values on the form and the names of the fields in your database are identical.** (It's case sensitive, and all quote marks and parentheses come in pairs.) Once you're getting data into your database, make three or four complete entries for later testing purposes.

You might have noticed the function addslashes. For reasons that I've never fully understood, apostrophes cause syntax errors in MySQL databases unless they're "escaped," which means putting a backslash (\) before the apostrophe. If you leave addslashes out, you'll get an error message when you try to put information containing an apostrophe into a DB. Symmetrically, you should include stripslashes when you pull content from a database that might have escaped apostrophes, as the presence of backslashes is distracting to human readers.

To get content out of a database and print it to the screen, you need to connect to the DB, select content from a table, and then print the content to the screen by wrapping the results in HTML. The code in the next section should do the trick.

File pull.php

File pull.php looks like this:

```
<?
include "db_connect.php";
 // Performing SQL query
$query = "SELECT * FROM reading_list order
by date desc";
$result = mysql_query($query)
     or printf ("database error: %s\n",
mysql_error ());
// Printing results in HTML
      while(list($book_id,$title,$author
,$summary,$published,$date)=mysql_fetch_
row($result)){
print "<b>". $date ." </b> --</br> ";
print "$author .","$title." </br>";
print "</br>";
print $summary;
print "<hr>";
}
// Closing connection
mysql_close($link);
?>
```

Basically all that means is get everything (* is everything) out of the database and
print it in order of the most recent entries (by date desc). You can make it
look anyway you like just by altering the HTML tags.

Finally, although you could see the contents of your database by pointing your
browser to pull.php, you can also include its contents inside another file. If, for
example, you wanted to share your current reading list with the world, then in your
index.php file (or any other .php file) you'd write an Include statement like this:

```
<? Include('pull2.php'); ?>
```

The file pull2.php is almost identical to pull.php, only the SELECT statement
looks like this:

```
$query = "SELECT * FROM reading_list order
by date desc LIMIT 3";
```

The LIMIT statement prints only three (or whatever number you choose) records
to the screen. That way you don't overflow the container or overshadow the other
information on your index.php screen. Alternatively, you could include the entire
DB in an <iframe>:

```
<iframe src='pull.php'></iframe>
```

That way your users could scroll through your entire reading list without it taking
up the whole screen. As is often the case, there are many different ways to do the
same thing. Think creatively. Keep an open mind. By the way, what do you figure
desc means in the SELECT statement and what would the opposite be? And
what effect would asc have on how the list gets printed to the screen?

At this point you have the very basics of a content management system. You have a connection to a database, a form for entering content into your database, and a file for pulling the content out of the database and printing it to the screen. Cool. And congratulations. But how do you edit an entry if you want to or delete one if you decide you need to? Well you could do either directly in PHPMyAdmin. In fact, you could enter data into your database use PHPMyAdmin instead of put.php. And you could read all of your entries in it as well, but we're all about creating custom interfaces and so we're making our own interface for our reading list instead of using PHPMyAdmin.

File reading_list.php

The code that follows puts all of the pieces together. We're going to leave put.php as is and just link to it in the file we're making now. We're also going to include db_coonect.php. The rest of the code we're going to write by modifying pull.php a great deal.

Because your summaries might be longer than a hundred words and so take up quite a bit of screen, we're going to pull only the first twenty characters and offer an option to read the whole entry. If you get it working, you'll see a table like the following, with content from your reading_list DB under each heading, with the capacity to sort by column heading, author, date, title, etc.

Author | Title | Summary . . . | Published | Date | Edit | Delete

What follows is the code that you can copy and paste from the website, but it's worth reading it here, I think, to get a sense of what's going on. Understand it will be valuable because you'll then be able to modify it rather than just replicating it. Replication is a decent start but no doubt you have some great ideas for your own content management system, and for that you'll need to be able to modify this. So read it through. Get it from the website and replicate it on your server, and then take it to your next level.

```
//print to the screen a link to data input
screen so user can click on that to access
form to enter a book summery into db
<a href="put.php">Add new entry</a>

<?
<?//Capturing data from user input and
associating each input //with a variable
$book_id = $_REQUEST['book_id'];
$title = $_REQUEST['title'];
$author = $_REQUEST['author'];
$summary = $_REQUEST['summary'];
$published = $_REQUEST['published'];
?$date = $_REQUEST['date'];
```

```
<?//connecting to database
<?include ("db_connect.php");

?//Creating SELECT query based on user
preference to enable sorting by author,
title, or year published

<?if(isset($author)){
     $order = 'author';
<?}

<?elseif(isset($title)){
<?    $order = 'title';
     }

elseif(isset($published)){
     $order = 'published';
     }
<?else $order = "book_id";

<?if($order=='book_id'){$desc = 'asc';
<?}
<?else $desc = 'desc';

<?//get the first 20 characters of a book's
summary, the author, title, date published
and date entered into db

<?$query= "select left(summary,20)
as summary, author, title,published,
date from reading_list ORDER BY $order
$desc";
<?$result = mysql_query($query);

<?//print data to screen as html with
links edit and //delete
<?echo "<table ><tr style='background-
color:#D7D7FF;'><td><a
<?href='reading_list.php?author'>author</
a> </td><td><a href='reading_list.
php?title'>title</a></td><td><a
href='reading_list.php?summary'>summary</
a></td><td><a href='reading_list.
php?published'>published</a></
td><td>entered</td><td>edit</
td><td>delete</td></tr>";

?while ($row = mysql_fetch_array($result))
{
```

```
<?echo "<tr>";
<?echo "<td>". $row['author'];
echo "</td><td>" ;
echo $row['title'];
echo "</td><td>" ;
echo $row['summary'];
echo "</td><td>" ;
echo $row['published'];
echo "</td><td>" ;
echo $row['date'];
echo "</td><td><a href='reading_list.
php?edit&book_id=".$row['book_id']."'>edit
</a></td>
<?<td><a href='reading_list.
php?delete&book_id=".$row['book_
id']."'>delete</a></td></tr>";
}
echo "</table>";

//get data for editing
$edit=$_REQUEST['edit'];
$update=$_REQUEST['update'];
$delete=$_REQUEST['delete'];

if(isset($edit)){
//print data requested into form for editing
print "<form method='post'
action='reading_list.php?update'><fieldset>
<legend>Edit Entry</legend>";
$query = "select * from reading_list WHERE
book_id = '".$_REQUEST['book_id']."'";
$result = mysql_query($query);
while($row=mysql_fetch_array($result)){
print "<input type='hidden' name='book_id'
value='".$row['book_id']."'>";
print "<p><label for='topic'>Author: </
label>";
print "<input type='text' name='author'
size='100' value='".$row['author']."'>";
print "<p><label for='title'>Title: </
label>";
print "<input type='text' name='title'
size='100' value='".$row['title']."'>";
print "<p><label for='summary'>Summary: </
label>";
```

```
print "<textarea name='summary' rows= 10
cols=50>".$row['summary']."</textarea><br>
";
print "<p><label
for='published'>Published: </label>";
print "<input type='text' name='published'
size='10' value='".$row['published']."'>
<br>";
print "<p><label for='entered'>Entered: </
label>";
print "<input type='text' name='date'
size='10' value='".$row['date']."'><br>";
print "<BR><INPUT TYPE='submit' name =
'update' value='update'>";
print "</form>";
}}

//process data edit upon user request
if(isset($update)){

 $book_id = $_REQUEST['book_id'];
  $title = $_REQUEST['title'];
  $author = $_REQUEST['author'];
  $summary = $_REQUEST['summary'];
  $published = $_REQUEST['published'];
  $date = $_REQUEST['date'];

$sql= mysql_query("UPDATE reading_list SET
author='$author',title='$title',summary='
$summary',published='$published',date='$d
ate' WHERE book_id =('$book_id')");
  if(!$sql) {
      printf ("Error : %s\n", mysql_error
());
 }
    else

//return user to original screen

print "<meta http-equiv='refresh' content='0;
url=http:reading_list.php?list' />";
}

//per user request, delete record

if(isset($delete)){
$sql= mysql_query("DELETE FROM reading_
list WHERE book_id =('$book_id')");
```

```
   if(!$sql) {
printf ("Error : %s\n", mysql_error ());
     }
  else
print "<meta http-equiv='refresh' con-
tent='0;  url=http:reading_list.php?list'
/>";
}
?>
```

By the way, instead of deleting a record you might add a database field called `archive` or something like that, and then instead of having a `delete` query, you'd have another update query that would set a record's archive field to 1 (the default being 0). And then pull data with `SELECT * WHERE archive=0`. You wouldn't be "deleting" a record but "archiving" it, hiding it from the screen but keeping it in the database. That way, of course, you can "undelete" if you change your mind or if you accidentally "delete" the wrong record. Life needs more undoes in general.

File login.php

The purpose of a login procedure is to verify that a user has the right to get inside and to assign the appropriate privileges to that user once identified. Your CMS might not require that general users login. Or it might require all to login. Presumably you'll want those who can add, edit, or delete database entries to login. The way login works is straightforward. You have a form that has, typically, email and password fields. When a user presses Submit, the machine goes to the database and checks to see if an email is there and the password is right. If all is well, it sets a session and sends the user to an interior screen. If authentication fails, it sends a user to the lost_login.php screen.

While I could easily reproduce login.php here, by now I think you have enough experience reading code to be able to read code from a screen, so head over to Sections/Memory+/Content Management/CMS Login to work out a login technique.

If you decide to cultivate users, to get them to provide content that helps develop a community, then you might want to switch your terminology, and thus your mindset, from "users" to "members" or "subscribers" or to "participants" and "observers" (noncontributing members). This shift from a functional projection onto your audience to a collaborative one signifies a change in your interaction style. Rather than developing content for people to use, you're creating a space for people to share.

While creating a shared space is a great way to build your reputation, maintaining order in a shared space can be very time consuming. You have to vet content provided by your members to make sure it meets the ethical standards of the community, that no one is trying to take advantage of others, and that there's no spam or machine-generated content finding its way onto your shared space. You also have to spend time cultivating relationships, getting people to post, connecting people to each other (via comments perhaps), and sharing what's happening in other related or similar communities. If your community takes off, you might want to think about deputizing others to moderate sections of the site. Before you get to that level, you might consider asking a few well-informed (preferably well-known) users to guest post. You could spend a few screens discussing the work of someone well known in the field and then ask that individual to comment or respond. The more participants you have, the more you'll attract.

In the meantime, your-online-self.com is about you, your brand, and your ethos, and as such your focus should be on cultivating a positive impression among your users by making valuable contributions regularly to the kind of work you all have in common. The more you give to the community you want to join, the better your chances of getting invited.

Schematic of a content management system

If you put readling_list.php into its own directory, and renamed it so that when your users go to your-online-self.com/reading they see a table containing a list of what you've been reading with access to summaries, then the file structure of that directory would be:

1. db_conntect
2. put.php
3. index.php

That's <litotes>all there is to creating a content management system.</litotes> In truth there's a great deal more for you to learn regarding databases and dynamic content management, but this, I hope, encourages you to believe that you can design and create your own CMS.

If you go the extra distance to write a login procedure and create a barebones but full-on content management system, then the file structure might look like the list of filenames that follows. If you were looking at the list of files in a directory, they'd be in alphabetical order, any numeric names preceding alphabetical names, capitalized preceding noncaps. The order that you see them in has nothing to do with how they function or relate to each other.

```
1. db_connect.php // makes the connec-
   tion to the database, enables logging
   in, adding, editing, deleting, and
   viewing db entries. Noncontributing
   users would have view privileges only
   but any file the results of which they
   can see on the screen would need to
   include('db_connect.php');
2. index.php // what everyone sees first.
   Pretty picture that fills the screen,
   20 words that says what's there,
   login. If noncontributing users don't
```

have to login, then it would have a
search function: sparse but vivid. Make
yours look any way you like. I'm just
describing today's dominant aesthetic

3. **Interior1.php** // what the noncontributing users see, would include('db_
connect,php'); include('menu.php')
or perhaps menu2.php, different from
what contributors see

4. **interior2.php** // what contributor sees
after login. This would include('db_
connect.php') include('menu.php') and
might include ('pull.php'); ('put.
php') or those functions might just
be in the file itself; and a list of
all db entries or all of the logged
in contributor's db entries if you
don't want everyone to see everything, i.e., you might have a super-
user with special privileges

5. **login.php** //might be included in
index.php, might be a separate
screen; would get user_id and role
(contributor or user) and let the
user or user/contributor in. It needs
include('db_connect.php') to work

6. **lost_login.php** // if you have contributing users, they will forget their
login and or password and you need to
automate the process of hooking them
back up. Safest way is with a randomly
generated password emailed to them

7. **menu.php** // you would include('menu.
php'); in any file that has the menu;
you might have one menu for users and
a different one for contributors

8. **signup.php** // users will need a login
and password. Signup.php will be just
like put.php, where the fields are
user id and password

9. **style.css** // you would use link
rel=style.css on all pages that use
the style

   Your best next step will be to imagine a project of your own and build
it. Start making a list of the kinds of digital objects you want to collect and

the kind of metadata you'll need to make the most use of each asset. Then make your database using each object type and each piece of metadata as a field. Then write put.php and pull.php, so you can get information in and out. Finally, consider making a variation on reading_list.php for your new CMS, so you can edit and delete (or archive) entries right from your website. By the way, if you want to keep images or other binary files in a DB, you need to identify the field type as BLOB (not VARCHAR or INT or TEXT). The same is true for .docx and .pdf files.

As you build, think about how much and what kind of user interaction you want to encourage. Are you building a community, providing a service, narrow-casting information? Do you want to enable comments? If so, from everyone or just those who sign up (do you want to start keeping an email database)? Do you want to enable user content? What about peer review of your content or of others? What's the best gift you can give the world to enounce who you are and where you're going?

Summary

Like all of our ancestors we have natural memories, powerful, fallible mental capacities to recreate past experiences. We've always remembered spontaneously. Like our preliterate ancestors, we can create memory palaces, although most of us would be very hard-pressed to carry a complete body of knowledge in our heads, accustomed as we are to our books and our ubiquitous connections to the Internet. As our literate ancestors, most of them anyway, replaced the memory palace with the practice of keeping commonplace books, regularly gathering and thinking about ideas to build a deep and interesting collection of pieces and parts that we might want some day to use, in some cases verbatim (mostly with attribution), so today we digital literates can create and maintain content management systems. Ours, however, can be instantly shared with the world and we can invite comment, peer review, and other forms of interaction and participation.

The CMS's greatest distinction, however, is that it's programmable, which means that we can tell it when to remind us of what. You can program your launch pad, for example, to pull from your database a story or image or item on a given day of the year, like your birthday or something less personal, like the anniversary of an important event in your field. You can also have your digital memory machine remind you periodically of something that would otherwise leave your conscious awareness. Maybe you want your reading list to pull old entries at random each time you go to your launch pad, to keep your mental library fresh. Maybe you have a digital archive of photographs you've taken over the years and you want to be reminded of a trip you took on the anniversary of the trip by having an image pulled and displayed on your launch pad for the relevant week.

From time to time, I've come across conversations in which people debate whether or not a well-stocked memory matters in the digital age. Why remember who produced which movie when you have the IMDB at your fingertips? I think that's a real question. Given the speed of our minds and the capacity to free up working memory for the task at hand if we don't have to keep looking things up, it seems like having a well-stocked natural memory remains important. I'm always amazed at how much experts remember about their craft or their discipline or their sport. It blows me away that a professional golfer can remember what iron she used on the approach shot on the fifth hole at [name golf course] on the Friday of a tournament three years ago. I've heard avid card players discussing hands they played months ago. Maybe one acquires such a memory in the process of becoming an expert. Maybe natural memory makes the expert. Or some combination. And then again, maybe careful note taking and constant review creates the readily accessible memory. If that's the case, then the IMDB is only the starting place. Do you remember Plato's perhaps ironic complaint that writing things down enables forgetting? Does having the IMDB mean you don't remember anything about movies anymore because you don't have to? Or does having it enable memorizing cool specifics of the movies and shows and actors you like?

I'm on the fence here. I can build a CMS over the course of a day now using the parts of the dozen or so I've made over the last few years, but if you told me I couldn't copy and paste, I'd be dead in the water. That seems like a significant limitation from a creative standpoint.

If you want to see what real programmers look like when writing in real time, head over to Livecoding.tv. That's a sight that does for coders what Twitch.tv does for gamers. We should build one for writers. **Imagine what we might learn from watching writers write instead of just reading what they've written.**

Where you are now

As far as your-online-self.com goes, at this point you should have:
1. Landing screen
2. About
3. Launch pad
4. Portfolio
5. Reading list (or other CMS)

If you have all five projects running, kudos. Now might be a good time to rethink the collection. You've got some serious digital skills at this point. Do you like the way your-online-self.com looks? Do you want to foreground one element, maybe combine pieces from other projects on it and hide the rest from general view? If you're underwhelmed with what you've made so far, you might decide to have a cool index.html page (a great picture, a handful of astute words, and contact info) as the only visible part, with everything else still hidden behind the wall that separates the general public from the heavy machinery and noise and confusion of a construction site in progress.

6

STYLE

Style, at least within the rhetorical traditions, has always been about fitting in while standing out, sounding and looking like someone who belongs, has the right to be there and knows it (getting the conventions right), while simultaneously appearing and/or sounding especially suited to the role one is expected and willing to play. Effortless performance takes a great deal of practice, training, and feedback. Even talented people have to work hard. The two previous rhetorical traditions have emphasized distinction via aesthetics, ornamental constructions, vivid descriptions, unexpected turns of phrase, striking metaphors, fascinating sounds (assonance, sibilance, rhyme, anaphora, epiphora, etc.), and conformity to the values and beliefs of the small group of educated elites who acquired books for libraries and taught literature at schools and universities, those which fit with tradition, in other words.

In the digital age, style has two meanings. There's the prose style, and there's the way in which information is displayed on the screen, such as fonts, text sizes, colors, word spacing, line height, padding, and so on—the visual characteristics of the content handled by CSS. This section of *Writing Online* discusses prose style, the linguistic characteristics handled by you the content provider.

We won't spend as much time on prose style as you might expect to find in a book on writing. We have a great many other things to discuss, for one thing. But also, the advice relevant for writing words meant to be read on a computerized screen can be reduced to the simplest set of guidelines: fewer words, shorter sentences, shorter paragraphs, with the main idea highlighted and, whenever appropriate, lists instead of paragraphs, pictures instead of words. All of this advice is predicated on two assumptions. People don't like to read from computerized screens and tend to scan content looking for the thing that they're looking for; they are task oriented and aren't interested in everything a site has to offer, only in the one thing the search engine that led them there promised was there. There are also a thousand alternative sites, in most cases, at the click of a button if what the user wants doesn't immediately draw his or her attention. The effect of these conditions is that online prose should be clear, direct, and brief, what the literate tradition called "the plain style."

[[Search: origin of laconic]]

An interesting side effect of getting used to writing in a plain style is that your work can be more readily translated by machines like Google Translate, making your work available to the world outside your primary language. The more idiomatic, not to say idiosyncratic, your prose style, the less well it travels.

The clarity and brevity machine

So in general the primary goals are brevity, clarity, and directness. How do you go about finding the least possible number of words for any given message? And what part can computer coding play in practicing precision and focus? There are several programs that will flag grammatical imperfections. Our word processing programs come with them, and there are standalone programs that offer even deeper levels of analysis. These programs can be useful if you already know the rules of grammar and have the patience to use the advice they offer so quickly. Grammar programs use complicated algorithms based on regular expressions, practices far beyond the level of coding we're trying to develop here.

There are, however, ways you can **use your own burgeoning computational skills to improve your prose style.** You can make filters, for example, that will automatically flag *your* writing's least desirable features and thus help you edit your own writing more quickly. For what I'm about to show you, dictionaries of unwanted expressions are key. The better your dictionaries, the more useful the process. It's up to you to make the dictionaries, although you're free to start building yours on top of mine.

You become a better writer by scrutinizing expressions and making choices, and you become a more efficient writer by making some of these choices habitually, so that you don't have to remember the rules for commas during each complex sentence, for example, but also so that you don't have to task your working memory with thoughts about nominalization and pretty pointless intensifiers, redundant expressions, clichés, week sentence opening moves, empty words like "thing" and "some" and "this," and all the other imperfect expressions we all grab so hastily while trying to keep our ideas from escaping.

It takes thousands of hours of practice with writing, revising, editing to make decent sentences on the first pass. One could argue in fact that the goal of fluency thus defined is a counterproductive goal, one that leads to cramped ideas and frustration. Still, if you decide in advance what expressions you want to avoid and create a bit of scripting to help speed-up finding them in your drafts, you can work toward internalizing the process of eliminating them before they show up on the screen. Even if you never internalize the phrases, your digital filtration process will keep you from publicizing your imperfections.

File stylechecker.php

Here, in digital detail, is how to write a prose-filtering program.
Below is a list of redundant expressions:

```
a bolt of lightning
advance planning
```

```
advance reservations
advance warning
final conclusion
final destination
free gift
general consensus
important essentials
invited guest
join together
just exactly
just recently
```

Below is a list of verbose expressions:

```
call a halt to
came at a time when
can be seen as
cannot be avoided
circular in shape
concerning the matter of
costs the sum of
due to the fact that
each and every
in a position to
in the event that
in the final analysis
in the same way
more and more
run counter to
keep in mind
Keep in mind
```

Notice that the last two entries in the second list are almost identical? What's the difference and why (computationally) might that difference exist?

For the stylechecker.php project to work, you need a file called verbose.txt containing verbose expressions. You also need a file called redundant.txt containing redundant expressions. The contents of these files would look like the lists above, one entry per line, a line break at the end of each line. Both files need to be in the same directory as the file below, called stylechecker.php.

```
<FORM METHOD="POST" action="<? echo
$PHP_SELF; ?>">
<textarea name="text" cols="50"
rows="15"><? echo stripslashes($text) ;?>
</textarea></BR>
<INPUT TYPE="submit" value = "submit"
name="submit">
</form>
```

```
<?
$submit=$_REQUEST['submit'];
if($submit){
$message = $_REQUEST['text'];
 $fh = fopen("verbose.txt","r");
 $fh1 - fopen("redundant.txt","r");
while($word = fgets($fh,4096))
   {
      $message = stripslashes($message);
      $message = ereg_
replace(trim($word),"<font
color='green'>$word</font>",$message);
   }
while($word = fgets($fh1,4096))
   {
      $message = ereg_replace
(trim($word),"<font color-'darkred'>
$word</font>",$message);
   }
echo $message;
?>
```

Can you read that? You don't need to be able to read it to make it work. Basically it says:

get the words the user typed into the
<textarea> called "text." Open file called
verbose.txt and read it into your temporary memory. Now open redundant.txt and
read it too into temporary memory. Then,
compare what the user cut and pasted into
the web form and wrap any phrase you can
match in verbose.txt with green font and
wrap any phrase you can match in redun-
dant.txt with dark red. Print the results
to the screen so the user can see where he
or she can reduce the words without reducing the meaning.

There's a bit more to it than that, but that's the gist of it.

The next step would be to see if you can add another dictionary. You could, of course, put every hated expression into a single dictionary, and thus reduce the number of lines of code the program needs to operate. Brevity-in-coding. Excellent. But then maintaining that ever-growing file of disparate words and expressions might be difficult. More choices.

Once you've got the script running, start adding to your .txt files, each word or expression on its own line. Every time you come across a redundant expression, add it to your collection. What are some other lists of frequent imperfections that might be worth keeping? What about clichés? What about vague words like "some" and "many" and "people" and "thing"? What about business jargon?

To see the script in action, go to Sections/Style+/Style Checker. For instructions about how to make your own, go to Sections/Style+/DIY Style Checker. You're welcome to copy and paste my files from that site as well, but **the real value is in making *your own* lists of expressions and words you want never to use,** to help you zero in on and zero out language that gets in the way of meaning.

Toulmin model markup tool

Style is about choice, consciously deciding to include and exclude for affect. One way to develop this kind of dexterity is to simply take a sentence and see how many different ways you can write it. There's an important Renaissance rhetorician, Erasmus of Rotterdam, who published a book on the subject, *De Copia*. The more ways you can think to say something, the greater your range of choices. If you only ever think to say the same things in the same ways, you have a very limited range of thought and expression. You can't consciously exclude what you don't notice, therefore getting good at identifying your blind-spots and dead-spots is important. One way to broaden your perspective is to get a meta-perspective on your writing by labeling the parts that a given structure should have and then seeing if all of the relevant parts are there and excluding any irrelevant or unidentifiable parts. For this practice, you need a document type definition. We'll start with a DTD for argumentation.

Stephen Toulmin was a British philosopher who felt that the traditional syllogism lacked real-life significance and so he offered an elaborated alternative that has become known as the Toulmin model. You'll see it in practically any book on argumentative writing. The basic parts of a Toulmin argument are claim, data, warrant, backing, rebuttal, and modal. The claim is an assertion that needs proof to gain acceptance from an audience. The proof consists of data, whatever kind of evidence, physical or logical, available. The warrant is anything that can be said to support the legitimacy of the evidence, some kind of support. The backing backs up the warrant. The rebuttal is the section where counterarguments and objections are dismissed. And finally, the modal asserts the level of assent the arguer believes the argument should obtain for the audience. Not all arguments are this fleshed out. And not all arguments really require all these parts. Some people think one should raise objections even if one can eliminate them. Sometime people create fake objections to make themselves look open-minded, only to demolish the fake objection (a.k.a. straw dog) and undermine their ethos.

You can take the Toulmin model as a DTD of an argument. In other words, you could create a semantic markup language out of it. That would look like this:

```
<argument>
<claim>  </claim>
<data>  </data>
```

```
<warrant> </warrant>
<backing> </backing>
<rebuttal> </rebuttal>
<modal> </modal>
</argument>
```

Given this markup, you could then evaluate any given argument according to how well it compared to the model. If one were in a strict markup situation, an argument missing a piece would be rejected or flagged as ill-formed. Arguments, however, come in lots of different forms, and a perfectly compelling argument might be missing a warrant because the value of the data is self-evident to the given audience, for example. Maybe all rebuttals are straw dogs, or maybe there's a rebuttal that can't be adequately addressed and thus one must tip-toe by the sleeping dog.

Despite the lack of required structure, you could learn something about arguments by marking them up using the Toulmin model. And you could write a JavaScript and CSS tool to enable the marking up of arguments. I've given you an example on the website under Sections/Style+/Toulmin Model. Go there. Copy and paste an argument either of your own composition or from something you've found in an editorial section of a digital magazine or newspaper, and see how well it can be marked up using the tool. Finding that a given argument doesn't quite match up with the markup doesn't prove it invalid or unconvincing. But it might show the existence of flaws. You could use a tool like this to get a meta-perspective on your own arguments.

If you're curious about the code that enables the markup, reveal the source code and copy and paste away (you can see the code for this file because it's JavaScript rather than PHP).

In case you aren't near a computer and you think a markup tool would be hard to write, here's the basic code. There really isn't much to it.

```
<html>
<head>
<script type="text/javascript">
function iFrameOn(){
    rte.document.designMode = 'On';
}
function claim() {
rte.document.execCommand("insertHTML",
false, "<span style='background-color:
blue; color:white;' title='The claim, an
assertion to be proven.'>"+ rte.document.
getSelection()+"</span>");
}
</head>
<body onLoad="iFrameOn();">

<input type="button" onclick="claim()"
value="claim">
```

```
<iframe name="rte" id="rte"
style="border:#000000 1px solid;"
width='60%' height='500px' ></iframe>
</body>
</head>
```

If you transcribe this code into a browser, you'll see a textbox input field and a Claim button. Put any text in the box; highlight some of it. Then press the Claim button, and the text will be highlighted blue, the text changed to white, and when you hover over it, the expression, "The claim, an assertion to be proven," will appear. With that bit of code as a starting place, you can design a markup tool for any kind of document as long as you've got a DTD or even just a list of recurring features you wish to identify (through their presence or absence) because doing so will help you, or someone you're working with, write a better document.

```
Replace function claim() with func-
tion whatever() and onclick="claim()"
value="claim" with onclick="whatever()"
value="whatever".
```

A markup DTD for exposition

You could design your own DTD for any textual object that has a regular form. If there are occasional differences among instances, the DTD might still be useful, but of course if every instance is unique, then there's no way to create a DTD. We could make our own DTD for expository paragraphs that might be useful. The best way to do this would be to generalize the standard parts of any given example of expository writing by comparing hundreds of samples. If we did that, maybe we might find that, generally speaking, all expository paragraphs have most of the following parts:

```
<expos>
<thesis></thesis>
<definition> of key term(s)</definition>
<example> </example>
<elaboration></elaboration>
<explanation> (origin, purpose, reason) </
explanation>
<exclusion></exclusion>
<caveat></caveat>
<digression> (factoid, mystery, adds flavor
but doesn't distract reader)</digression>
<transition></transition>
</expos>
```

Any given expository paragraph might be missing one section and still be for the most part properly formed; maybe there's no caveat, for example. But any paragraph that didn't have a thesis statement might be considered malformed and therefore broken; the thesis statement being a minimum requirement for a complete example of an expository paragraph.

If you were to come up with such a DTD and used it to mark up an essay you were working on, then you could apply a special style sheet to each element. Thus, for example, you could collapse each paragraph to display only the thesis statement, so you could read the whole document as an outline, or expand each paragraph to see if they all had examples, or have only digressions displayed, or only those paragraphs that contained digressions, or display only those paragraphs without digressions to see what effect that had on the reading experience.

Given the DTD for exposition, you could rewrite the Toulmin markup tool to label parts of an expository paragraph and then use the markup as a way of deciding if a given paragraph is sufficiently developed, if anything important is missing, if irrelevant details obscure the message, and so on.

Writer's feedback markup tool

If coming up with a DTD of another genre isn't interesting or is a bit too abstract for you, consider applying the same JavaScript/CSS technique to a less formal kind of markup.

An interesting project that might help prove to you that you understand the code and also help you write more effectively would be to create a markup tool for identifying problems in your prose. Anyone who writes knows how hard it is to make what's on the paper match what's in one's head. Getting both of those to coincide with what happens in someone else's head as they read what you wrote is even harder (let's deny its impossibility on principle). The only way I've ever improved as a writer is by getting and making good use of good feedback. Over time I've internalized that feedback, and now I can do some of it for myself before I share what I've written with others. When I do, I often get pretty much the same comments in the margins that I would have written for myself if I'd noticed the need for them. I had failed to notice the need because my working memory was full already. That's why we ask other people to give us feedback as a regular part of turning good ideas into words worth reading and computer programs and apps worth using.

If you end up teaching writing or doing research and writing in a corporate or nonprofit or small business setting, then you're going to need an efficient and effective feedback process. What follows will help you think through the design of such a process. This tool doesn't automate the process of offering feedback so much as it regularizes and speeds up the process. You still need a human doing the reading and the marking up.

Make a list of every kind of writing imperfection you search for when you're revising your own writing, the kinds of <vague>things</vague> you've seen written in the margins of your papers, as well as the kinds of things you write in the margins of drafts others have shared with you. What might that list look like? Here's a start:

1.   New paragraph
2.   Is this the right word?

3.   Do you have evidence of this?
4.   Why might someone disagree?
5.   Citation needed
6.   Unwarranted assumption
7.   Editorializing
8.   Ambiguous
9.   Not following you here
10.   Transition?
11.   Why?
12.   Proof?
13.   Something's missing here
14.   Provide an example
15.   Be more specific—what kind of X is this X?

This is a small sample. You might have twenty items. The more you have, however, the more cluttered the feedback screen will be: twenty buttons is a lot of buttons. You have to search for the one you want, and that takes time. On the other hand, only a few buttons means you have to spend more time typing comments by hand. If any of those comments is a comment you'll write more than once, maybe it deserves a button. Once you have a good list of canned comments and queries, you'll need to spend some time thinking about how best to organize the buttons. Grouping them into kinds of problems makes sense.

If you aren't sure what your list of chronic imperfections should look like, re-read everything you've got in your portfolio and think about how you'd advise the author were you their editor. Resist the urge to just start editing. Your task is to abstract the advice, making it generally applicable in any given piece of writing, not to improve that particular piece of writing. If you saved the papers your teachers gave you over the years, look back over what they wrote in the margins. Again, you're looking for the generalizable. Finally, get together with some writerly friends and read some of one another's pieces. See if together you can work up a list of feedback cues that you all agree would help increase the efficiency of communication.

Once you've got a good list, make a markup button for each one. Now you've got a writer's feedback markup tool. Of course, this tool isn't automated. It has to be applied by a human being. All it can do is speed up the process of offering feedback by quickly attaching a comment to a section of text. Timely feedback is critical for making sense for others. And resisting the urge to just dive into a bit of broken prose at the point where you see the break can facilitate the distance that clarity requires. The markup tool will keep you at a distance for a little while.

I encourage you to share your markup tool with others. For those of you who are really getting into the construction of writing environments, I encourage you to extend the markup tool to provide a way to pass the marked-up texts back and forth, perhaps via email (not that hard, see Sections/Rhetoric+/Communications) or, if you're really feeling it, via a data-based writer's workshop content management system of your own design. The discussion and examples for CMSs are in Chapter 5 on digital memory.

I've left an alternate explanation of the markup tools and several different examples on the website (Sections/Style+/Composition Markup). Because these markup feedback tools are written in JavaScript, you can just reveal the source code and copy and paste. But remember that while applying what I made to your own writing will be useful, making your own markup tools and keeping your own dictionaries of imperfect expressions will be far more beneficial for your prose style.

Paragraph scrambler

Clarity isn't just about getting the words right. It's also about getting the sentences in optimal order, so that the reader can clearly understand the relationship among the sentences within a paragraph. The difference between a draft and a final copy is often a matter of turning associative thinking into linear prose—that is, sifting through all of the things you wrote down as they occurred to you and grouping them according to some principle of arrangement and then resorting and organizing what you have so that it makes sense to other people.

I've found over the thirty years I've been teaching rhetoric and composition that novice writers find tinkering with the order of their ideas difficult. It's like they're chiseling stone or something. To help them develop a great flexibility of mind, I wrote a script that scrambles the order of sentences in a paragraph and thus gives them a chance to ponder the idea of order without having to mess with their own sentences right away. We start by scrambling other people's paragraphs, which takes the threat out of the experience. Eventually they get to scramble, or hopefully unscramble, their own.

On the website under Sections/Arrangement/Scrambler you'll find a PHP script that will take a paragraph, scramble the order of the sentences at random, and then print the randomized version back to the screen. On the same screen, you'll see the PHP code that randomizes the sentences by finding each period, treating everything to the left of that period as a unit, shuffling the sentences it has thus identified, and finally printing the result back to the screen.

Outliner tool (vaporware)

While we're on the topic of writing environments, I'd like to suggest one more project. One of the comments I write most often in the margins of papers written by novice writers is "new paragraph." Why? Because most people learn to write in school and schools inevitably fall back on timed writing assignments, mostly for efficiency in grading but also for anti-cheating control. Therefore, people get the mistaken impression that fluency equals effective communication and mistakenly define fluency as writing sentence by sentence. I've conducted experiments where students and grad students sit down to write an essay in a timed environment with screen-casting software running in the background while they write, and I've consistently observed that while novices write in a linear fashion, one word after the other from capital to period, followed by the next sentence, followed by the next, from beginning to end, reviewing what they wrote and fixing up a spelling or punctuation error only at the end, graduate students tend to make lists of topics or keywords, and build sentences up around the keywords. Then they ponder the optimal order of the paragraphs. They aren't writing as they expect their intended reader to read. They're writing toward a clarified view of what the readers need and when they need it. So the expert's writing process is about ideas, questions, revised ideas, then sentences, then collections of sentences, then paragraphs, and so on. This process is iterative rather than linear, and it can't really take place in a single hour, unless the person is trying to write just one or two paragraphs.

Here's how to design a writing environment that might help you develop a more sophisticated perspective on your writing. We're going to use the JavaScript hide/show technique.

Effective paragraphs develop one idea completely. Or so we're told, and the idea makes sense on paper. It's hard to hold more than one idea at a time in working memory. When you write linearly, you dot down every idea as it comes to you, and so you often get more than one idea per paragraph. Hence the new paragraph feedback comment option. The next time you have something to write at length, wrap the topic or thesis or main idea sentence in the show tag, and the rest of the paragraph in the show on click tags. That way you end up with an expandable and collapsible version of your work. Click a topic sentence and the supporting material, or what's supposed to support it, will be revealed. Now you can survey the whole piece topic sentence by topic sentence, to see if it holds together like an elaborated syllogism or recipe, with the option to click down to see the details.

Here's the bit of JavaScript magic:

```
<script>
function toggle(e) {
if (e.style.display == "none") {
e.style.display = "";
} else {
e.style.display = "none";
}}
</script>
```

You put that at the bottom of the file, above the </body> tag. Then you code your paragraphs as follows:

```
<span onClick="toggle(document.all.
HideShow0);"><a href="#">Thesis statement
one</span></a><br>
<span style="display: none;"
id="HideShow0">Sentences supporting thesis
statement one.  </span>

<span onClick="toggle(document.all.
HideShow1);"><a href="#">Thesis statement
two </span></a><br>
```

```
<span style="display: none;"
id="HideShow1">Sentences supporting thesis
statement two.</span>
```

Notice that each `HideShow` pair has a unique number. It won't work if they don't. To see what the JavaScript show/hide looks like in action, go to Sections/ Rhetoric+/Reading (Q&A). That's a slightly different application of the same script.

Cumbersome, I admit. So here's the challenge. Can you figure out how to design a form that would offer a writer an input box `type=text` for a topic sentence and then a `<textarea>` for the subsequent sentences, followed by another input box and `<textarea>` pair, and so on? Then when the writer presses Submit, a PHP file takes what he or she entered and wraps the topic sentence in the show/hide code and the subsequent sentences as a span to be revealed on click. It then prints the newly marked-up text to the screen so the writer can expand and contract and think about how the topic sentences fit together without being distracted by the rest of each paragraph. Remember you need to make sure that each clickable instance has a unique number, which means that you have to use an incrementing loop of some kind when you wrap the incoming text in show/ hide JavaScript.

What? No copy and paste code? Just a challenge? Yeah, that's why I called it vaporware. All promise, no code.

Summary

Style is and always has been about fit with the nature of the content, the occasion, the expectations of the audience (genre conventions), and the speaker's/ author's/provider's ethos and goals. In the context of *Writing Online*, we've assumed information-rich discourse, where the content provider is nearly invisible, with the goal of purveying useful and interesting information in smart but unobtrusive ways. You may prefer a more personal style, where you're a visible participant in the communication. That's of course up to you. Just remember to keep your goals in mind, and remember that a thousand alternatives are a click away.

I've emphasized brevity and clarity because I believe that effort leads to keener insights and more critical thinking. Still, as a rhetorically astute writer, you know that whereas brevity can be quantified as number of words, clarity is purely metaphorical. Words are not windows onto an actual world. Clarity is an illusion created by using words exactly as the people reading (using) them do, in their prevailing sense, as Aristotle wrote. Adding or subtracting something important and previously unnoticed creates distinction. Critical thinking is hard. Effective writing is even harder.

Once you've got a complete draft, something you think "says" what you want to say, reduce the number of words by ±10%. Here's some simple word-counting JavaScript:

```
<textarea name="laconic"
onkeyup="wordcount(this.value)">
</textarea>
<script type=""text/javascript"">
var cnt;
function wordcount(count) {
var words = count.split(/\s/);
cnt = words.length;
var ele = document.getElementById
('w_count');
ele.value = cnt;
}
document.write("<input type=text
id=w_count size=4 readonly>");
</script>
```

Where you are now

At this point, in addition to all the other projects, you have two writing tools you designed specifically to help you with your writing style. You've created a semi-automated style checker that uses dictionaries you maintain to highlight features of your work you might like to revise, thus saving you time while editing and making you more conscious of your choices, while ultimately making unconscious the process of eliminating imperfect expressions. You've also created a markup tool that speeds up the process of offering feedback. If you're really on fire, you'll have used email.php to turn your markup tool into a peer review tool.

7

DELIVERY

Oratorically, delivery was about stance, tone, volume, modularity, accent, pronunciation, gesture, pace (speeding up to signal urgency, slowing down to suggest deliberation, pausing for effect, etc.), humor, responding appropriately to current conditions, being present and aware, within but above the moment, not getting emotionally involved, but not coming across as cold or indifferent. A great deal of rhetorical training was devoted to this element of oratorical performance. As Demosthenes was recorded as saying, when asked what the three most important elements to rhetoric were, "Delivery, delivery, and delivery."

Delivery in this sense remains important, both because public speaking still happens and because many rhetors need to look presentable on camera. One way to get a handle on contemporary representations of delivery in the traditional sense is to watch television with the sound off. Music videos can be especially instructive. You should also make a point of speaking on camera from time to time, even if you have no intention of providing video content, just so you can get an external perspective on what you look and sound like to others. You'll quickly notice your verbal ticks (ums, likes, rights?) and your physical tells (touching your hair or your nose, looking at your slides instead of the audience, and so on). You'll do a much better job with oral delivery if you suffer through watching yourself from time to time. If you can rid your speech of verbal ticks, you'll greatly outpace your competition in job interviews and when giving presentations that might lead to a job offer.

In the literate world, members of the book trades, typesetters, binders, paper makers. and so on handled delivery. The author just supplied the text, often in manuscript (handwritten). With the advent of personal computers, laser printers, and high-resolution color monitors, increasingly sophisticated word processing software and eventually desktop publishing software, it became possible although ill-advised for a writer to take on some of the roles once held by book professionals. When a wide array of fonts, for example, first became readily available, in the late 1980s, it was not uncommon to see printouts that looked like ransom notes, a jumble of randomly mixed font families and sizes. Given the power of typography, one had to learn something of design aesthetics. One also had to learn how to layout columns of text, design interesting pages, and provide effective photographs. With the advent of relatively inexpensive color laser printers, it became possible to produce slick publications in-house, and more and more companies were doing it.

Hence, for a while, at least in the 1990s and early 2000s, a person who wanted to write for a living could get a foot in the door knowing the basics of layout and his or her way around InDesign.

Now, with digital publishing, you need to know the basics of design and typography and photography as before, but with a special attention to the screen or rather the various screens on which your work might be delivered. CSS handles these elements of layout. You also need to know something of the composition of photographs, how to get them, and how to make sure they both look good and load quickly to a screen. You need to know something of video and the graphic representation of data as well. Large organizations still have a few specialists, but increasingly fewer people are required to do and therefore know more. As a person focused on writing and research, it nevertheless behooves you to know something of all of the elements of creative expression, because in many cases, you'll need to provide all of them, and besides, you may need to communicate effectively with those providing the rest.

As is often the case, there are two poles of ideal design. On the one hand you have the ideal of universal design, where anyone regardless of limitations in equipment or physical ability (dexterity, vision, hearing, etc.) should be able to get the same information from a site. At the very least, one strives for cross-browser compatibility and uses such aides as the title and the alt tag for images, so that screen readers can articulate what people with imperfect eyesight can't see. **Movies should be captioned and transcripts provided.** If you use color to signify meaning, you need to keep in mind that <vague>some</vague> 8% of men and something like 0.5% of women are color-blind and so may be disadvantaged by your color scheme. Anyone over the age of forty can't read blue text on a black background, by the way. So don't just use color because you like the color scheme or because it evokes the emotions you want to evoke. There are cultural conflicts between color and evocation anyway—white signifies purity in some cultures, but death in Japan, for example. Think about color primarily from a functional perspective. Go for high contrast and minimal interference.

This goes for fonts as well. While you can use a wider variety of screen fonts today (Sections/Delivery+/Fonts), and more all the time, what you choose won't match what the users see unless they too have that font on their computer, not guaranteed, and their default settings might override your choices anyway. Any design that's truly font dependent will fail frequently. Generally speaking, you can stick to serif and sans serif.

When it comes to universal design, less is always more. Keep the design and navigation simple, unadorned, obvious, and robust. Don't use menu schemes that require dexterous use of a mouse or other pointing device (the menu on our website fails this test). And provide alternatives.

Because the minimalism of universal design requires the least amount of scripting and CSSing, and because it's nondiscriminatory, it's a great aesthetic to aspire to as you get started. But just like the newbies of desktop publishing created unintentional ransom note effects with their first font sets, so your burgeoning capacity with CSS and JavaScript will lead you down more than a few ugly paths. That's actually okay, good even. You need to practice and stretch if you're going to learn. Just think twice about making your newest designs public. And always separate form and content so you can quickly unstyle when the flaws of your design become apparent.

The other aesthetic is dynamic visualization, where the meaning is contained in the motion and the imagery. Information-rich sites often make understanding what they offer accessible, to the visually inclined at least, by using sophisticated graphics and imagery. Your progress chart project is a very simple example of the approach. The more data you have, the more effective it can be if it can be represented visually.

To get effective with designing effective layouts, you have to both develop an eye for design and become proficient with CSS. That's a tall order and one that will take some serious bench time. The designs I've given you on the website should be enough to get you started, but you'll have to spend considerable time honing these skills. Below are a few concepts that will be useful places to start.

Cognitive processing and design

The best way to learn how to design screens is to scour the web for what you like, reveal the source code, and see if you can mimic what you like. If the code behind the site is too complex, as will often be the case, see if you can identify the attractive feature and describe it well enough for Google to find an example you can understand. Learn, in other words, experientially. All the same, there's a relevant body of theory about cognitive processing and usability that you should be aware of. What follows is a brief description of some key terms. In general, with visual design as with prose composition, you want to **keep the noise-to-signal ratio as close to zero as possible.**

Interference effects

Given that a message is what you want your users to receive, and the signal is the means by which you convey the message, then **if the signal interferes with the message, your users will be confused.** Confusion happens either because the message doesn't fit the signal, or the audience's expectations about how to interpret the signal aren't the same as yours. An iconic sign, like the winding-road-ahead sign, perfectly matches message to signal. If your goal is to facilitate other people getting their work done, as it is typically when you're writing for digital delivery, allowing the signal to interfere with the message is counterproductive. By contrast, a green stop sign will confuse people because it sends conflicting messages.

People become accustomed to doing things in a particular way and will be perplexed if a site doesn't conform to those expectations. If you don't make the logo a link back to the index page, they may be unhappily surprised. If you give people a search box, they may prefer it to the menu system. If you make the menu system overly complicated by linking to everything directly, they'll find it bewildering and annoying. If you can anticipate a path, you can deliver well.

Affordance

Affordance refers to the level of correspondence between an object's design and its function. Round wheels have a greater affordance for rolling than square wheels. A corollary of affordance is that things that look like they do what they do are easier to use than things that don't. **Effective designs signal their function.** Seems obvious, and yet when you're enthralled by the latest script or CSS technique, it's tempting to design for the sake of design without regard for function. It's hard to be self-effacing, but **effective designs are invisible.** Imagine a door that has Push written on it and a handle to pull. Now image a door that says Pull but only has a flat panel where you would put your hand to push. If the instructions (or assumptions) don't match the design, you confuse your users.

Constraint

A constraint is a limitation that can't be overcome without breaking the object or confounding a convention. You can't put six syllables into an iambic pentameter line. A rhyming couplet that doesn't rhyme isn't one. Boat anchors make terrible paperweights. Long sentences are hard to read on a phone. You can't type on a watch face. You need to consider how the interface and the information interact with each other, and you need to keep in mind what kind of devices and in what circumstances you're delivering your information to. If a person needs to make a decision quickly, history and backstory and justification are useless. If they have to get the information off their phone, a navigation scheme that requires multiple layers will be useless and frustrating. You have to design within the limits of the environment, both physical and psychological.

   While constraints are a universally relevant element of existence, when it comes to writing online, screen size and resolution are the most relevant constraints. You have to think about what you want to say, but you also have to think about how your words will appear to your users and in what context. Writing Twitter posts is one way to practice compressed prose, but in general, you should practice brevity and clarity using the tools outlined in the section on style. Screens may have no edges but users tend to be impatient and abrupt.

Cohesion

Similar things are found close together (proximity) and look alike (familiarity). If you want to cohere disparate things, group them; put them close together and give them a common set of recognizable characteristics (put a boundary around them, or make them all the same color).

The bucket examples on the website exemplify cohesion (Designs/Buckets+).

Size and movement

Bigger things are perceived as more important, or at least they tend to attract the eye. So place important elements prominently. **Don't bury the lead.** Movement also attracts the eye and offers the possibility of fitting a great deal of information into a small space (by scrolling it across). You see this on news programs and on some news websites. Auto-scrolling using JavaScript is a relatively easy technique to master, but people often find movement distracting and they tend to dislike ceding control to the machine (maybe they read faster or slower than you scroll), so think before you scroll. You see scrolling a great deal on TV these days but it's pretty much out of favor online, near as I can tell. Consider using the CSS overflow auto-declaration so that if you end up with more text in any given region, the user can choose to scroll to see all of it.

Responsive design

One of the interesting things about digital rhetoric is that you have to be more broadly context-aware to be effective. In oral rhetorical situations, the audience is right there and you can, if you're adept and permitted to ad lib a bit, adapt as you notice them responding. Most spokespeople today are trained to stay on message, to answer every question with exactly the same information, to avoid sending mixed messages, creating potential legal problems, or otherwise straying the course. Still, a real audience is really present. A literate readership isn't present and they may be both temporally and geographically distributed.

As an author you can't respond to an audience's reaction; you can only anticipate based on your knowledge of what has worked in the past (history of literature) and your knowledge of literary conventions and beliefs and mores and so on. If the written communication has a short time dimension—that is, it will be acted on within days or weeks or months—then you can adapt the message based on feedback. But if the piece is written for an indefinite timeframe, like *belle lettres* and history, and even certain kinds of journalism, then you have to rely on your intended audience sharing with you a common understanding of conventions and expectations and knowledge of previous work like the work you're writing. Either that or the audience is willing to suspend their disbelief and accept you as a temporary maestro of their experience, until you're finished and they're satisfied or you fail to meet their needs and they leave early.

In a digital setting you have both distributed and immediate users, people needing something in the present moment and others who are days or months away from your context. Because websites can be instantly "republished" (an anachronism, in many ways), the information on them can change regularly and sites that matter to an enterprise tend to change frequently, the content anyway, but also the design might change every few years. Other sites are historical records only, collecting dust for years, but they're not the norm these days. In the publishing industry, a book that's a year or two old is a recent publication. On the web, content two years old is historical. There's nothing necessarily wrong with old material on the web. Just because it's digital doesn't mean it has to have a short half-life.

One way to parse the differences is by the device used. If a person is viewing your site on a large monitor (1086), then they're likely sitting at a desk. If they're on a small screen (200 × 400), they're on a phone. The user on a phone may be like one sitting at a desk, just browsing about, but, because the interface he or she is using is mobile and therefore the user might be out and about, depending on the nature of your site, he or she may be looking for something with some urgency, such as your location, your operating hours, your phone number, or some other way to get in touch. You need to think about delivering different content based on usage cases, often triggered by the device being used.

A common technique is what's known as **fluid design, where you define screen spaces by percentages.** 100% percent of 1086 and 100% of 200 is still 100%. That can work. Ideally you want to decrease the number of words and amount of information available as the screen size goes down, but fluid design alone isn't enough. What you offer is the same, just wider or narrower, stretched or compressed, as the screen changes size. For greater responsiveness, you need to know what the user is using to view your site so you can alter not only the appearance of the interface but the interface itself. More than likely, you'll also want to reduce the amount of content as well.

Given the goal of flexibility based on what kind of equipment a user happens to be using, you might consider designing not only a liquid site but in fact two variations of the same site, one mobile and one standard. For example:

```
If wide - www.gpullman.com
If phone - m.gpullman.com
```

A few years back you might have used a JavaScript "browser sniffer" technique to make the initial decision about which site to send a given user to. This practice is generally deprecated now in favor of what CSS3 calls @media queries.

Using @media you can offer different style sheets for the same content based on the orientation (landscape or portrait), pixel density, and the dimensions of the screen users are using.

[[Search: @media query]]

A few years from now you may need a new technique.

Usability

For the last fifty years or so, it has been a commonplace of rhetorical history and theory to assert that if the rhetors of Socrates' day were alive today they'd be working on Madison Avenue, in advertising. A great many of them might now be working on the other side of the country, in Silicon Valley. Some of those might be doing usability research. Usability is the study of how people interact with and make use of objects, both virtual and real, as a way of designing tools that are easier to use. The goal is intuitive design, a design that doesn't require any instructions for use. Generally speaking one unobtrusively observes people using the object you're interested in to see how quickly they succeed with the given task, what frustrates them, what features they miss, what alternative uses they discover, and so on. Often usability research includes feedback from users as well, although if you listen too closely to what people want you'll find your product a victim of feature creep quickly. Also, there's often a gap between what people think they do and what they actually do, so you need to back up feedback with direct observation and data analytics when they're available.

Usability testing for your-online-self.com might be overkill, but you should look at your site in all browsers and on as many different machines as you can get your hands on: phones, tablets, widescreens, and so on. You should also ask a few friends to view the site and offer observations. If you're trying to decide between two different designs, you might try what's known as A/B testing, where you offer different people one of two different versions and see which version seems to suit the users' needs better. For this to work, you need to have some way to measure user need, how quickly they find what you want them to find, for example, or how long they stay on your site. These kinds of observations are available through your server's analytics.

If you find yourself really getting into designing and programing content, you should make a separate study of usability, and even if you remain a casual content provider, you should keep up with the big trends and pay attention to new developments.

[[Search: design thinking]]

Summary

Delivery is still about looking the part you want people to let you play. When it comes to designing screens for conveying information efficiently and interestingly, you need clean, well-organized designs, with the newest information at the top. People need to know at a glance what's there and how to get at it. Emphasize imagery. Use words sparingly. Make sure that the person or people behind the site are prominent and available. This advice is generally true, but as far as your -online-self.com is concerned, you want to convey industry and competence. You want fresh content appearing as often as you can make it happen. And you want to provide a service to others in the discipline(s) you want to join. Your-online-self .com is an advertisement, but one that proves by demonstrating ability rather than crowning achievement.

Once you have a malleable layout for the different parts to your site, a look and feel that indicates the parts are related but serve different functions, you need to start thinking about how you're going to serve content. How often are you going to update your site and where will the content come from? As you finish new projects, you'll want to consider including them in your portfolio, but there might be quite some time between the completion of one project and the completion of another, making your site seem abandoned. Keeping a running list of things you're reading is a solid strategy for keeping the site looking fresh without having to create new content from scratch all the time. You can just read interesting books and articles and then provide the world with a gist of the content and whatever reflection on that content you have to offer.

You might also consider offering a more curated version of dir.php. Since you're in the habit of finding interesting CSS, JavaScript, and PHP techniques anyway, rather than just stashing them in a directory, you might consider a show-case for each, perhaps containing a link to where you found it, when you found it, what you think is interesting about it, and some initial thoughts about how you might use the snippet, in what context and for what purpose. A curated list of parts will show you working constantly toward developing your skills, as long as you're in fact collecting and curating regularly.

Where you are now

This chapter was more conceptual than productive, but you've had a chance to encounter the @media CSS declaration and to think about usability, so hopefully you've started thinking about how your-online-self.com looks on a mobile device.

Because you're using your-online-self.com for marketing more than sales, I assume, you don't need to have a mobile-first attitude toward design, your potential "customers" being less like people trying to find you to buy something from you as potential colleagues or employers searching for talent, a less mobile device–centric activity, these days at least. That may change tomorrow or the day after.

CONCLUSION

What unifies the three rhetorical traditions, from the pedagogical perspective at least, is the persistent desire to educate people to be effective citizens, emphasizing the medium that dominates the day. In the past a person needed basic logic and basic prose composition, first spoken and later written rhetoric, to be an effective member of their world. Today basic programming is just as foundational an intellectual discipline.[1] Although knowledge of how any art or science is done can increase a person's appreciation for the results of either, actual practice provides deeper understanding. It's true that digital products are getting easier to use but ease of use brings helplessness and dependence. You have to be able to program it, even badly, to understand a technology's benefits and its costs, what it enables and what it disables or limits, which means among other things that any technology you adopt should be open source or at least highly customizable. People who don't have this level of understanding are at a disadvantage when it comes to personal and public decision making in the digital age.

In addition to gaining hands-on insight into digital rhetoric through the creation of your-online-self.com, you've created a digital presence for yourself, a brand, if you like, a representation of your professional value as exemplified by your work and your ongoing projects and interests. People will find you by means of all of your social networking profiles, but at your-online-self.com you're in complete control. When you design the interface, you control the information.

Rhetorical practice revised for the digital age

Given everything in *Writing Online* to this point, I'd like to suggest the following as a preliminary revision of rhetorical practice customized for the digital age, preliminary because while we're living within the digital age, we're not yet exactly of it. There are youngsters about to join us who are of it, but really it will be their descendants who are fully digital, and by then changes we can't anticipate will be done deals.

In the oratorical past when preparing to give a public (socially significant) speech, one worked out the topics to cover in advance, arranged them in optimal order based on

1. I hasten to add that just as freshman speech and freshman composition fail to adequately provide the necessary rhetorical capacity, so a freshman class in programming will fail. All three need to adumbrate all curricula. Writing doesn't belong to English. Speaking doesn't belong to communication. Logic doesn't belong to philosophy. Programming doesn't belong to computer science. We're all in this together.

an intuitive understanding of the people one was about to address, and embedded the whole in memory by performing it over and over in one's head, tweaking the language, polishing the sentences. When the moment of delivery arrived, one performed fully focused on the people present, the audience, attuned to what was needed as the event unfolded, making certain to strike the correct demeanor and attitude—distraught, humble, impassioned, vindicated, triumphant, even the full range if necessary—whatever the audience signaled and you inferred from the context was needed. You learned how to do this by watching the polished performances of others and by talking with others about how they do it. To succeed you needed access to the group that held power and you needed courage, ambition, and luck. If you were successful, you had a reputation for success combined with virtue, what the Greeks called *arête*.

As the need for public speaking to affect change gave way in more and more instances to written documents, rhetoric shifted its emphasis away from delivery and memory toward invention, increasingly focusing on research in the form of searching through existing written records and doing scientific research. The writing relevant to those enterprises had profound social consequences. Traditional political speeches remained a part of the dominant class's repertoire of rhetorical practices, but more and more rhetorical work was written rather than spoken. Sometimes there was a performance of the written, a reading, but those were a gloss on the main work that remained in writing.

You became literate through attendance at school, progressing up the levels as your aptitude and financial backing warranted. You read in libraries and took notes and met others along the same path. To succeed you needed access to great libraries and for that you needed credentials and letters of introduction supplied by the professoriate and the literati. You built a vita, a bibliography of your own work, and upon it you created further opportunities. Even today a budding politician will write a book as a way of asserting his or her worthiness of election.

In the digital age, **we still have oral and literate rhetoric,** the canons of rhetoric and <oversimplification>the writing process</oversimplification>, **but we also now have a continually evolving workflow.** We can keep our own ever-expanding collections of ideas and forms of expression (we don't need libraries, or at least not the stacks) as well as code pieces and design patterns to facilitate delivery of them. We also have access to a constantly expanding network of similar repositories kept by others, both people working in our fields and those by others in contiguous fields. In the digital age, the time for rhetorical performance never arrives because it's always now. **Your-online-self.com is always on.** Your actions, intentional and unintentional, are always public.

In addition to deciding what to present, you need to consider how to present it in different ways for different people and set up the interface to seamlessly accommodate those differences. Digital arrangement becomes a matter of multiple navigation routes. The novice gets the explanations of relevance, the context, the definitions, the conclusions; the experts get the methodology and the results; the journalists get the implications dramatized. The Internet gets the compressed, 140-character Twitter version. Instagram gets the pictures. Facebook gets the social announcement. And so on. You generate and store all of this rhetorical activity on the content management system that is your-online-self.com. You tailor that information based on server analytics and user awareness and your understanding of your users based on persona generation, scenarios, and ethnographical inquiry, when possible.

Every document you make for whatever purpose, you markup for metadata as well as structure and store for future use, reuse, and repurposing. Your CMS also regularly receives information from your RSS feeds that you can review and archive, in part or in whole, adding more to your storehouse of material. Thus, you design it to accommodate information as it comes and goes, dynamic deliver. Your memory, both of what you yourself created and what you gleaned from other's creations, is expansive, stored in databases and recalled via database queries, some user triggered, others event triggered. You can deliver that information repackaged for context of reception (text message, email alert, Twitter feed, small square on index.php, large central section in index,php, or tease fragment on index,php with a link to the full article, hyperlinked so that people can choose what to read and what to ignore and what to skim and still make sense of the work). **Rather than a single speech or a single document, you're offering multiple variations of the thinking and research in different forms of expression** and even perhaps in different media. You could offer a podcasted version. A video press release on your CMS is also always an option.

Your CMS is in essence a personal library and code warehouse. It can become a collaboration hub. If you invite others to contribute, either by commenting on your work or by offering their own, or both, then you've got a digital equivalent of the marketplace of old, an agora, a forum. You might get enough traffic eventually to start offering advertising, turning your CMS into a full-on silk road.

What you've learned so far amounts to the first hundred miles on a thousand-mile journey that will become even longer if you choose to really make something of your-online-self.com. You may be content with a manicured portfolio of your own work. You may have grander ambitions. How far you go is entirely up to you now that you have a foundation of code-informed rhetoric to build on.

Where you are now

I wrote at the outset that working through this book would change your mind, teach you to read and write and think and learn differently (digitally). The truth, of course, is that I have no idea if (or if how) you're different now. If you came this far (and didn't start with the conclusion, which of course you might have), I imagine you think differently in the ways listed below. I've use a list instead of paragraphs here because I'm pretty sure, regardless of anything else, that by now you prefer lists to paragraphs.

Digital thinking

1. You teach yourself new digital communication techniques daily using free online resources.
2. You have project management and self-motivation skills.
3. You produce more, consume less.
4. Computers don't mystify you.

5. You're discontent with defaults.
6. You make your own digital writing environments because you know that tools constrain and enable work and you don't want others telling you what to think by dictating how you work.
7. You can think outside the Internet's ec(h)o system.
8. You have disciplined troubleshooting skills.
9. You can think in both literate and digital ways, but you don't use literate assumptions or practices to make digital assets.
10. You know that the next generation may not think in literate ways.
11. You're designing with an eye toward replacing books.
12. You never type the same thing twice (the DRY principle).
13. You automate. You make databases do the counting, the sorting, the organizing, the filtering.
14. You know that everything you do and say online is part of a permanent public record and that even real life can find its way online.
15. You know how you're being marketed to and that you're being marketed, and thus you have taken control of your brand via your-online-self.com.
16. You know that products are now services, artifacts are commodifiable assets.
17. You know that history is history—what's important today will be useless tomorrow and meaningless the day after that, but impending obsolescence makes you want to keep learning, reinventing, and redesigning.
18. You know that education is neither a product nor a service but rather, like health, a state achieved and maintained through daily effort.
19. You've abandoned nostalgia.
20. You've fully embraced being digital.

Digital invention

1. You spend some time every day foraging for new ideas and perspectives.
2. Your digital content is constantly growing in multiple dimensions, some shared with the world, some only with a select few (password protected), and some hidden from all but your own awareness.
3. You know how to recycle and repurpose your own content and that of others. You know how to mine the Creative Commons for work to supplement and enhance your own.
4. You know how to phrase questions so precisely that rarely does an Internet search require more than the first or second click to find what you were looking for and sometimes you don't need to search at all because clarity brought insight.
5. You're a self-directed, self-motivated, lifelong learner.

Digital arrangement

1. You think navigation rather than arrangement.
2. You offer an infinite surface covering readily accessible depths.
3. You know how to let your users decide what to view when.

4.   You know how to let the machine decide what to show when.
5.   You know how and when to use random as a method of engagement.

Digital memory

1.   Everything you learn now finds a rediscoverable place in your ever-expanding digital archive, your dynamic memory palace.
2.   You memorize new bodies of information efficiently using memorization tools you made.

Digital style

1.   You're brief, specific, and precise. No one will ever say of you TL;DR.
2.   You separate structure and appearance.

Digital delivery

1.   Your content is direct and efficient: device agnostic and device aware, multimodal, dynamic, and responsive.

Coda: Revisit the three epoch tables

Now that you have some serious coding skills, I'd like to suggest you indulge in a brief thought experiment before you turn your attention to version 2.0 of your -online-self.com. Have another look at the table of epochs from the Introduction (repeated below) and think again about how I characterized the distinctions among the oral, literate, and digital. To what extent do you disagree with my characterizations? In particular, reconsider the dimension called character traits. Imagine those three boxes as forming a continuum. Where do you fall on the line? You can't be on the far left, chin deep in the oral tradition, because you're literate, but to what extent do you consider yourself digital now?

Character traits fostered and required of sender but receiver also	Deep focus, presence (of mind and body, a good memory), pragmatic, decisive, quick-witted, extroverted (good with people and crowds)	Deep concentration, absence (reflective, meticulous), resilient (to criticism), deliberate, conscientious (dedication required to learn letters and literature and history, but also writing is more durable than words), introverted (more scholar than politician), historical perspective	Shallow/broad awareness caused by constant stimuli (email, Twitter, Facebook), less reflective, more immediate, but not always present; focus and concentration still required of makers, much less so users, video games being liminal; networked—ambiverted

Which mixture of traits best describes you, and what assets in your-online-self .com demonstrate those traits? What about a year from now?

GLOSSARY[1]

Sarah Murphy

A

`<a>`:
the `<a>`, or anchor tag, is the HTML element used to define/mark up hyperlinks

accordion menu:
a vertically expandable/collapsible menu type; typically requiring JavaScript for the show/hide functions

`addslashes`:
a PHP function used to prepare an entry for processing and storage by adding a backslash (\) before certain punctuation marks (like 'single quotes' and "double quotes"); PHP processing is punctuation sensitive—adding the slashes *escapes* whatever follows (meaning that it tells the machine to ignore whatever follows because it was part of an entry and not part of the PHP instructions)

Adobe:
a multimedia software company (Adobe Systems, Inc.) responsible for the .pdf file type and for popular programs such Acrobat Reader (.pdf viewer), Photoshop (graphics editor), InDesign (desktop publishing), and Dreamweaver (web development)

algorithm:
any series of operations used to solve a problem

`alt` tag:
an attribute of the `<img>` element used to provide an alternate description for an image whenever the actual image fails to display to the screen

---

1. Many of the terms in this glossary required outside research. For these, I consulted a minimum of three references each—often including, but not necessarily limited to, W3Schools.org, Wikipedia.org, Techterms.com, Webopedia.com, Techopedia .com, and StackOverflow.org—and consolidated information as relevant for this book. For some, I have also included personal examples, code snippets, and cropped screenshots.

alternative story form (ASF):
refers both to the practice of offering users alternative approaches to and paths through content and to the means through which the alternatives are supplied (hybrid compositions of textual, visual, and/or digital elements); examples include anything from "choose your path" novels; to database documentaries, diagrams, charts, and calendars; to Q&As and checklists

Amazon Cloud Services (ACS):
an online, cloud-computing web-hosting service offered by Amazon.com featuring pay-as-you-go pricing; aws.amazon.com

Apache:
refers to the Apache HTTP Server, a popular, open source web server software system that's supported and maintained by the Apache Software Foundation (ASF)

Apple:
an innovative multinational technology company (Apple, Inc., founded in 1976) responsible for a vast line of popular products including the iPod, iPad, iPhone, and Apple Watch, and a diverse range of online services such as iCloud, iTunes, and the App Store

> *"Think different." (2015)* www.apple.com

Arrangement.
the rhetorical canon referring to the means and methods of organizing, presenting, and navigating through whatever is being said/written/designed/coded

array:
a type of data structure used to create variables, assign their values, and define their relationships; arrays are built out of $strings of key-value pairs, which are assigned either indexically or associatively

Types of PHP arrays:

1. *indexical arrays*: assign an explicit numerical order to key-value pairs based on the order listed:

```php
<?php
$appeal = array("ethos", "Pathos",
"logos");
echo "Aristotle's rhetorical appeals are
". $appeal[0] .", ". $appeal[1] ." and ".
$appeal[2] ".".";
?>

//prints the following to the screen:
```
Aristotle's rhetorical appeals are ethos, Pathos, and logos.

2. *associative arrays*: assign an implicit order based on how the pairs are asso-
    ciated; there are two ways to create associative arrays:

    Option 1: with a list of `$array['key'] = "value"`
    pairs, separated by semicolons:

    ```php
    <?php
            $appeal['ethos'] = "to character";
            $appeal['pathos'] = "to disposition";
            $appeal['logos'] = "to logic";

    echo "\"Logos\" is defined as the appeal"
    . $appeal['logos'] . ", according to
    Aristotle.";
    ?>

    //prints the following to the screen:
    ```

    "Logos" is defined as the appeal to logic, according to Aristotle.

    Option 2: with a series of `"key" => "value"` pairs
    separated with commas and grouped within the ( ) of a single
    `$string: $array = array("key0" => "value0",
    "key1" => "value1"); :`

    ```php
    <?php
    $appeal = array("ethos"=>"to character",
    "pathos"=>"to disposition", "logos"=>"to
    logic");

    echo "Aristotle defines \"Ethos\"  as the
    appeal " . $appeal['ethos'] . ".";
    ?>

    //prints the following to the screen
    ```

    Aristotle defines "Ethos" as the appeal to character.

attributes:
bits of information that are embedded into the `<open>` tag of an element to
further markup/define the element's contents:

```html
<element attribute="value" >contents</element>
<a href="www.funnysite.com" title="for some
giggles" target="_blank">FunnySite</a>
```

Azure:
Microsoft's cloud computing platform used for building, hosting, and managing
various services, analytics, and applications across a global network of Microsoft-
affiliated data centers

B

_blank:
the value assigned to the `target` attribute of a hyperlink telling the machine to open the link in new browser tab

```
<a href= "www.somesite.com" target= "_
blank">Opens SomeSite in new tab</a>
```

BLOB:
stands for binary large object and refers to the data-type specification for a field that accepts and stores complex data-like images, audio, and other multimedia files; widely (but not universally) supported across database platforms

Bluehost:
a server-based web-hosting company and domain registrar (sister companies include HostMonster, FastDomain, and iPage); www.bluehost.com

bot:
a web robot (really, a software application) that runs automated (usually mundane and highly repetitive) tasks over the Internet

branching:
a programming structure that offers a range of further options once a certain condition has been met:

```
(if not A, then no offer)
if A is met, offer A1, A2 and A3
if A1, do action X
if A2, do action Y
if A3, do Z
```

browser:
a downloaded and installed software program used to view and interact with web pages; examples include Firefox, Chrome, Safari, and Internet Explorer

C

charset:
refers to the intended character-encoding system as defined in the metadata for digital documents; affects the use and display of letters, accent marks, symbols, and other characters

Creative Commons (CC):
nonprofit organization dedicated to enabling and supporting the legal sharing of creative content and knowledge; go to www.creativecommons.org for more information and to search for CC licensed material

Creative Commons licenses:
a genre of free, public copyright licenses that allows creators to give the public permission to use/reuse their work; also protects the public from copyright infringement

checkboxes:
an HTML form input type that allows users to select multiple options simultaneously:

```
<h4>Make it your own</h4>
<form>
<input type="checkbox" name="customize"
value="add_shot">extra shot of
espresso<br>
<input type="checkbox" name="customize"
value="add_wc">whipped cream, please<br>
<input type="checkbox" name="customize"
value="cr_sauce">caramel drizzle<br>
<input type="checkbox" name="customize"
value="m_sauce">chocolate drizzle<br>
</form>
```

Make it your own

- ☑ extra shot of espresso
- ☑ whipped cream, please
- ☐ caramel drizzle
- ☑ chocolate drizzle

CHAR(N):
stands for "character" and refers to a data-type specification for a database field that accepts only entries of a predetermined length (N); practical for things like phone numbers, CHAR(10), or zip codes, CHAR(5)

cloud server/hosting: (see "virtual server")

CMS, content management system:
any software tool that enables users to create, edit, publish, delete, and otherwise manage web content from a central interface

code:
instructions written to the computer

code repository:
an archive of source codes

computational thinking:
a way of thinking diagnostically about how code works and how programs operate

content creation:
refers to the contribution and cultivation of digital content (info, images, data, etc.)

content management:
refers to the collection, organization, management, navigation, and presentation of digital content

cookies:
little bundles of information exchanged between a server and a browser that can track/remember user activity

CPanel:
a "control panel" made up of a graphical interface containing a set of tools intended to simplify the process of hosting a website and managing a hosting account

crowd sourcing:
a term referring to the practice of soliciting information, data, services, and/or other sought-after resources from the vast, unnamed, unpaid digital crowd

CSS, Cascading Style Sheets:
CSS is the language of display; style sheets are used to format how elements are designed and displayed on the screen; CSS can be either:

1. written as a separate .css file, saved, and linked to within in the head of another file:

```
<html><head>

<link rel="stylesheet" type="text/css"
href="filename.css">
</head><body>
```

2. written as a part of a single file, within the head between the `<style>` `</style>` tags:

```
<html><head>
<style>
body {
width: 80%;
height: relative;
background-color: black;}
H1 {
font-size: 3em;
color: grey;
text-align: center;}
</style>
</head><body>
```

D

data:
moveable, searchable, reformattable, and repurposable units of information

database:
a dynamic, searchable repository of information units

data mining:
the process of gathering data and cross-analyzing for patterns, trends, and other correlations

debugging:
finding and fixing errors (a.k.a. bugs) in a source code

decision tree:
a branching schema used to represent a situation's various possibilities and their respective outcomes

dedicated server:
a physical computer reserved for/dedicated to running web server software (e.g., Apache), which serves hosted files to the web; companies offering dedicated servers include Bluehost, GoDaddy, and Dreamhost

Delivery:
the rhetorical canon concerned with the sensory modes through which communicative content is transmitted

desktop:
a convenient, conceptual metaphor that's often intended to familiarize users with the interfaces of various operating systems

development environment:
refers to the practices, processes, and programming tools used in software development (as well as to the atmosphere of the developers' physical settings); an integrated development environment (IDE) is one that coordinates and assembles tools and processes together with a graphical interface for users' convenience

digital rhetoric:
refers to the practices and intellectual habits that foster effective online content creation, sharing, and management; often used in this book to talk about, characterize, and distinguish digital practices from oral and literate traditions; digital rhetoric is inherently multimodal, revolves around data, favors alternative paths, and adapts to real users

directory:
a folder of digital files

distributed revision control:
programs and practices that foster developer collaboration across networks by
keeping a cloud-based record of all incremental revisions to a project

.div:
.div's are author-defined tags used to divide up portions of content for display;
.div's are styled using CSS and are opened/closed within the body of an HTML;
there are two varieties:

1. an id (for a unique component on a page)
    • which takes a #name { } in the CSS and <div id="name">
      in the HTML
2. a class (for a grouping of elements you want to behave alike)
    • which takes a .name { } in the CSS and a <div class="name">
      in the HTML

    *the distinction between id and class is relatively trivial
    for CSS/HTML; the distinction becomes more significant in
    JavaScript

```
<HTML><head><style>
#header {
color: white;
background-color: grey;}

.blockquote {
border: solid black 3px;
padding-left: 100px;
font-style: italic;}

</style></head><body>
        <div id="header"><h1>Aristotle: On
Rhetoric</h1></div>

        <div class="blockquote">rhetoric is
identifying the means of persuasion</div>
</body></html>
```

DOM, document object model:
a programming interface that displays the hierarchal structure of HTML and XML
documents using a family tree of nodes to map the relationship among elements

domain name:
the unique, owned, and registered name that identifies the location of a website (including the suffix ".com/.edu/.net/.etc" but excluding the "http://www.")

download:
to pull a file from somewhere else and put it onto a local device; to receive a file from another computer

Dreamhost:
a web-hosting company and domain registrar; see "web host" for more; www .dreamhost.com

Dropbox.com
a web-based service offering cloud storage, file sharing, a collaborative platform, and local-directory synchronization

> "Good things happen when your stuff lives here:
> Dropbox keeps your files safe, synced, and easy to share." (2015)
> www.dropbox.com

dropdown selection list: (see "select")

Drupal:
an open source software package for content management; distributed under the GNU General Public License; used as the backend framework for anything from personal blogs to government websites

DTD, document type definition:
defines elements and their attributes in XML or HTML documents; refers to both standard markup and semantic markup

E

echo:
a command that tells the computer to display contents to a screen that would otherwise be hidden; synonymous with the `print` command

element:
refers to content jurisdiction of an element—includes the opening <tag>, everything in the middle, and the closing </tag>
- the body element is the `<body>` tag, plus everything in the body (including all other sets of tags therein), plus the `</body>` tag
- an anchor element is the open `<a href="linkfile.html" target="_blank" other_attributes= "their values">`, plus its link text, plus the closing `</a>`

entry:

a term used rather loosely to refer to the input point for a unit of information (can refer to a specific form field, entire forms submitted elsewhere, or the moment at which a program begins operating)

F

Facebook.com

an online, social networking service structured around user profiles and "friends" circles, and using communication types including posting, messaging, status updates, liking/disliking, and picture tagging

Fantastico:

a commercial "script library" of commonly used scripts that can be set to auto-install web applications on a website using the hosting service's CPanel

field:

a unit of data input and storage; often refers to a single entry point on a web form; also refers to a column in a database

file:

a digital document (word doc, image, audio file, etc.); a collection of data stored as a single unit identified by a filename plus file extension

file extension:

the three to four characters to the right of the . in a filename (e.g., .doc, .dox, .htm, .html, .jpg, .pdf); tells the computer what program to open the file with

file manager:

a system that organizes (and allows for the reorganization, renaming, deleting, and copying) of files and folders on a computer

form:

an HTML element composed of various input types such as blank fields (`input type="text"`), checkboxes (`input type="checkbox"`), radio buttons (`input type="radio"`), and other selections/inputs that a user fills outs and submits (`input type="submit"`)

```
<form action="classlist.php">

First name:<br>
<input type="text" name="firstname"
value=""><br>
Last name:<br>
<input type="text" name="lastname"
value=""><br>
Gender:<br>
```

```
<input type="radio" name="gender"
value="m">male
<input type="radio" name="gender"
value="f">female
<br>
<input type="submit" value="Submit">
</form>
```

> `<input type="submit">` gives you a button for
> *submitting* a form with; the destination, often a file or
> a database, is determined by the value assigned to the
> form's action attribute at the top

First name:

Last name:

Gender:
● male ● female
Submit

FrameMaker:
a popular document-processor program by Adobe that facilitates structural coherence in format, content, and design across multiple web pages

FTP, File Transfer Protocol:
the customizable protocol, or set of rules and practices, for transferring files over
the Internet; regulates uploads and downloads and administrative access

G

Git:
a speedy and efficient, open-source distributed revision control system

GitHub:
a web-based Git service offering clients access to a repository of source codes, a collaborative platform, a user-friendly graphical interface, and other programming perks

> "Build software better, together." (2015) https://github.com/

GNU General Public License (GPL):
a free software license guaranteeing users the right to copy, share, modify, or
otherwise utilize a program's code, as well as any code derived from it; originally
authored by software freedom activist Richard Stallman in affiliation with the
GNU Project (a free, mass-collaboration project initiated by MIT in 1983)

GoDaddy:
a web-hosting company and domain registrar often known for their spunky TV ads
"It's Go Time" (2015) www.godaddy.com

god-term:
an ultimately compelling term, one of the highest value, for a given culture (as opposed to "devil-terms," which are ultimately repulsive); the concept of god-terms derives from the early 1950's scholarship of both Kenneth Burke and Richard Weaver

greeking:
a term used to describe the process of using *lorem ipsum* "dummy text" as a place-holder during the structural design phases; allows clients and developers to focus on the structure, layout, and function for a site's contents without getting caught up on the content itself

H

hamburger menu:
a navigational menu type that collapses into a square icon with three horizontal lines, typically found floating in the top corner of mobile-ready web pages

hardware:
the material/physical substance of computers (keyboards, screens, batteries, chips, motherboards, etc.)

"Hello world" program:
any computer program that, when successfully executed, returns the message "Hello, world" to the screen; commonly used for an introductory lesson to a new programming language

HTML, HyperText Markup Language:
a markup language that defines/labels the content of web documents using sets of tags that tell the browser how to structure a page

HTTP, Hypertext Transfer Protocol:
the underlying data protocol system of the World Wide Web; it defines how mes-sages are formatted and transmitted

href:
an attribute of the <a> element that indicates and assigns a link's destination

hyperlink:
a link; a way to get from one web page to another (or to jump from one place to another place on the same page)

I

InDesign:
an Adobe desktop publishing program used to create and edit various professional documents, both printed and digital (posters, flyers, brochures, books, and tablet-compatible ebooks)

inline style:
line-specific style directions for individual elements, embedded inline within the element tag

```
<p style='font-size:24px; text-
indent:20px' >makes this one p different
than all the other p's</p>
```

Instagram.com
a social networking service allowing users to take pictures and videos and share them across a variety of other social media platforms

INT:
stands for integer and refers to a data-type specification for a database field set to accept only integers (whole numbers, both positive and negative)

interface:
the point of contact/communication between a user and a computer program

Invention:
the rhetorical canon concerned with how we come up with the appropriate things to say/write/make within any given context

J

JavaScript, JS:
a client-side programming language that facilitates user interaction with computers; often required for animations and effects (like show/hide toggles, slideshows, and fade in/out)

Java Script Object Notation, JSON:
a language-independent, lightweight data-interchange format (much like XML) that uses a relatively simple set of structures including objects, object members (such as strings and values), and arrays

jQuery:
a free and open source library of common Javascripts intended to simplify HTML client-side scripting

jump-to:
often used synonymously with "hyperlink" or "link" to refer to the movement from one page to another; sometimes used to refer specifically to internal links that jump from one place to another place on the same page

K

Khan Academy:
a nonprofit educational institution that produces and distributes a host of free educational resources (including YouTube videos, practice exercises, and other tools for students and educators)

> "A free, world-class education for anyone, anywhere." (2015) www.khanacademy.org

Klout.com
a social media analytics service that measures users' social prominence by tracking their social media presence and comparing it against their influence in the digital community (based on their follows, re-tweets, pins, likes, links, search hits, etc.)

> "Be known for what you love." (2015) www.klout.com

L

language:
a way of communicating with a machine; predicated on patterns of syntax and other formalized, grammatical rules

LAMP stack:
a type of web stack using Linux (as the operating system), Apache (as the web server), MySQL (as the RDBMS), and PHP/Python/Perl (as the scripting language), and offering a platform for open source web development and application deployment

link:
a clickable reference to another web page; a hyperlink

LinkedIn.com
a social-professional networking site where employers post jobs and screen candidates, and users search job listings, set up notifications, and "link in" with their contact networks

link rot:
when a link stops working because the target file/page has been renamed, moved (or deleted), or has been otherwise altered such that the URL has changed (or been erased); a.k.a. linkrot, link death, and reference rot

literate rhetoric:
refers to the practices and intellectual habits that lead to effective written communication; used in this book to talk about and characterize the practices peculiar to literate traditions (like linear arrangement, avoiding repetition, appealing to an imagined/universal audience, and being concerned with intellectual property)

loop:
a type of programming structure that continues to execute and reexecute an action, or set of actions, until satisfactory conditions have been met and the action is no longer required

Lynx:
an early textual-based, hypertext web browser created in 1992; still in limited use today

M

@media queries:
used to determine the display capabilities of a device (width and height, landscape versus portrait, pixel resolution) and assign the CSS accordingly

machine learning:
refers to the ability of machines to study algorithms and make intelligent predictions based on data patterns

mail-to forms:
used to send emails via a web form (rather than email client)

markup:
the process and conventions of "marking up" a document using <tag></tag> to label contents and define structure

Memex:
the hypothetical machine (named for "memory" plus "index") imagined by Vannevar Bush that would allow people to store, connect, and recall every bit of information ever encountered; the concept is credited for having inspired the development of hypertext systems

Memory:
the rhetorical canon concerned with the means and methods of memorization and remembering

menu:
a list, dropdown, or other set of selectable navigational options; often use the HTML list <li> element together with the unordered list <ul> element to organize the menu options

```
<li>
<a href="#">Portfolio &#65516;</a>
<ul class="hidden">
<li><a href="#">Essays</a></li>
<li><a href="#">Web Design</a></li>
<li><a href="#">Graphic Designs</a></li>
</ul>
</li>
```

metadata:
data about data

Microsoft:
a multinational technology company responsible for the widely used line of Windows operating systems (including Microsoft Office and Internet Explorer)

mockup:
a rough draft of a web design or a navigational schema

Mosiac:
the first web browser capable of displaying images inline with text (rather than on a separate page as with earlier hypertext browsers)

multiple selects:
an HTML dropdown element that allows users to select more than one option (by holding the ccntrl on Windows, or the command on Mac, when clicking)

```
<select multiple>
<option value="pep">pepperoni</option>
<option value="sausage">sausage</option>
<option value="mush">mushroom</option>
<option value="x_chz">extra cheese</option>
</select>
```

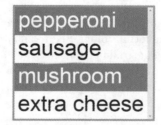

MySQL:
a free, open source, relational database management system (RDBMS); pronounced "My Sequel"; used frequently with PHPMyAdmin

N

namespace:
namespaces avoid ambiguity in data by ensuring that tags, which may be repeated in different settings with different meanings (e.g., `<table>` for a data table and `<table>` for a furniture item), are unique by assigning them a unique namespace (e.g., `<h:table>` or `<f:table>`); all subsidiary components of those tags would also take the identifying prefix (e.g., `<f:name>` `<f:width>` . . .)

node:
an individual data point on a larger network

NoSQL:
a term (often interpreted as "non SQL" or "not only SQL") referring to a variety of database technologies that transcend the (storage capacity and retrieval speed) limitations of relational SQL/MySQL databases management systems

O

open source:
any source code that's available to the general public and licensed for legal reuse and modification; a certification standard; also, the social-political movement advocating and promoting open source values

Open Source Initiative (OSI):
a global nonprofit dedicated to the promotion and protection of open source software communities (see http://opensource.org/ for more information)

operating system:
software for your software (and hardware); operating systems are programs like Windows or Apple OS that manage and maintain everything else going on in a computer (other programs, applications, devices, equipment, etc.)

oral rhetoric:
refers to the practices and intellectual habits that lead to effective spoken performance; in this book, the term is often used to talk about and characterize the practices peculiar to preliterate traditions, such as borrowing from a storehouse of "communal knowledge," training in memory techniques, practicing public speaking, and emphasizing physical delivery (speaker's voice, stance, and attractiveness)

P

PageMaker:
one of the first desktop publishing programs; used to create pamphlets, brochures, newsletters, flyers, and other professional, hard-copy documents

parse:
to divide a communicative whole into its constituent parts; refers to the process of receiving input, identifying patterns, and arranging constituent parts into a hierarchy according to syntactical rules; word derives from early English grammar studies

path:
defines the location of a file within a local system or hosted domain; can be either relative (to a current directory) or absolute (from the root directory of a system or website)

PHP, Hypertext Preprocessor:
a server-side scripting language used to create dynamic websites; PHP code is parsed by the server and returned to the screen as HTML; this means that .php files must be uploaded to a server and viewed in a browser to display correctly

PHPMyAdmin:
a popular web tool intended to handle the administration of MySQL databases; allows users to create, modify, edit, and otherwise manage databases and tables; offered as a part of most hosting services

Pinterest.com
a social media site geared toward saving, sharing, and inspiring crafty ideas through pins and pinboards
> "Discover all the things that inspire you" (2015)
> www.pinterest.com

plain text editor:
any program that processes plain text files without embedding formatting information (unlike word processors); common examples include TextEdit and NotePad

platform:
what something is built on; can refer to devices' underlying hardware and software systems and their corresponding program compatibilities (iPads and Apple apps); can also refer to programs' underlying structure and their corresponding environments (i.e., collaborative platforms)

"point your browser":
to fill in the complete URL path to a file and jump directly to it; can be used to access files that are hosted but not linked to

plugin:
a small bit of software that can be added to web files to enable a specific feature or function

portfolio:
a collection of sample work intended to showcase one's skills

Prezi.com
a web-based presentation tool capable of zooming in/out and panning across a layered background of "slides" and images; requires user signup (basic package is free, upgrades and privacy options available for purchase)

`print`:
a command that tells the computer to display contents to a page that would otherwise be hidden; synonymous with `echo`

program:
a set of instructions telling the computer to perform a specific task

programming language:
a language that communicates directions to a computer about how to run applications, execute scripts, and otherwise perform computational actions; for example, include JavaScript, XML, PHP, and SQL

prototype:
a preliminary model

pseudocode:
a conceptual outline for a program using everyday language but modeling the logical steps necessary for the actual program code

pull:
information transmission that solicits content from somewhere else

push:
information transmission that sends content to somewhere else

Python:
a type of programming language designed to make code more readable and to condense concepts into fewer lines of code

Q

QuarkXpress:
a desktop publishing program (compatible with both Windows and Mac OS X) for designing and editing professional documents (like flyers, brochures, pamphlets, etc.); created, owned, and published by Quark, Inc.

query:
a request for/to request information from a database or a server

R

RackSpace, Inc:
a computing company offering various web-hosting packages (including both cloud server hosting and dedicated server hosting)

radio buttons:
a set of mutually exclusive user options (e.g., age or income ranges); selecting one radio button will automatically deselect the others

```
<h4>Choose your milk</h4>
<form action="">
<input type="radio" name="milk"
value="whole">whole<br>
<input type="radio" name="milk"
value="2">2%<br>
<input type="radio" name="milk"
value="skim">skim<br>
<input type="radio" name="milk"
value="soy">soy<br>
</form>
```

Choose your milk

whole
2%
skim
soy

README file:
a file, included in software download/installation packages, that contains licensing information and specifics about files in a program's directory

relational database management system (RDMS):
a type of database system built on fluid, yet logically structured, correspondences among relational, tabular data; most RDMSs require SQL for definition and query

repository: (see code repository)

"revealing a source code": (see source code)

reverse engineering:
taking something apart to see how it works so that you can replicate it or make
something like it; for example, revealing and repurposing a source code

revision control:
the automated versioning of (saving copies of revisions to) a file—saves a new version after each change, attaching a timestamp and editor ID stamp, and stores a
record of it all

rhetoric:
refers to a set of practices and intellectual habits that develop in a person the
capacity to think clearly and communicate effectively within a given setting

RSS:
Rich Site Summary (originally RDF Site Summary), commonly referred to as
Really Simple Syndication; a method of sharing web content from one source site to
infinite other sites using feeds that pull and display selected source data

S

script:
a sequence of programming commands/functions written to either a browser or
a server; enable more animated display options and more dynamic data processes
than HTML-only files

scripting languages:
are high-level, formalized programming languages that execute scripts on one of
two sides
  1.   *Client-side* (a.k.a. frontend) scripts are read by browsers after a web page
       has been loaded; affects what a user sees on the screen; JavaScript
  2.   *Server-side* (a.k.a. backend) scripts are read by servers before a web page
       is loaded; affects how a server interprets and manipulates data (e.g., in a
       database); PHP

select (dropdown selection list):
the HTML <select> element is used within a form to create a list of option
values that drops down after clicking an initial option; allows users to *select only a
single option* value

```
<form>
  <select>
<option>Select your status:</option>
      <option value="fresh">Freshman</option>
    <option value="soph">Sophomore</option>
    <option value="jr">Junior</option>
    <option value="senior">Senior</option>
```

```
<option value="grad">Graduate</option>
</select>
</form>
```

*to *select multiple options,* use the `<select multiple>` attribute; see "multiple selects"

```
Select your status:
Select your status:
Freshman
Sophomore
Junior
Senior
Graduate
```

semantic markup:
a type of markup used to identify and label content according to its semantic meaning (rather than its structural function)

SEO, search engine optimization:
the process of optimizing search engine returns, getting higher rankings, and increasing site traffic by using strategic HTML title tags and metadata contents

sequence:
a logic structure in programming that establishes a series of actions/events to be executed in predetermined order (with no branching off or skipping ahead)

SHG, segmented hypergraphic:
an image with coded hotspots that, when hovered over, popup some additional content

social media:
refers (often vaguely) to the tools and programs (and ideologies) that solicit content from users, encourage exchange, and foster social networking among users

social networking sites/services (SNS):
any website, program, or application designed to cultivate an online community; examples include Facebook, Twitter, Instagram, LinkedIn, Klout, and Pintrest

software:
the immaterial, abstract substance of computers (programs, concepts, algorithms) that code for and carry out processes and actions

SME, subject matter expert:
someone with specialized knowledge on a particular subject; often consulted in the process of developing products and services to help ensure integrity, usability, and practicality

source code:
the code "behind" any given web page; revealed by right-clicking (Windows) or two finger–clicking (Mac), and selecting "view page source"

splash page/screen/message:
a page/screen/message that temporarily displays over another page (often used to alert, inform, or advertise)

spans:
much like .div's (both are user-defined, combine CSS and HTML, and take both #ids and .classes) but used to style elements across a single line of code (rather than a block of screen)

SQL, Structured Query Language:
a standardized, special-purpose programming language for working in/with relational database management systems (RDMS)

`stripslashes`:
a PHP function used to remove slashes from a data entry for display; see "`addslashes`" for explanation of how they got there in the first place

Style:
the rhetorical canon concerned with how certain manners of communication (be they verbal, visual, sonic, or digital) will be better or worse depending on purpose and context; considers things like brevity, clarity, and embellishment, and about knowing when to opt for simple style versus embellished style, and when to use generic hyperlink versus animated on hover popups

switching:
programming that prompts a single action based on the satisfaction of a single condition (if A, do B; if light switch up, turn lights on)

syntax:
the meaningful patterns of punctuation, spacing, spellings, and other characters of a language

T

`table`:
an HTML element used to arrange data into rows `<tr>` and columns `<td>`

```
<table border="solid black 2px">
  <tr>
    <td>small</td>
    <td>12oz </td>
  </tr>
  <tr>
    <td>medium </td>
    <td>16oz </td>
        </tr>
  <tr>
    <td>large</td>
    <td>20oz </td>
        </tr></table>
```

small	12oz
medium	16oz
large	20oz

tags:
pairs of open <tags> and close </tags> that sandwich and define documents,
marking them up for function, display, and/or semantics; may or may not include
extra attributes for the elements

template:
a prefabricated, ready-to-go design (along with its various customization choices)
that users simply fill up with content

title attribute: `<tag title = " ">`
used to add more information about an element using a tooltip that pops up on
hover; often used with `<a>` elements to offer a description about a link; values
can be read by screen readers

```
<a href="www.domain.com/file.html" title="a
little more about the link">link text</a>
```

`<title>` element:
the portion within an HTML `<head>` marked-up with `<title></title>`
tags and used to define a label for the little tab on a browser window

```
<html><head>
    <title>BPE: Best Page Ever</title>
</head><body>
```

title tag:
refers, in the strictest sense, to the open `<title>` and close `</title>` tags that
sandwich the `title` element; however, the term is often used ambiguously to
refer to the value of an element's `title` attribute

toggling:
switching (back and forth) between conditions/effects/states; toggles are the buttons that facilitate this on-click switching; a common feature of JavaScript and
JQuery plugins

tooltip:
an on-hover, popup display box used for supplying more detail about an element;
can be styled with CSS

Twitter.com
a free social media microblogging site where users send their "followers" brief
"tweets" that can be categorized with #hashtags and/or directed @other_users

> "Connect with your friends—and other fascinating people."
> (2015) www.twitter.com

U

"unzip a file":
to decompress a compressed file (files are often compressed to increase download
and processing speeds, unzipping them allows a user to view, edit, or otherwise
manipulate individual files)

URL, universal resource locator:
the specific address of a web page; takes the form http://www.example.com
/folder/filename.html, which indicates the protocol type (http), the domain name
(example.com), and the path to the specific web page (/folder/filename.html)

usability:
refers to the ease, intuitiveness, and learnability of a software program or computer application (or, any other designed product like a cookbook, can opener, or
car dashboard)

user:
anyone (or anything) viewing/interacting with a website; the digital descendent of
the literate reader and the oral audience member

upload:
to send, post, copy, or otherwise move a file from a local device up onto another
system (e.g., to a server)

V

VARCHAR:
stands for "variable character field" and refers to a data-type specification for a database field that accepts any combination of letters and numbers of a variable length

versioning:
the practice of saving multiple drafts along the way during development and revision; often an automated process in software programs, especially collaborative platforms

virtual (cloud) server:
a "spun up" web server that shares computing resources with other operating systems such that a separate dedicated server isn't required to host pages; examples include Amazon Cloud Services (ACS), Microsoft's Azure, and RackSpace

W

W3Schools.org
a web developer site with resources and tutorials on topics such as HTML, CSS, JavaScript, PHP, SQL, and JQuery

web host:
a company that leases space on a web server, stores documents and presents web pages to the web

web page:
any single file hosted online

web server:
a web-hosting software (such as Apache or Microsoft IIS) that provides global Internet access to hosted web pages; refers to both dedicated (physical) servers and virtual (cloud) servers

website:
a file or set of related files supplied by a single domain and served to the web

WHOIS:
ICANN's (Internet Corporation for Assigned Names and Numbers) query and response system, which utilizes a cross-database platform of domain registrations, IP addresses, and other registrant information with the goal of answering the question "who is" responsible for any given web page

widgets:
small, limited-capacity software applications that allow users to handpick programs, customize usability options, and personalize their preferences on a web page

wireframe:
a skeletal mockup of a website's essential framework; a.k.a. page schematic or screen blueprint

WordPress:
a free, online, open source, PHP- and MySQL-based content management system offering a range of free and for-purchase templates, plugins, and other customizations; used by individuals, organizations, and businesses for blogging and/or creating websites

WYSIWYG:
acronym for "what you see is what you get"; pronounced wizz-ee-wig; refers to any editing platform where the working environment resembles the finished product (e.g., Microsoft PowerPoint)

X

XML, Extensible Markup Language:
a markup language intended to describe data; uses self-defined, text-based tags to identify data for both humans and machines

Y

your-online-self.com
a term used in this book to refer to how you represent yourself online as a member of the digital community—your registered domain, your hand-coded website, your digital ethos

Z

zebra stripes:
alternating row colors on a table; often improves usability; the following bit of CSS gives every other row <tr> in the body of a table a gray background

```
tbody tr:nth-child(odd) {
background-color: gray;}
```

Miscellaneous symbols

! =	means "not equal"
=	means "is"
==	means "equal"
===	means "identical"
//	used to insert natural language explanations and comments about a piece of code
$	symbol used to create/name a string; creates and names a variable

WORKS CITED

Alcidamas. "On the Sophists." Trans. LaRue Van Hook. *The Classical Weekly*. Vol. 12, 1919. Retrieved Sept. 3, 2015 from http://www.classicpersuasion.org /pw/alcidamas/alcsoph1.htm.

Aristotle. *On Rhetoric: A Theory of Civic Discourse*. 2nd ed. Trans. George Alexander Kennedy. New York: Oxford University Press, 2006.

Bavota, C. "An Easy Way to Display an RSS Feed with PHP." July 15, 2010, Web Tutorial. Retrieved Sept. 3, 2015 from http://bavotasan.com/.

Burke, Kenneth. *A Rhetoric of Motives*. Berkley: University of California Press, 1969.

Center for Disease Control. "FluView." Retrieved Sept. 3, 2015 from http://www .cdc.gov/flu/.

Cortazar, Julio. *Hopscotch: A Novel*. Trans. Gregory Rabassa. New York: Random House, 1966.

Dynamic Drive. Script Library. Retrieved Sept. 3, 2015 from http://www .dynamicdrive.com/.

Eckersley, Peter. "A Primer on Information Theory and Privacy." *The Electronic Frontier Foundation*, 2010. Retrieved Sept. 3, 2015 from https://www.eff.org /deeplinks/2010/01/primer-information-theory-and-privacy.

Erasmus, Desiderius. *The Adages of Erasmus.* Compiled by William Barker. Toronto: University of Toronto Press, 2001.

——. *The Collected Works of Erasmus.* Trans. Margaret Mann Phillips. Compiled by R. A. B. Mynors. Toronto: University of Toronto Press, 1982.

Havens, Earle. *Commonplace Books: A History of Manuscripts and Printed Books from Antiquity to the Twentieth Century.* New Haven, CT: Yale University Press, 2001.

IBM, and The Institute of Culinary Education. *Cognitive Cooking with Chef Watson: Recipes for Innovation from IBM & the Institute of Culinary Education*. April 14, 2015. Print and web, https://www.ibmchefwatson.com/.

ICANN WHOIS. The Internet Corporation for Assigned Names and Numbers, 2015. Retrieved Sept. 3, 2015 from http://whois.icann.org/en.

Kim, Joshua. "iPads, Hotels, and Learning." *Inside Higher Ed.* Jan. 4, 2015. Retrieved Sept. 3, 2015 from https://www.insidehighered.com/blogs/technology-and-learning/ipads-hotels-and-learning.

Lidwell, William, Kritina Holden, and Jill Butler. *Universal Principles of Design.* Gloucester, MA: Rockport Publishers, 2003.

Lorem Ipsum. Lipsum. Retrieved from Sept. 3, 2015 from http://www.lipsum.com/.

Live Coding. Livestreaming platform. Retrieved Sept. 3, 2015 from https://www.livecoding.tv/.

National Oceanic and Atmospheric Organization. United States Department of Commerce. Retrieved Sept. 3, 2015 from http://www.noaa.gov/.

Plato. *Phaedrus.* Trans. Alexander Nehamas and Paul Woodruff. Indianapolis: Hackett Publishing Company, 1987.

Pope, Alexander. *An Essay on Criticism.* London: Printed for W. Lewis in Russel Street, Covent Garden; and Sold by W. Taylor at the Ship in Pater-Noster Row, T. Osborn near the Walks, and J. Graves in St. James Street. 1711. Retrieved Sept. 3, 2015 from http://www.gutenberg.org/ebooks/7409.

Pullman, George. *Persuasion: History, Theory, Practice.* Indianapolis: Hackett, 2013.

Quintilian. *Institutio Oratoria.* Trans. H. E. Butler. Cambridge, MA: Harvard University Press, 1980.

Schwencke, Ken. "Earthquake Aftershock: 2.7 Quake Strikes Near Westwood." Algorithm. *LA Times*, March 17, 2014. Retrieved Sept. 9, 2015 from http://articles.latimes.com/2014/mar/17/news/earthquake-27-quake-strikes-near-westwood-california-rdivor.

"The Beta Test Initiation." *The Big Bang Theory.* Television episode. Directed by Mark Cendrowski. CBS, Jan. 26, 2012.

Toulmin, Stephen E. *The Uses of Argument.* Updated ed. Cambridge: Cambridge University Press, 2003.

Twitch. Livestreaming platform. Retrieved Sept. 3, 2015 from http://www.twitch.tv/.

Tzu, Lao. *Wen-tzu: Understanding the Mysteries.* Trans. Thomas Cleary. Boston: Shambhala, 1991.

UC Berkeley Labor Center. "The High Public Cost of Low Wages: Poverty-Level Wages Cost U.S. Taxpayers $152.8 Billion Each Year in Public Support for Working Families." UC Berkeley Center for Labor Research and Education, April 2015. Research Brief by Ken Jacobs, Ian Perry, and Jennifer MacGillvary. Retrieved Sept. 3, 2015 from http://laborcenter.berkeley.edu/the-high-public-cost-of-low-wages/.

Weaver, Richard M. *The Ethics of Rhetoric.* Davis, CA: Hermagoras, 1985.

INDEX

Alcidamas, 39, 41–44, 110

arrangement
  dynamic, 42–44, 79, 86–88,
    96–103
  random as method, 100, 103–04,
    141

audience
  community dynamics, 49–50,
    56–57
  location awareness, 58–59
  oral, literate, and digital, 51–52,
    54–56, 59
  and personas, 65–67
  See also user feedback

branching, 96–98, 103, 104;
  decision tree, xxvi–xxix, 68, 96

copyright, 48–49

CSS
  about, 11, 13–14, 18–19, 35
  with HTML, 19–21, 23–24,
    29–31
  inline style, 18, 105
  include a relative style sheet, 19
  <style> tag, 5–6

domain names, 1, 6–8, 24–25

DTD (document type definition)
  for argumentation, 136–138
  for exposition, 138–139
  See also markup

errors
  sources of diagnostic error, 31–34
  syntax errors, 121

file
  404.html (file not found), 4, 6,
    113
  extensions, 4, 80–81
  security, 57–58
  upload to server, 12
  See also path

forms
  checkbox, 61, 68
  dropdown, select, 72, 76–78
  email form, 62–64
  radio buttons, 34–35, 68

Havens, Earle, 48–49

hooks for headlines, 93–96

HTML
  getting started, 2–6
  styling elements, 30–31
  what you need to know, 10–15,
    23
  See also forms; linking; markup

hyperlink. *See* linking

images
  dynamic display, 97, 114
  embed, 4–5
  and memory, 110–12
  open source, 48–49

188